Trolling Ourselves to Death

Oxford Studies in Digital Politics

Series Editor: Andrew Chadwick, Professor of Political Communication in the Centre for Research in Communication and Culture and the Department of Social Sciences, Loughborough University

Advance Praise for *Trolling Ourselves to Death*

"When assessing online toxicity, violence, and manipulation, it's tempting to frame them as creatures of the platforms' lagoons: 'new' problems caused by digital technologies. In this provocative analysis, Jason Hannan shows that there are creatures in the lagoon, yes, but those waters are older, murkier, and much more steeped in analog dysfunction than we might care to admit. Identifying these origins is the first and most critical step to understanding how we arrived at such a precarious political moment—and what we can, and must, do next to begin undoing the damage."

—Whitney Phillips, author of *This Is Why We Can't Have Nice Things: Mapping the Relationship Between Online Trolling and Mainstream Culture*

"Almost forty years after Neil Postman's seminal work, Jason Hannan analyzes the profound problem of a poisoned public sphere in a platform society. His new book offers a deeply insightful analysis of the transformation of online culture, in which trolling, disinformation, and conspiracy theories are increasingly normalized. Essential reading for all teachers and students who believe that education can serve as a civic counteroffensive against the massive pollution of our online channels."

—José van Dijck, co-author of *The Platform Society: Public Values in a Connective World*

"Democracy comes with an abundance of enemies, and lately with trolls. In this engaging read, Jason Hannan historicizes trolling with and without technology and walks us through its impact on civic cultures. This lucid and informed book is a must-read for those curious about what trolling is, why and how it manifests, and how we may survive it."

—Zizi Papacharissi, author of *After Democracy: Imagining Our Political Future*

Trolling Ourselves to Death

DEMOCRACY IN THE AGE OF SOCIAL MEDIA

JASON HANNAN

Oxford University Press is a department of the University of Oxford. It furthers
the University's objective of excellence in research, scholarship, and education
by publishing worldwide. Oxford is a registered trade mark of Oxford University
Press in the UK and certain other countries.

Published in the United States of America by Oxford University Press
198 Madison Avenue, New York, NY 10016, United States of America.

Library of Congress Control Number: 2023040389

ISBN 978–0–19–755777–8 (pbk.)
ISBN 978–0–19–755776–1 (hbk.)

DOI: 10.1093/oso/9780197557761.001.0001

Paperback printed by Marquis Book Printing, Canada
Hardback printed by Bridgeport National Bindery, Inc., United States of America

Contents

Acknowledgments

This book, like all books, has a history. The core idea behind it originated during a panel discussion on post-truth politics at Deutsche Welle's annual Global Media Forum in Bonn, Germany, in 2017. Shortly thereafter, I published the first iteration of the main argument as "Trolling Ourselves to Death in the Age of Trump" for *The Conversation Canada*. I then published an expanded version of the argument as "Trolling Ourselves to Death? Social Media and Post-Truth Politics" for the *European Journal of Communication* in 2018. After letting that article sit and gestate for a year, I finally decided to submit a book proposal to Oxford University Press in early 2020. Three years and several revisions later, this book is the final product.

I have many people to thank for helpful discussions and constructive feedback throughout the different stages of the writing process: Salam Al Sayed, Adina Balint, Stephanie Behl, Matthew Bost, Christopher Breu, Julie Chamberlain, Dana Cloud, Stephen Coleman, Bruno Cornellier, Sara Flynn, John Gregson, Josh Hanan, Robert Hariman, Mohammed Hashemi, Peter Ives, Rebecca Janzen, Jordan Kinder, Anna Kornbluh, Leigh Claire La Berge, Elisha Lim, Helmut-Harry Loewen, Sabrina Mark, Mark Martinez, Andrew McGillivray, Jaqueline McLeod-Rogers, Alina Moore, Robert Neubauer, Rachel Nixon, Victor Prado-Cajina, Richard Raber, Cassidy Rempel, Donovan Schaefer, Jacob Scheier, James Stanescu, Robert Tally, Brad Vivian, Tracy Whalen, and Jenny Wills.

I have benefited enormously from presenting much of the material in this book at the annual conferences for the Rhetoric Society of America, the National Communication Association, and the Canadian Communication Association. I was also very fortunate to have been invited to present some of my arguments as public talks to the University Women's Club of Winnipeg, the Canadian Federation of University Women, and the North Dakota–Manitoba Chapter of the Association of College and Research Libraries at the University of Manitoba. The thoughtful feedback I received at these events has made this a stronger book.

The various arguments presented here are based on my course lectures and classroom discussions at the University of Winnipeg. It is a real honor and privilege to have so many brilliant and civically engaged students who genuinely care about the quality of our public discourse and the health of our civic culture. It is an understatement to say that their highly original and perceptive research papers have helped me think through many of the issues addressed in this book.

At Oxford University Press, I am sincerely grateful to Andrew Chadwick and Angela Chnapko for believing in this book and for being so supportive throughout the writing and publication process. Writing a book is never easy. However, writing a book during long periods of social isolation in the middle of a global pandemic has been, at times, positively agonizing. I want to thank Andy and Angela for being so understanding and encouraging during an extremely difficult time for everyone. I want to thank Alexcee Bechthold for overseeing the many different stages of the production process so thoroughly and professionally. Also, it would be thoughtless of me if I did not also thank the two anonymous peer reviewers, who provided extremely detailed and helpful comments on both the proposal and the manuscript.

For institutional support, I wish to thank my longtime department chair and close friend Jaqueline McLeod-Rogers. Jaque has been a strong advocate and reliable mentor ever since I joined the University of Winnipeg in 2013. Angela Failler, Director of the Centre for Research in Cultural Studies at the University of Winnipeg, has built a truly one-of-a-kind scholarly community, where I am lucky to be a member. CRiCS has become an invaluable space in which to share my work and to learn from others, especially during our summer writing cafés. I also want to thank the University of Winnipeg, which granted me a six-month sabbatical for the latter half of 2020, during which I completed the bulk of the first draft of this book.

Chapter 1 previously appeared as "Trolling Ourselves to Death? Social Media and Post-Truth Politics" in *European Journal of Communication* 33, no. 2 (2018): 214–226. Portions of this book have also been used with permission of ABC-CLIO, LLC from my chapter "Truth and Trolling" in Carlos G. Prado ed., *America's Post-truth Phenomenon: When Feelings and Opinions Trump Facts and Evidence*, (Santa Barbara, CA: Praeger, 2018), pp. 126–140; permission conveyed through Copyright Clearance Center, Inc.

Introduction

The horrifying events of January 6, 2021, in which thousands of loyal Trump supporters descended upon the United States Capitol Building in a spectacular, if ill-coordinated and ultimately bungled, attempt at an armed insurrection, marked the culmination of the most bizarre and chaotic administration in American history. For four straight years, Donald Trump bombarded America, along with the rest of the world, with one shocking statement after another, with one brutal and inhumane policy after another, and with perfect indifference to colossal human and ecological suffering. He actively fed the worst possible human instincts, unleashing a homicidal orgy of racial hatred and violence among his ardent admirers. His governing style has justifiably been termed "psychological terrorism."[1] A sadist to his very core, he relished the thrill of scandalizing, exasperating, and horrifying "liberals," an all-purpose designation for everyone he regarded, implicitly and explicitly, as the enemy. Whether through Twitter or his executive pen, Trump savored the twisted pleasure of being the world's loudest and most obnoxious troll, tormenting the public psyche without pause or mercy. Like trauma victims, our memory of Trump's four years in office is one long blur, a dark and painful period we have tried to bury into the deepest recesses of our minds. His electoral defeat in 2020 delivered a widespread sense of relief and numbness. In the early months of 2021, we emerged from a nightmare. We experienced the strange feeling of not having to endure the daily mind-numbing and soul-deadening shock and awe of the man's outrageous and semiliterate tweets. In our exhaustion and delirium, in our desperation for something resembling normalcy, it was tempting to think that the chaos was finally over, that the nadir had finally passed, and that political sanity had been restored. That conclusion, it is now clear, was gravely mistaken. Trump lost the 2020 presidential election. But the monster he unleashed is very much alive and flourishing.

It will be some time before we are able to make proper sense of the Trump era. His sole term in office will undoubtedly become a standard reference point

Trolling Ourselves to Death. Jason Hannan, Oxford University Press. © Oxford University Press 2023.
DOI: 10.1093/oso/9780197557761.003.0001

for social, political, and media analysis. That Trump should have been elected at all has raised grave concerns about the fate of contemporary democracies. There is now a burgeoning literature about the crisis of democracy—the historical forces that lead modern democratic states to fall into disarray and degenerate into authoritarianism.[2] Not surprisingly, a central theme in this recent concern about the viability of democracy is the effect of digital technology upon the public sphere.[3] Commentators emphasize that our political discourse is becoming increasingly antisocial, paranoid, combative, and violent.[4] It is no longer just digital platforms like Facebook, Twitter, Instagram, Reddit, and YouTube that have been overtaken by angry and sanctimonious culture warriors of various ideological stripes. Life offline appears also to have fallen into the same caustic and corrosive patterns.

The emergence of demagogues and reactionary populist movements has sparked a growing fear that the political fabric of modern democracies might be coming undone. This fear has led *New York Times* columnist Michelle Goldberg to diagnose a new condition she calls "democracy grief," the political counterpart to what environmental scientists call "climate grief."[5] Democracy grief can be understood as the sense of frustration, anger, and despair over the loss of a democratic culture to the forces of political, ethnic, and religious fanaticism. While Goldberg's diagnosis of democracy grief might at first seem premature, the concern about the increasing toxicity of the public sphere is not lacking for evidence. Contemporary democracies do indeed appear to be undergoing a profound historical mutation in which the basic norms of public discourse are rapidly breaking down. In addition to the 2017 election of Donald Trump, the elections of populist leaders such as Boris Johnson, Viktor Orban, Giorgia Meloni, Narendra Modi, and Rodrigo Duterte and the rise of nationalist parties and movements like Brexit, Austria's Freedom Party, Alternative for Germany, Brothers of Italy, India's Hindutva movement, and Canada's Freedom Convoy can be seen as a testament to this breakdown. How, then, do we explain this historical shift in contemporary democracies? What are the primary drivers behind the deterioration of the public sphere, the proliferation of trolling into the political realm, and the disturbing growth of reactionary populism and violent demagoguery?

Of the many possible angles for analyzing the acidification of the public sphere, this book focuses on social media, arguably the dominant media of communication today. Social media have come to play a powerful role in shaping our culture, politics, institutions, and social practices. Social media are many and diverse. They make up a dizzying array of platforms. They spark new trends and movements. They shape the way we think and speak. They redefine love and hate. They make and break relationships. They set the terms for much of our social world. They determine, limit, distort, and obstruct how we apprehend social and even physical reality.[6] Social media notably generate new personalities and even new personality disorders.[7] This book is about one such personality. It tells the story of a creature who has emerged from the unique environment made possible by social media, a creature who has grown in power and multiplied in number, and who has become an intimately familiar character on our cultural and political landscape: the troll.

We have been living with trolls for literally decades. We encounter them each time we open Facebook, Twitter, YouTube, and Instagram. We take their presence in our digital lives for granted. We are intimately familiar with their habits, patterns, quirks, and idiosyncrasies. We can spot their antics in real time, their signature tactics for luring unsuspecting users into their noxious and fetid traps. We have become accustomed to warning each other about taking their bait. "Don't feed the trolls," we say. We know all too well their love of the "lulz," their habit of "shitposting," their obsession with semiliterate memes, their penchant for discord, their delight in provoking, mocking, humiliating, and abusing others online. We know their infernal psychology, the "dark tetrad" of narcissism, Machiavellianism, psychopathy, and sadism.[8] We know Trollface, the demonic black and white cartoon image forever seared into our psyches as the transcultural avatar of trolling. We know famous trolls like Andrew "weev" Auernheimer, Milo Yiannapoulos, Alex Jones, Laura Loomer, Andrew Tate, and now Elon Musk. We have even lived through famous historical episodes of mass trolling, including Gamergate, Comicsgate, and the bullying of mass shooting survivors.[9] Trolling has sadly become a familiar part of everyday social life. But what exactly is trolling? How do we demarcate it from other forms of antisocial behavior?

Making Sense of Trolling

How we make sense of trolling depends on whether we examine its beginnings or its origins. These are not the same questions. As Edward Said has insightfully shown, beginnings and origins are very different things.[10] In the realm of human culture, beginnings are active. They denote consciousness. They mark a moment of the will. Beginnings imply personal agency in the course of human history. To ask when and where trolling began is therefore to ask at what point in time and in what medium trolling first became a self-conscious activity and a distinct and recognizable subculture. Origins, by contrast, denote passivity. Origins are the conditions under which something comes into being. Unlike beginnings, origins concern causation—historical forces, social circumstances, chains of events, lines of continuity. To ask how trolling originated is to inquire into the historical, cultural, and economic conditions under which trolling could arise. When it comes to trolling, we are good at asking about beginnings, but not so good at asking about origins.

The Beginnings of Trolling

Media scholars typically trace the beginnings of trolling to Usenet. A portmanteau of "user" and "network," Usenet is a still-extant digital communication system first established in 1980.[11] Usenet was originally conceived as a medium for exchanging information between members of different university campuses. By the late 1980s, Usenet had become a global network and a formidable competitor to postal mail, fax machines, and even telephones. In its heyday, Usenet was known as an "electronic news magazine" and a "world town meeting."[12] The main appeal of Usenet was its newsgroups. Modeled after the ubiquitous corkboards that line the halls of schools, universities, and corporate offices, newsgroups were digital bulletin boards to which users could post messages, announcements, requests, questions, and the like. The key difference between a newsgroup and a corkboard was the reply function. Newsgroups created the endless possibility of exchanging messages. They enabled rich discussions among a global community of users about any topic under the sun—something inconceivable on the physical surface of a humble corkboard. Early users were thrilled to be able to share information with searching minds from around the world. Because of its exhilarating power to facilitate the exchange of information, Usenet was seen as a tool for education and even a medium of grassroots democracy.[13]

But as a digital network, there was a downside to newsgroups. The communities that formed around them were disembodied.[14] Instead of a flesh-and-blood presence, users appeared as a mere screen name, stripped of their facial expressions, vocal cords, intonations, accents, bodily gestures, inadvertent movements, clothing, accessories, hairstyles, and scents—all the subtle and complex elements of face-to-face communication that we so often take for granted. The immaterial presence of a mere username created a problem for identification. How could you really know that the person behind the screen was who they said they were? Newsgroups thrived on an honor system, in which users were expected to present themselves truthfully.[15]

But this honor system was threatened from the start by allowing users to select their own username. The veil of anonymity opened the temptation to deception. You didn't *have* to use your real name. You didn't *have* to be truthful about your A/S/L (age, sex, and location). A young man from Seattle could pretend to be an elderly grandmother from Orlando. The temptation to fabricate one's identity proved to be all too enticing for all too many newsgroup users. If they could hide behind a false persona, then they were no longer bound by the basic social norms and expectations that governed their lives offline. They were free to be someone else. They could speak and behave in ways they ordinarily would not. Together, immateriality and anonymity were an invitation to test social limits and boundaries. Like infants learning to make their way about the world, these newsgroup users explored the contours of the new digital realm by experimentally transgressing social norms. Liberated from the personal repercussions and consequences of life offline, some newsgroup users discovered a sordid pleasure in transgression for its own sake.[16]

Trolls first emerged as social parasites, digital delinquents who abused the collective trust of an online community. By posting manipulative questions and provocative comments as bait, they lured unsuspecting users into arguments and then relished the ensuing flame wars. In essence, these early trolls were pranksters who got a kick out of sowing discord online. Good-faith users dubbed their disruptive behavior "trolling." There are two competing etymologies for this term. According to one, trolling was originally a fishing metaphor, a technique in which a fishing line is pulled back and forth along the edge of a boat in the hopes that some unlucky fish will take the bait.[17] According to another, trolling refers to the unpredictable behavior of the cave-dwelling, club-wielding, and human-devouring monsters of Norse mythology.[18] Regardless of how the term originated, "trolling" fast became the accepted designation for a distinctive form of juvenile and sociopathic behavior online. That behavior later spread to other early online platforms popular in the 1990s, such as Internet Relay Chat, ICQ channels, AOL chat rooms, message boards, and blogs. Trolling underwent a dramatic rebirth in the mid-2000s with the introduction of social media platforms like Facebook, Twitter, YouTube, Instagram, Reddit, and especially 4Chan. Today, trolling thrives on a newer generation of platforms like Rumble, Gab, Telegram, Twitch, Discord, and TikTok. Despite their more sophisticated user interfaces, social media platforms share one basic characteristic with the early Usenet newsgroups: the ability to be faceless and anonymous, and therefore deceptive and manipulative.

Media scholars who have attempted formal definitions of trolling almost always stress the element of anonymity. In her classic account of identity and deception on Usenet newsgroups, Judith Donnath describes trolling as "a game about identity perception, albeit one that is played without the consent of most of the players. The troll attempts to pass as a legitimate participant, sharing the group's common interests and concerns."[19] Trolls thus take advantage of the identity cues implicit in an online community. They specialize in infiltration by wearing the false mask of community membership. As Donnath explains, guardians of online communities learned early on how to identify imposters by looking out for deviations from social cues.

In an anthropological study of the hacktivist group Anonymous, Gabriella Coleman traces the origins of Anonymous to the early trolls of 4chan's notorious /b/ board.[20] Similar to Usenet newsgroups, 4chan is an image-based message board. Instead of posting comments, however, users post images. In the mid-2000s, the /b/ board was infamously dubbed the "asshole of the internet," a space in which anonymous users posted some of the most shocking, disgusting, horrifying, and traumatizing content online. The /b/ board was a space for experimental transgression, provocation, and tasteless humor. What we today know as memes—images from popular media captioned with ironic jokes in big white fonts—originated on /b/. Notably, some of the first orchestrated trolling campaigns were also launched through /b/. It is not an exaggeration to describe /b/ as the onetime global epicenter of trolling, a status overtaken by its far more notorious, vulgar, and lawless successor, 8chan. Based on the antics so distinctive of /b/, Coleman defines trolling as "an activity that seeks to ruin the reputations of individuals and organizations and reveal embarrassing and personal information." Trolls seek to get a rise out of their victims "by spreading grisly or disturbing content, igniting arguments, or by engendering general bedlam."[21] What enables this behavior is anonymity. As Coleman observes, "On 4chan, there is an interplay between the *function* of anonymity (enabling pure competition without the interference of reputation or social capital) and the *effects* of anonymity (the memes, hacks, and acts of trolling) that emerge and have real impact on the world."[22] Only rarely do 4chan users register faithful screen names. Typically, they do not bother with personalized screen names at all. Rather, they go by the default "Anonymous." Hence the name of the eponymous collective.

In what is the most authoritative study of trolling to date, Whitney Phillips describes trolling as a unique and self-conscious subculture. She proposes that we define trolling "according to trolls."[23] Following this approach, Phillips identifies several distinctive characteristics of trolling. First, trolls are driven by the "lulz," the peculiar and perverse form of glee and laughter enjoyed at the expense of others. The "lulz" signify that nothing is sacred, that everything, even the worst forms of human suffering, misery, violence, and tragedy, are potential objects of laughter and derision. Second, trolls target groups with overt moral and political commitments. This includes marginalized communities fighting for equality and dignity: racialized minorities, feminists, and the queer community. It also includes right-wing Christians who suffer from a persecution complex. Both communities betray a vulnerability that makes them prime targets for trolling. Lastly, Phillips emphasizes that trolls revel in anonymity, preying on those who display their real identities. Trolls thus thrive on a fundamental asymmetry between themselves and their victims.[24]

Anonymity is thus a core element in standard scholarly definitions of trolling. Although the standard definition has served us well, we still need to explain the widespread phenomenon of trolling beyond the self-conscious subculture of anonymous trolls. Something has arguably changed about trolling. Defying our familiar picture of the troll as a strictly anonymous online prankster who hides behind a clever avatar and screen name, an entire army of trolls has emerged from the cave, so to speak, and now walks in the clear light of day. This new species of troll has shed the veil of anonymity and no longer fears being named or seen. Trolls now include politicians, performers, patriots, protesters, and professors. What was once an alien, cryptic, and mysterious phenomenon limited to the darker corners of the Internet has since gone mainstream. We are surrounded by trolls, online and offline. Trolls have invaded every aspect of social and political life. They have shaped the way we engage each other in the public sphere and changed the norms of democratic politics. We are now arguably immersed in a new political language game, in which the speech act of trolling has become a normalized part of public discourse.

  How did this come to be? Is the proliferation of trolling into the general culture attributable solely to the effects of digital technology? Or are there deeper historical roots to trolling as a broader cultural phenomenon? This book conceives of trolling as more than a digital subculture limited to social media platforms. It departs from the standard picture by telling a story about origins, the historical conditions that gave rise to this distinctively antisocial mode of communication. By telling a story about origins, this book seeks to reconceive trolling in more expansive terms and acquire a better understanding of its proliferation and variety in the public sphere. Trolling, I will argue, is a logical, if extreme, expression of a widespread cynicism, suspicion, and paranoia deeply rooted in a culture of possessive individualism.[25] Although trolling as we know it was born on digital platforms, the seeds for this sociopathic behavior were sown long before the rise of digital technology. To use a familiar metaphor, technology pulls the trigger, but culture is the gun. This book presents the figure of the troll not as some sort of cultural aberration but rather as the logical expression of a culture that valorizes the sovereign individual. When politicians, including a former president of the United States, become trolls, we urgently require a new understanding of trolling. This book answers that need.

From Television to Social Media

The title of this book is an obvious play on Neil Postman's *Amusing Ourselves to Death: Public Discourse in the Age of Show Business*. In that now-classic book, Postman argued that public discourse had been reshaped in the light of television and its central ideology: entertainment. As Postman took great pains to show, the emergence of entertainment as the reigning ideology of the age had devastating consequences for democracy. Contrary to a common misreading, *Amusing Ourselves to Death* is not a critique of entertainment television. Postman bore no animus against amusement per se. Rather, his critique concerned the extraordinary power of television to redefine serious content—politics, religion, health, education, science—in the light of entertainment. As Postman demonstrated, we have come to expect that topics of great political urgency, such as the economy, foreign policy, and nuclear war, should be presented in entertaining form. Nothing should be so serious, detailed, or complex as to strain a broken attention span nourished on a mental diet of sound bites, commercials, mottos, jingles, and punch lines. The result, Postman argued, was a severe degradation of public discourse: a loosening of our standards of truth and accountability, a disturbing tolerance for logical contradiction and semantic incoherence, a loss of historical memory, a severely warped sense of political judgment, and mass submission to the ideology of entertainment. Postman wrote with great shame and embarrassment for what America had become in the age of television. Would that he had lived to see what America would become in the age of social media.

It has been almost forty years since the publication of *Amusing Ourselves to Death*. Although dated in many obvious respects, it remains a remarkably relevant book. It is impossible to read Postman's description of the effects of television on public discourse and not see the striking parallels with social media. Cultural and political commentators have similarly looked back upon *Amusing Ourselves to Death* with understandable amazement over its prescient insights.[26] In his eerie and unforgettable prologue, Postman drew our attention to a crucial but overlooked difference between the two most influential dystopian visions of the future: George Orwell's *1984* and Aldous Huxley's *Brave New World*. As Postman wrote:

> What Orwell feared were those who would ban books. What Huxley feared was that there would be no reason to ban a book, for there would be no one who wanted to read one. Orwell feared those who would deprive us of information. Huxley feared those who would give us so much that we would be reduced to passivity and egoism. Orwell feared that the truth would be concealed from us. Huxley feared the truth would be drowned out in a sea of irrelevance. Orwell feared we would become a captive culture. Huxley feared we would become a trivial culture. . . . This book is about the possibility that Huxley, not Orwell, was right.[27]

With the election of a former host of *The Apprentice* to the most powerful office on earth, it is tempting to conclude that Huxley was indeed right—that we have entered a more extreme version of the beguiled and benumbed world that Postman described in 1985. Yet any such assessment is complicated by the prevailing mood of the day. In a world of viral outrage, Twitter feuds, Facebook fights, Zoom gloom, anti-vaccine protests, and mass shootings, would we really describe our mood as one of amusement? Although we enjoy the new forms of cheeky and ironic humor so distinctive of TikTok and Instagram, would we really say that we are amusing ourselves to death?

There is some reason to reject parts of Huxley's dystopian vision. *Brave New World* depicts a totalitarian society whose inhabitants are perpetually narcotized by soma, the "ideal pleasure drug" that has "all the advantages of Christianity and alcohol" but "none of their defects."[28] Soma is an apt metaphor for the stupefying effects of mass media and popular culture. To be fair, we do enjoy binge-watching our favorite TV shows on Netflix, Amazon Prime, and Apple TV, whose soma-like powers leave us tranquilized and spellbound for hours on end. But we are also in the habit of doom-scrolling before bed, looking for news of the next fresh hell: the latest political outrage, another COVID wave, the latest mass shooting, another climate catastrophe. We are more addicted to our smartphone screens today than we were to our television screens in 1985. Yet the effect of smartphone screens isn't that of an opiate but rather that of an amphetamine, one that induces anxiety, aggression, paranoia, and psychosis. *Brave New World* seems more applicable to the television society of 1985 than to the social media society of 2023.

And what are we to make of the nightmarish world that Orwell envisioned in *1984*? Is it possible that it was Orwell, and not Huxley, who was right? Unlike *Brave New World*, *1984* depicts a totalitarian society whose wretched masses are subjugated by fear. The citizens of Oceania are conditioned to respond reliably to state power and control like the dogs of Ivan Pavlov's experiments. Each day, the citizens of Oceania attend Two Minutes Hate, a public assembly in which they are whipped into a terrifying outburst of mass rage at an imaginary enemy:

> The horrible thing about the Two Minutes Hate was not that one was obliged to act a part, but that it was impossible to avoid joining in. Within thirty seconds any pretence was always unnecessary. A hideous ecstasy of fear and vindictiveness, a desire to kill, to torture, to smash faces in with a sledge hammer, seemed to flow through the whole group of people like an electric current, turning one even against one's will into a grimacing, screaming lunatic. And yet the rage that one felt was an abstract, undirected emotion which could be switched from one object to another like the flame of a blowlamp.[29]

To be fair, Postman didn't witness anything like Two Minutes Hate in the years leading up to 1985. But for four years, we witnessed public spectacles very much like Two Minutes Hate—ritualized, all-American hate fests, in which Donald Trump repeatedly drove his supporters at campaign rallies into an irrational frenzy by reciting a long list of imaginary grievances, leaving them chanting hateful absurdities like "Lock her up!"[30] We now have real-life versions of doublespeak in the form of "fake news" and "alternative facts."[31]

But whether Huxley or Orwell got it right is beside the point. Our present historical moment is a mixture of the most disturbing elements of both dystopian visions. What matters now is to make sense of this moment with the help of Postman's insights. This book is premised on the claim that we have undergone a second transformation in our public discourse: the rise of social media has once again changed the terms on which we communicate in the public sphere—and once again for the worse. In the spirit of Postman's prescient analysis, it is necessary to apply his framework to our current media ecosystem. That task, however, requires coming to terms with a critical limitation of that framework. For all of Postman's strikingly accurate insights, it needs in fairness to be noted that something crucial is missing from *Amusing Ourselves to Death*—namely, a historical understanding of how our reigning economic ideology has shaped our practices of communication and warped our sense of self.

Communication Under Capital

This book synthesizes Postman's insights with those of another cultural critic: Alasdair MacIntyre. A prominent figure in the 1960s British New Left, MacIntyre is one of the most important political theorists of the last half century. Although MacIntyre is not a household name in media studies, his analyses of moral language under capitalism complement Postman's analysis of public discourse under television. In his classic work *After Virtue: A Study in Moral Theory*, MacIntyre diagnosed a crisis of communication in modern democracies. He observed that public discourse had become fragmented and disordered. Public reasoning had come to follow a hopelessly circular pattern of assertion and counterassertion. Interlocutors in public debate, he noticed, became uneasy when pressed to justify their moral standpoints, and tended to veer into loud, sanctimonious, and defensive speech. At some point, democratic citizens were no longer talking to each other but seeking to unmask and expose each other's ulterior motives.

The root of this impasse, MacIntyre argued, was the absence of a shared morality and moral language. As he observed, we each speak in our preferred moral idiom. We each invoke our preferred moral premises. But we lack a shared framework for public moral reasoning. Our culture has therefore become deadlocked in intractable disagreement. MacIntyre argued that this deadlock would only intensify with time. He warned of the "coming ages of barbarism and darkness" and urged us to construct "new forms of community" so that "both morality and civility might survive."[32] MacIntyre presented a dire reading of the state of modern democracies. Looking back upon his argument some forty years later, it would not be an exaggeration to say that MacIntyre predicted our current political chaos with surprising accuracy.[33]

This book suggests that we can make better sense of the rise and proliferation of political trolling by incorporating MacIntyre's analysis of ethics and language under capital. Writing in the tradition of Georg Wilhelm Friedrich Hegel, MacIntyre tells an original and provocative story about the degeneration of public discourse. That story is notably the opposite of Hegel's own story about the development of *Geist*, a term that can be translated as both "spirit" and "mind."[34] According to Hegel, reason unfolds, or develops, over the course of history. It does so not unlike a seedling that develops into a tree. Reason, on this view, becomes more self-aware with time. Just as a seedling strives to flourish, reason strives to grow and be free. Reason and freedom are of a piece. The growth of the one is coterminous with the growth of the other. The endpoint can be succinctly described as the full realization of freedom through absolute reason.[35]

When MacIntyre writes about the degeneration of public discourse, he, too, tells a story that proceeds in historical stages. But this story is the opposite of the one that Hegel tells about reason. MacIntyre's story is one not of development but of decline, not of growth but of decay. It is the story of the unfolding not of reason but of unreason, a process of putrefaction that ends in the collapse of communication. Our present historical moment—the plague of trolling, the loss of trust, the epidemic of paranoia and antisocial hostility, the deterioration of public reasoning, the mass contempt for truth, the spread of conspiracy theory—can be seen as the fulfillment of MacIntyre's dark and foreboding warning forty years ago.

When read together, Postman and MacIntyre emerge as surprisingly complementary thinkers. They help us understand the degeneration of public discourse. Postman attributes that degeneration to our technologies of communication. MacIntyre attributes it to the language, values, and ideology of liberal capitalism. Although they come from very different vantage points, Postman and MacIntyre nonetheless describe one and the same phenomenon. In fact, their descriptions are strikingly similar. In some sense, each represents the blind spot of the other. Because of his exclusive focus on technology, Postman underestimates the role of possessive individualism in feeding the fragmentation and disorder of our public discourse. Similarly, because of his exclusive focus on ethics, MacIntyre lacks an appreciation for the role of communication technologies in feeding that same fragmentation and disorder.

When read together, however, Postman and MacIntyre tell a more compelling story than either of them could tell alone. This is a story about the emergence not of *Geist* but of *Ungeist*, not of Spirit but of Demon. This is not a literal demon, of course. In German, *der Ungeist* translates as both "demon" and "unreason." In the context of this book, *der Ungeist* can be understood as the collective unconscious of a growing culture of irrationalism: the rabid, sordid, and twisted psyche of the troll; the hivemind of neofascists, white nationalists, QAnon conspiracy theorists, and the Boogaloo Bois; the mass delusion of anti-maskers, anti-vaxxers, and climate change deniers; and the mania of gun-toting, flag-waving, and Bible-wielding proponents of "liberty" and "freedom." *Der Ungeist* is the monster that Trump awakened and actively fed for four straight years. It's the monster that will survive long after he recedes into political oblivion.

The Approach of This Book

This book follows Fredric Jameson's oft-cited dictum: "Always historicize!"[36] It narrates the *longue durée* of the phenomenon of trolling. It seeks to understand trolling as more than a mere digital subculture by placing it within a larger historical materialist frame. A primary focus of this book is the doctrine of liberal individualism, the moral core of a free market society. Liberal individualism is a philosophy of social division. It is not an abstract value floating in the ether. Rather, the logos and ethos of liberal individualism are materially encoded into our dominant modes and relations of production, our laws and institutions, our political language and rhetoric, and our technologies of communication, often in vague, subtle, and implicit ways. By historicizing trolling, this book shows how our most popular social media platforms are the technological embodiments and expressions of the antisocial values of market competition and the quest for individual capital. Digital technology merely unleashes corrosive instincts and impulses that have long been encouraged and fortified under the economic logic of private gain. By situating trolling within an expansive frame, we can recognize the historical emergence of ur-trolls who crafted an abusive rhetorical style well before the age of social media. A larger historical context can therefore help us understand the phenomenon of deanonymized political trolling today. We can see why political trolling has become so prevalent, extreme, hateful, sadistic, and violent. Perhaps most importantly, we can better understand the disturbing popularity of conspiracy theory, the assault on truth, the resurgence of demagoguery, and the rapid proliferation of neofascist movements, all of which are today bound by the common thread of trolling.

Chapter Breakdown

In Chapter 1, I build upon *Amusing Ourselves to Death* to explain how and why we are trolling ourselves to death. Just as Postman argued that television brought about a fundamental transformation in public discourse by elevating entertainment to the status of a supreme ideology, I argue that social media have brought about a second transformation by normalizing the speech act of trolling in public discourse. No technological medium is ideologically neutral. To put a twist on one of Marx's famous precepts, it is not our consciousness that determines our social media use but, on the contrary, our social media use that determines our consciousness.[37] Because of their interface design, social media devalue the norm of truth and effectively reduce public discourse to a popularity contest. If television turned politics into show business, then social media have arguably turned it into a giant high school, with a familiar cast of characters to boot: cool kids, losers, cheerleaders, and bullies. This explains the social media popularity of Donald Trump and Elon Musk, whose immature personalities fit squarely within the juvenile moral universe of social media.

In Chapter 2, I situate trolling in a metahistorical and metaethical context. I explore MacIntyre's thesis that public discourse today is "in a grave state of disorder" and his description of the public sphere as an arena of interminable and acrimonious moral conflict.[38] MacIntyre traces this interminability and acrimony to the failure of the Enlightenment to formulate a secular foundation for morality. In theory, morality is a medium of human relationships. It provides impersonal standards for negotiating moral conflict and disagreement. Without such standards, however, our relationships are liable to become instrumental and manipulative. The chapter discusses moral order in the premodern world and moral theory during the Enlightenment. The two key paradigms discussed are those of David Hume (the passions) and Immanuel Kant (transcendental reason). I then discuss MacIntyre's explanation for why Enlightenment moral theory failed and what took its place: capitalist individualism and the ethic of moral instrumentalism. As I argue, this is where the seeds for political trolling lie.

In Chapter 3, I explore the historical and ideological link between conservatism as a political tradition and the contemporary phenomenon of right-wing trolls. "Moderate" conservatives like David Frum, George Will, and Rick Wilson have adamantly insisted that Donald Trump and his army of trolls are not true conservatives, that they are a grotesque deviation from the spirit of conservatism. In this chapter, I show why this argument is false and misleading. Revisiting some of the key ideas in the political thought of Edmund Burke, widely regarded as the founder of the conservative tradition, I argue that political conservatism is congenitally oriented toward political trolling. Burke celebrates "veils," "illusions," "prejudice," and "ignorance" as the core components of "tradition." These components are precisely what animate conservative political trolls today. I look at the examples of two of the most toxic media personalities in recent memory: Rush Limbaugh and Ann Coulter. As I argue, Limbaugh and Coulter were early trolls, specializing in the political art of shocking and offending the liberal enemy. Limbaugh and Coulter were "trolling the libs" before "trolling the libs" became an everyday feature of life on social media.

Chapter 4 seeks to make sense of the explosion of conspiracy theory in the digital age. The opening case study concerns COVID-19 conspiracy theories, which have resulted in the abuse of, and even death threats against, healthcare workers and scientists. COVID-19 conspiracy theories pose a twofold problem for public health: combatting disinformation and understanding its underlying motivation. One common view maintains that we can effectively combat medical disinformation by educating the public. Against this view, I argue that the popularity of conspiracy theory reflects not public ignorance but rather distrust. The loss of trust is one of the symptoms of a culture of widespread alienation, atomization, loneliness, cynicism, and paranoia. I explore the relationship between the political emotion of loneliness and the fragmentation of the self. The power of conspiracy theory, I argue, is that it enables the alienated and fragmented subject to achieve a sense of wholeness once again, but only by severing the subject's relationship to reality.

Chapter 5 explores the phenomenon of "cancel culture," the scourge of conservatives, liberals, and leftists alike. Much of our popular commentary on this curious practice has focused too narrowly on free speech and the excesses of so-called social justice warriors. The problem with this extremely myopic focus is that it falsely construes the act of canceling as a predominantly or exclusively left-wing phenomenon, failing to appreciate how the very design of digital platforms creates the conditions for intolerant communities and encourages sanctimonious and uncompromising judgment toward alleged wrongdoers. This chapter therefore offers a different perspective on the entire phenomenon by drawing from Friedrich Nietzsche's historical analysis of the link between guilt and debt. I argue that social networks are predicated upon debt, the debt that comes from relying upon a social network for one's digital existence. With debt comes the possibility of guilt and punishment through the ritual of online shaming. Drawing from Michel Foucault's history of the prison and Martha Nussbaum's philosophical analysis of shame and humiliation, I argue that online shaming is best understood as a return to premodern spectacles of public torture.

In Chapter 6, I take up the question of how we might confront the problem of trolling. I first revisit the conclusions of *Amusing Ourselves to Death* and *After Virtue*, respectively. Postman makes a desperate plea for turning to public schools as a mass medium for teaching television literacy and resisting the ideology of entertainment. MacIntyre calls for building local forms of community to resist the corrosive influence of liberal individualism upon our public reasoning. In this chapter, I synthesize their complementary pleas. Taking inspiration from Robert Brandom's innovative reading of Hegel's *The Phenomenology of Spirit*, I make a case for building a "spirit of trust" to counter the culture of mass distrust that feeds the problem of political trolling. I further draw from Paulo Freire and bell hooks to propose what I call a pedagogy of trust. As I argue, classrooms can play a powerful role in countering the epidemic of distrust that lies at the heart of political trolling.

In the conclusion, I offer some reflections on where we appear to be heading. I discuss the decline of Facebook, the chaos of Twitter under Elon Musk, and the persistence of trolling in both its original and political forms. Whatever we might say of our rapidly evolving social media ecosystem, we can say with certainty that political trolling will continue to pose a serious danger to the culture of democracy.

A Final Note

As any media scholar will attest, writing about social media is no enviable task. It demands that we strike a critical balance between a journalistic focus upon the endlessly quirky and bewildering details of the platforms and a scholarly focus upon overarching historical and cultural patterns. Because our media ecosystem is constantly changing, it has proven to be enormously challenging to pinpoint those overarching patterns with any degree of precision. In the time it took to conceive and write this book, our social media landscape has changed dramatically. Facebook appears to be dying, while Twitter has plunged into disarray. These changes have led media scholar Ian Bogost to declare that the age of social media is coming to an end.[39] Whether we are really witnessing the beginning of the end of social media is unclear. What is clear is that our public discourse is becoming more violent by the day. My hope is that this book will offer some worthwhile and lasting insight into why that should be the case.

1

Technology

In July 2017, the *New York Times* took on the seemingly impossible task of counting the lies of Donald Trump. To make this task manageable, it counted all the lies over the course of his first six months in office. The *Times* arrived at a grand total of one hundred lies. That number would have been far higher had they included in their count such categories as "dubious statements" and "careless errors," categories that might well have made their task effectively impossible.[1] By January 2021, that number had reached over thirty thousand.[2] It is difficult to imagine a more bizarre and depressing job than counting the lies of the most powerful figure on earth, a man commonly labeled a pathological liar. For those who could not turn away, the sheer number, rapidity, and vileness of the man's lies ambushed the mind like a rapid-fire assault weapon. The lies had left us numb. We had grown accustomed, passive, and helpless before them. We fully expected the lies as surely as we expected the sun to rise and fall. Indeed, we would have been shocked and disoriented if Trump had ever told the truth.

Although Trump was defeated in the 2020 general election, the damage he left behind remains. How, then, did we get here? How did we arrive in a twilight zone in which the norms of public discourse have broken down, an alternate universe in which brazen lies and grotesque spectacles of immaturity, incivility, and obnoxiousness have become the new normal? There are at least two ways of framing this problem. One is to focus on *the media*—that is, on journalism. This way of framing the problem sees fake news as the primary culprit. If only we could find some way of keeping fake news in check, this way of thinking goes, we could restore some order and rationality to our public discourse.[3] Presumably, then, the answer lies in more aggressive fact-checking on the part of traditional journalism and greater media literacy on the part of the public.

A second way of framing the problem is to focus on *media*—that is, on technologies of communication. This way of framing the problem regards the dominant media of the age, not their content, as the primary culprit. According to this second way of thinking, if only we could understand how our dominant media

Trolling Ourselves to Death. Jason Hannan, Oxford University Press. © Oxford University Press 2023.
DOI: 10.1093/oso/9780197557761.003.0002

shape not just their content but the entire affective structure of public discourse, we might come to appreciate the nature and severity of our present chaos.[4] Both ways of framing the problem have their respective merits. But between *the media* and *media*, which, if either, can be said to be the driver behind our post-truth world?[5] This chapter follows the latter framework, locating the problem of post-truth politics in social media, arguably the dominant media of our age. It seeks to make sense of the way that truth operates on popular social media platforms like Facebook, Twitter, Instagram, and YouTube. It argues that the logic of public discourse has been restructured in the light of social media. This chapter further suggests that trolling has gone mainstream, shaping politics and even legislation. Adding a twist to Neil Postman's classic thesis, I argue that we are not so much amusing as trolling ourselves to death.

Background: Postman on Television and Public Discourse

In *Amusing Ourselves to Death: Public Discourse in the Age of Show Business*, Postman argued that television had severely degraded the quality of public discourse. The ascendance of television to the status of the preeminent medium of the age had the effect of recreating public discourse in the image of television. In doing so, it turned democracy into entertainment, thereby heaping farce upon tragedy. Postman turned to Marshall McLuhan, who, in *Understanding Media: The Extensions of Man*, argued that the key to understanding a culture lies in its dominant media and that the study of media *forms* is more profitable than the study of media *content*.[6] According to McLuhan, the form communicates more than the content, the latter being of negligible significance to the meaning of the overall message. Hence, McLuhan's provocative and familiar aphorism: "The medium is the message."[7] Postman took up this classic insight to make sense of contemporary public discourse. He argued that the form of television (i.e., entertainment) negated the seriousness of its ostensibly serious content, such as news and political debates. To appreciate this provocative thesis, it is necessary to review a critical distinction that lies at the heart of Postman's analysis.

Television, as Postman pointed out, can be understood in one of two ways. It can be understood as a technology, a device for the transmission of moving images through a screen.[8] It can also be understood as a medium, the culturally defined purpose to which the technology is put. To help explain the difference between a technology and a medium, Postman drew a distinction between brains and minds. The first is an anatomical concept, the latter a cultural one. How the mind is understood will vary from culture to culture. Similarly, how television is understood will vary from culture to culture. In the United States, the country with which Postman was principally concerned, television serves to amuse and entertain. To understand a medium, he said, it is necessary to understand the type of discourse it promotes. The discourse promoted by television is different from that promoted by books. Television promotes a discourse of dazzling and enchanting visual content, which takes little time and even less mental energy to process. The fragments of information, the fleeting images, and the rapid transition from one bit of data to the next are conducive not to deep, critical, and challenging reflection but rather to its opposite—to shallow, uncritical, and unchallenging mental preoccupation. Television discourse is a contest not of ideas but of visually induced sensations. Entertainment, in this sense, is not laughter per se; it is any sensation that can be excited through passivity and minimal thought.

Postman's concern was not that television is entertaining but rather that public discourse had been reinvented in the light of television. Every subject of public discourse, including politics, religion, health, and science, had been converted into a form of entertainment. To compete for the public's increasingly short and fragmented attention span, it was necessary to conform to the medium to which those attention spans are most accustomed—television. For this reason, Postman claimed that entertainment had become the "supra-ideology" of all discourse, the invisible ground on which public reasoning was conducted.[9] The effect of this conformity to television was that we came to treat public discourse much like the way we treat television, as something that requires minimal effort to grasp, that must be presented in an entertaining format if it is to be given the time of day, and that can be switched off and disregarded as it suits us.

By way of illustration, Postman described an eighty-minute debate on ABC in 1983 on the topic of nuclear war, featuring such prominent figures as Henry Kissinger, Robert McNamara, Elie Wiesel, Carl Sagan, William F. Buckley, and Brent Scowcroft, each of whom had a reputation for being a serious (as opposed to entertaining) intellectual figure, someone whose *ideas* actually mattered. Yet, as Postman observed, the debate was remarkable for its lack of substance and depth. Each guest was given only a few minutes to answer questions about some really quite grave matter, forcing them to offer superficial comments that failed to do justice to their subject matter. The result was something other than a debate: a fast-paced roller coaster of disjointed comments that followed no conceivable order. Postman added that the problem of extreme time constraints was only further compounded by an intolerance on the part of the show for the very act of thinking itself. Serious thought, as he took great pains to show in his account of the Age of Typography, is slow and methodical.[10]

Television discourse, by contrast, is fast and chaotic. The key attraction of a television debate is not thought but excitement, which must be maintained at all costs, including at the cost of the very act of thought itself. From the stand-point of a television producer, slow and methodical thinking is not just a mood killer but also a ratings killer. Television debates are therefore theatrical arenas for the *performance* of thinking, not the actual act of thinking itself. The drama of discussion sells, and the more superficial and meaningless the discussion, the better. Postman found an extreme version of this kind of empty and superficial discussion in the public debates between presidential candidates, debates that barely conceal their intention to entertain and amuse and which more closely resemble a boxing match than a serious discussion. The highlight of a televised presidential debate is not principled agreement or even principled disagreement but rather a dramatic, knockdown one-liner that leaves the opponent bloodied and defeated.[11]

In his description of the "Now . . . this" phenomenon, the magical words that newscasters routinely recite to signal a break for commercials, Postman observed how the transition from one topic to the next had the effect of trivializing all topics.[12] Each instance of "Now . . . this" simultaneously carries the viewer to the next topic while severing the connection with the last. "Now . . . this" creates the impression of continuity while dividing content into discontinuous, self-contained moments that vanish from memory with the power of two words. The consequences of "Now . . . this" for truth lie in what passes for credibility on television. In a "Now . . . this" mental universe, which shuns serious thought and erases mental content as fast as it produces it, credibility becomes a matter of performance. The newscaster, the politician, and the talk show host must all appear sincere, authentic, and likeable to be taken seriously. The content of their words matters less than the likeability of their personalities. The more likeable the personality, the more likely they will be believed. In a "Now . . . this" universe, truth is determined by whether you might like to sit down and have a beer with someone.

While books create the expectation of continuity of tone, subject matter, and logic, repeated instances of "Now . . . this" dissolve that expectation altogether, normalizing discontinuity and fragmentation instead. The effects of such discontinuity and fragmentation on public discourse are severe. In one of his most prophetic observations, Postman wrote, "I should go so far as to say that embedded in the surrealistic frame of a television news show is a theory of anti-communication, featuring a type of discourse that abandons logic, reason, sequence, and rules of contradiction."[13] Postman observed that the more Americans watch television news, the more misinformed they become about the world, leading him to suggest that what television news disseminates is not information but disinformation. The force of "Now . . . this" to sever the connection from one moment to the next, to change the mental frame from matters grave to matters silly in a few seconds, fosters a worldview in which "contradiction is useless as a test of truth or merit, because contradiction no longer exists."[14] This, Postman believed, explains why Ronald Reagan's innumerable misstatements and contradictions did little to unsettle the American public. Americans had, apparently, been rendered insensitive to contradiction.[15] The internalization of a "Now . . . this" worldview is the beginning of what we today, extrapolating from Postman's analysis, might call our post-truth world.

From Television to Social Media

If we apply Postman's insights into television in the hopes of making sense of public discourse today, then it is necessary to develop his analysis in light of the new dominant media of the age. Television arguably no longer exclusively holds that status. Rather, social media have become a powerful competitor. Just as we should draw a distinction between television as a technology and television as a medium, we would be wise to do the same for social media. That is, we should ask what purpose social media serve and what type of discourse they create. If television turned politics into show business, then social media might be said to have turned it into a giant high school, replete with cool kids, cheerleaders, losers, and bullies. The metaphor of high school for politics and public discourse is all the more fitting given the origins of Facebook, the paradigmatic social medium, as an interactive digital student directory akin to a high school yearbook. The logic of social media can best be illustrated by the presidencies of Barack Obama and Donald Trump. Both are very much social media presidencies. Yet they tell two very different stories.

Barack Obama was not just America's first Black president. He was also America's first social media president. Obama's candidacy in 2008 set itself apart from the competition by its robust social media presence. His communications team created a social networking system on his campaign website, enabling a powerful grassroots movement to develop in support of his candidacy. Supporters made use of this network to hold local meetings, organize canvassing projects, and conduct outreach campaigns. Obama was also an incredibly popular figure on Facebook and YouTube, and later on Twitter and Instagram, quickly building a formidable following in the tens of millions.[16]

But it was not just Obama's presence on social media that ensured his victory. His political messaging and image branding very much reflected the world of social media. Obama was keen to share his tastes in popular music and television shows. He shared photos of himself in everyday settings. He demonstrated his command of hipster humor and irony, poking fun at himself and never taking himself too seriously. His amiable personality boosted his appeal among the then-young audience of Facebook users. His interviews and speeches were peppered with memorable, witty lines that were easily disseminated on YouTube. His friendships with numerous celebrities, including Beyoncé, Jay-Z, Bruce Springsteen, Ellen DeGeneres, and Oprah Winfrey, demonstrated his unprecedented cool factor. He appeared on *The Daily Show with Jon Stewart*, once a rite of passage for any candidate hoping to establish their credibility with the new generation of young voters. Obama was not an ordinary political candidate. Voting for Obama was like voting for class president, a candidate whose sheer coolness and hipness certified his political ethos. Indeed, Obama's coolness was his credibility. It mattered more than the actual substance of his political platform. His coolness was the "truth" behind his words.[17]

Obama's stunning victory established new rules for democratic politics. He demonstrated that politicians could no longer be the dry, boring, and humorless personalities of the past. Rather, they had to exhibit qualities that would enable them to stand out constantly on social media. They had, in effect, to reinvent themselves as cool kids. Obama's success on social media, however, turned out to be a curse for his party. His fellow Democrats wrongly assumed that social media were the terrain of a younger generation of liberal hipsters, fluent in irony, memes, hashtags, acronyms, grumpy cats, filtered pictures of chai lattes, and an ever-growing urban dictionary of cyber words and phrases, all the while assuming that conservatives were a largely clueless generation of technologically challenged old people scarcely able to make sense of the bright, colorful, and exotic world of "Facebooks," "Twitters," and "Snapchats." Those fellow Democrats could not have been more wrong.

Reversal of the Culture Wars

What Obama's Democratic colleagues failed to recognize was the rise of what was then known as the alt-right, a new generation of conservatives equally as cyber-savvy as their liberal counterparts but whose politics were driven by a burning, insatiable rebellion against liberal orthodoxy. We have seen a reversal in the popular narrative of the culture wars: the cultural rebels of yesterday are now said to be the mainstream, while conservatives have become the new rebels.[18] The alt-right grew out of the subversive culture of 4chan, the obscure image board on which anonymous users freely post images, no matter how graphic, vulgar, and offensive. The anonymity of 4chan early on fostered a spirit of rebellion against authority. What we today know as memes originated on 4chan. Anonymous, the anarchist-hacktivist collective known for its distributed denial of service (DDoS) attacks on government websites, also originated on 4chan. But the same spirit of rebellion that gave birth to Anonymous also gave birth to the alt-right, which formed in reaction to feminist critiques of video games and gamer culture.[19] One of the most vocal supporters of the Gamergate movement was Milo Yiannopoulos, who was to become the most prominent face of the alt-right.

It is not for nothing that Yiannopoulos, a self-identified and quite proud troll, led the new generation of conservative rebels in support of Donald Trump, in whom they saw the most effective and consistent force against the liberal tyranny of political correctness. The rest of the 2016 Republican field was just too tame, too civil, and too submissive before the enemy to warrant their allegiance. Donald Trump, however, was the real deal: a man whose irreverence and absolute lack of principle made him the perfect instrument against the liberal enemy.

The Dark Side of Social Media

If Facebook is a high school popularity contest, then Twitter is a schoolyard run by bullies. Twitter is the medium in which both Yiannopoulos and Trump honed their craft as trolls. Although originally designed as a social tool, Twitter has since devolved into an antisocial hellscape.[20] The 280-character limit, even with endless threads, is hardly conducive to civil disagreement. It does, however, lend itself to reactionary and paranoid behavior: vicious insults that seek to hurt and offend, to get under another's skin, to find their weak spot and then to stick the knife in and violently twist it to exact the maximum degree of psychological pain. Twitter has a unique way of bringing out its users' inner sadists. It is difficult not to get pulled into the black hole of Twitter trolling. Even the most dignified users will feel tempted to respond to vicious personal attacks. Twitter wars have become a type of media spectacle in themselves, worthy of full-blown news coverage, often with headlines like ". . . and Twitter Lets [him/her/them] Have It."[21]

If we take high school as a metaphor for contemporary politics, then we need to confront the dark side of this metaphor. If Obama represents the class president, then Donald Trump represents the high school bully. Trump epitomizes the dark side of social media, their capacity to be used as a tool for harassment and abuse. It is no secret that Trump was the inspiration for a fictional high school bully, Biff Tannen from Back to the Future Part II.[22] Like Tannen, Trump is a petty, deeply insecure, hypersensitive, and impulsive narcissist obsessed with being loved, admired, and worshipped by everyone around him. Everything Trump says and does revolves around his narcissism, his constant, desperate need to feed his ego through exaggerated praise. Just as he is perfectly willing to live on a mental diet of lies and wild exaggerations, he is even more willing to disseminate lies about his "enemies," anyone who threatens his extremely fragile and sensitive ego. In addition to his attacks on fellow politicians, including those who are no longer in office, Trump has viciously attacked journalists, musicians, late night comedians, athletes, union leaders, the European Union, and even private citizens. That such a volatile and unstable personality was able to thrive on social media reveals something disturbing about social media: it is a breeding ground for trolls, maladjusted sociopaths who find psychological nourishment in the abuse of others. Despite Trump's stint as the host of *The Apprentice*, his electoral victory in 2016 is perhaps the starkest lesson that show business is no longer the appropriate metaphor for politics and public discourse. Rather, the schoolyard and the figure of the bully are far more appropriate metaphors.

Trolling: From Obscure to Mainstream

Trolling first emerged in the darker corners of the internet. It was epitomized by anonymous users in newsgroups and the comments section of blogs, where certain users would leave deliberately cruel and callous comments that served no purpose other than to hurt, shock, offend, and sow discord. The protection of anonymity offered the benefit of unaccountability. From behind the veil of a fake profile, anonymous users were free to unleash the worst possible instincts: irrational hatred, racism, misogyny, homophobia, transphobia, Islamophobia, and the like. Anonymity brought out their inner sadists—repressed monsters who delighted in watching others suffer under relentless psychological abuse. Trolls operated both alone and in packs, on the prowl, seeking prey, waiting in the shadows for unsuspecting victims, and then moving in for the kill at just the right moment.

But what began as an anonymous practice has since become so normalized that anonymity is no longer a necessary condition of possibility. Trolling is now an open practice, in which many trolls no longer bother hiding behind fake names and fake pictures, feeling ever more confident about making abusive comments against people they know and do not know alike. The atmosphere of social media has become so poisoned by incivility that trolling can rightly be said to be the new normal, as regular to our political atmosphere as the air we breathe. It is a tense environment in which disagreements, even between friends, quickly descend into vicious battles, very often destroying those friendships in the process.

Disagreements on social media reveal a curious epistemology embedded within their design. Popularity now competes with logic and evidence as an arbiter of truth. In a discursive economy in which the basic unit of currency is a status update, popularity often carries more persuasive power than the appeal to impersonal fact. Indeed, being too factual, too thorough and meticulous, in a disagreement on social media is a recipe for "tl;dr" ("too long; didn't read").

Lengthy, detailed disquisitions do not fare very well against short, biting sarcasm. They also do not fare well against comments that, however inane, rack up a far greater number of likes, hearts, and shares. In the mental universe of social media, truth is a popularity contest. And if a troll amasses a substantial following, that popularity can be put to malicious ends, including pushing falsehood as truth and responding to criticism with merciless abuse.

Trolling is also no longer confined to everyday citizens. It has become a mainstream political practice. Politicians now routinely troll each other online. Citizens troll politicians, and politicians increasingly troll them back.[23] Trolling as a new genre of political speech has become so common that new norms and expectations have quickly developed around it. Political trolling has become a media spectacle, worthy of full-blown news coverage. Media commentators now distinguish better trolling from worse trolling. Partisan news sources celebrate with glee when their preferred politician "expertly trolls" a rival politician.[24] Trolling is no longer seen as a necessarily bad thing. In a deeply divided and highly toxic political atmosphere, trolling is all well and good if the troll belongs to "our" side. Although this new discursive environment is not entirely chaotic, it is nonetheless a race to the bottom. The one common denominator in all of this angry white noise is the logic of the insult: whoever insults hardest wins.

Government by Trolling

Trolling has become normalized through the rise of a disturbing new practice: government by trolling.[25] In the United States, it is becoming more common for Republican and Democratic lawmakers to propose legislation that serves no purpose other than to troll the other side. So-called satirical bills, which were never expected to pass, have been dressed up as though they had some noble, principled intention behind them—to enlighten the other side through biting wit. In 2012, a Republican member of the Alaska House of Representatives, Kyle Johansen, proposed a bill to declare New York City's Central Park "a wilderness area and to prohibit any further improvement or development of Central Park unless authorized by an Act of Congress." Johansen's bill was intended to mock very serious efforts to prevent oil drilling in Alaska's Arctic National Wildlife Refuge.[26] Shortly thereafter, members of Wyoming's state legislature proposed a similar bill with the same wording.[27] This satirical bill was proposed in solidarity with Johansen's bill.

Also in 2012, Steven Holland, a Democratic member of the Mississippi House of Representatives, proposed a bill that would officially rename the Gulf of Mexico the "Gulf of America," a move intended to mock his Republican colleagues for their hostility to everyone and everything Mexican in the state of

Mississippi.[28] That year, too, Oklahoma state senator Constance Johnson proposed an amendment to Oklahoma's so-called Personhood Bill, which reads,
"Any action in which a man ejaculates or otherwise deposits semen anywhere
but in a woman's vagina shall be interpreted and construed as an action against
an unborn child." The "Every Sperm Is Sacred Amendment" was designed to
mock attempts by Republican lawmakers to police women's bodies through
regressive abortion legislation.[29] In a similar spirit, Virginia state senator Janet
Howell proposed an amendment to an anti-abortion bill that required women
to be subjected to a sonogram before undergoing an abortion. Howell's amendment would have required men to be subjected to a rectal exam before being pre-
scribed medication for erectile dysfunction.[30] Again in the same spirit, Yasmin
Neal, a Democratic member of the Georgia House of Representatives, proposed
a bill that would seek to limit vasectomies, because of which, she said, "thousands of children are deprived of birth"; Neal's bill would have limited the procedure to life-threatening circumstances.[31] In 2017, Jessica Farrar, a Democratic
member of the Texas House of Representatives, proposed a bill fining men $100
for masturbation, deeming it an "act against an unborn child."[32] Satirical bills
have rightly been designated as a form of trolling.[33] However clever, biting, and
imaginative, legislative trolling signals a breakdown in the deliberative process
and an increasing sense of frustration, impatience, and exasperation between
lawmakers. In this respect, they appear to be mimicking the communication
breakdown on social media.

Social Media and Right-Wing Populism

Because social media feed a hyperemotional environment of visceral reactions
and paranoid instincts, they encourage the psychology of reactionary right-wing
movements. This is true not just in the United States but in Europe as well, which
has seen a surge in right-wing populist movements in recent years. In France, for
example, the anti-immigrant National Front has amassed a legion of far-right
cyber activists and dutiful far-right trolls, who fought, though ultimately failed,
to bring Marine Le Pen to power in 2017. The National Front would have been
too scattered and weak even for this limited political success, however, were it
not for social media, which enabled otherwise isolated xenophobes and right-
wing populists to gather online and build a sense of ultranationalist solidarity.[34] Le Pen and her online supporters created a nightmare for rival candidate
Emmanuel Macron by spreading disinformation claiming that Macron held a
secret bank account in the Bahamas. Macron was forced to file a defamation suit
against Le Pen. Although Macron eventually won the election decisively, it was
clear that online trolling had become a serious problem in French politics.[35]

In the United Kingdom in 2016, the anti-immigrant U.K. Independence Party (UKIP) similarly proved to have a strong social media presence, with typical Facebook posts being liked and shared by the thousands. Nigel Farage, the former leader of UKIP and one of the central faces of the Brexit campaign, has a long record of telling brazen lies, which have been disseminated by UKIP and its followers on social media. These lies include Farage's claims that Barack Obama "can't stand Britain,"[36] that the European Commission acts arbitrarily,[37] that 75 percent of Britain's laws were designed by the European Union (EU),[38] and that the EU costs Britain £350 million every week.[39] Farage's lies, amplified through social media, helped secure a parliamentary vote in 2016 in favor of the United Kingdom withdrawing from the EU.

Even Germany, which has long been sensitive to far-right political rhetoric, has in recent years witnessed the disturbing rise of Alternative for Germany (AfD), a far-right, nationalist party whose political platform includes opposition to immigration, opposition to refugees, explicit hostility to Islam and Muslims, and even teasing expressions of sympathy toward Germany's Nazi past. The AfD has enjoyed the enthusiastic financial backing of American philanthropist Nina Rosenwald, whose Gatestone Institute[40] supplies German social media with endless disinformation about the threat of Islam, the extinction of Christianity, and stories of German homes being confiscated for "hundreds of thousands of migrants from Africa, Asia, and the Middle East." The Gatestone Institute has also spread false reports of non-European migrants raping German women, migrants bringing deadly infectious diseases into Germany, and German neighborhoods being turned into "no-go zones" by immigrant gangs. The Gatestone Institute has gone so far as to promote Björn Höcke, a prominent AfD leader who has criticized Berlin's Holocaust Memorial for perpetuating a collective sense of German guilt. Gatestone stories are routinely picked up by German blogs and circulated on German media. Although the AfD could not compete with Olaf Scholz, who succeeded Angela Merkel to become Chancellor in 2017, it has nonetheless built a large social media following.[41] As of June 2023, the AfD surpassed Scholz's Social Democratic Party in national polls, second only to the conservative CDU/CSU parties.[42]

Trolling Ourselves to Death?

The unusual danger posed by social media, not just for local politics but also for global peace and stability, is most disturbingly illustrated by the heated war of words between Donald Trump and North Korea's Kim Jong-un in 2017. In May 2017, Trump said in an interview with Bloomberg News that he would be "honored" to meet the North Korean leader. Then in July, after North Korea launched a test missile directed near the coast of Japan, Trump tweeted, "Does this guy have anything better to do with his life?" CIA director Mike Pompeo later suggested at a public forum on security issues that Kim Jong-un should be "separated" from his nuclear weapons program. Shortly thereafter, North Korea issued a statement saying, "Should the U.S. dare to show even the slightest sign of attempt to remove our supreme leadership, we will strike a merciless blow at the heart of the U.S. with our powerful nuclear hammer, honed and hardened over time." In August 2017, after the United Nations Security Council voted to impose sanctions on North Korea, the state media of North Korea issued another statement: "We will make the U.S. pay by a thousand-fold for all the heinous crimes it commits against the state and people of this country."[43]

None of this violent rhetoric bothered Trump in the slightest. Rather, he responded in kind, seeking to outdo his North Korean rival. After hearing reports that North Korea had managed to modify intercontinental ballistic missiles to fit miniaturized nuclear warheads, Trump told reporters that "North Korea best not make any more threats to the United States. They will be met with fire and fury like the world has never seen." Trump then took to Twitter to say, "Military solutions are now fully in place, locked and loaded, should North Korea act unwisely. Hopefully Kim Jong Un will find another path!" In September, Trump mocked Kim Jong-un on Twitter, saying, "I spoke with President Moon of South Korea last night. Asked him how Rocket Man is doing. Long gas lines forming in North Korea. Too bad!" In a speech, just days later at the UN General Assembly, Trump repeated the "Rocket Man" insult:

> The United States has great strength and patience, but if it is forced to defend itself or its allies, we will have no choice but to totally destroy North Korea. Rocket Man is on a suicide mission for himself and for his regime.[44]

In response, North Korean foreign minister Ri Yong-ho told reporters that "it would be a dog's dream if he intended to scare us with the sound of a dog barking." Kim Jong-un later said in a direct statement to Trump himself that North Korea would respond to any threats with "a corresponding, highest level of hard-line countermeasure in history." He went on to say, "Whatever Trump might have expected, he will face results beyond his expectation. I will surely and definitely tame the mentally deranged U.S. dotard with fire." Once again, Trump took to Twitter to insult and provoke the North Korean leader, saying, "Kim Jong Un of North Korea, who is obviously a madman who doesn't mind starving or killing his people, will be tested like never before!"[45]

It is not an exaggeration to say that Trump's trolling actually increased the threat of nuclear conflict. Trolling now shapes the discourse and the practice of lawmakers and now defines the political style of powerful political leaders, including those with access to nuclear weapons and who threaten each other and the rest of the planet through pett and most irresponsible wars of words. While insults and threats of violence between national leaders are nothing new, the bizarre public drama of national leaders openly threatening each other with nuclear war and the paranoid habit of publicly insulting each other through childish name-calling have been decisively exacerbated by social media. There is little that is entertaining or amusing about open threats of nuclear annihilation. If Postman were alive today, he might say that we are not so much amusing as trolling ourselves to death.

Birth of a New Political Language Game

With the rise of social media, we have witnessed the birth of a new political language game, in which one of the primary moves is the speech act of trolling. In a discursive space unregulated by shared standards of truth, logic, evidence, and civility—in effect, a kind of Wild West of communication—trolling functions as a nuclear option, metaphorically speaking, for public discourse that all too often breaks down over political disagreements. While television might have turned politics into entertainment, social media have turned it into a global schoolyard, but one without any teachers to uphold rules or to put the bullies in their place. We have watched the practice of trolling migrate from anonymous comments on newsgroups and blogs to open comments by users with no wish to hide their identities, from citizens who troll politicians to politicians who troll them back, and from lawmakers who troll each other through legislative trolling to national leaders who troll each other with the threat of a literal nuclear option.

If we wish to understand why truth and reason have become casualties in contemporary politics, we should carefully examine the dominant media of our age, social media. The form through which we communicate on social media plays a powerful role in what gets communicated. The social aspect of social media decides matters of truth on the basis of popularity and social affinity rather than impersonal logic and evidence. The problem with zeroing in on fake news as the culprit for a post-truth world is that it does not explain what is driving the fake news. It would be naive to think that fact-checking can somehow contain the problem of fake news. The problem, I want to suggest, is much deeper. A focus on the dominant media of our age can go a long way in explaining not only the proliferation of fake news but also the political factionalism currently tearing democratic societies apart at the seams.[46]

While an analysis of social media can help us understand the more disturbing patterns in our public discourse, that analysis can only take us so far. Social media might have catalyzed the violent forces of political unreason today, but those forces have historical origins that long predate social media. We can get a fuller picture of political trolling by situating it historically and seeking to understand its origins in the distant past. This is the focus of the next chapter.

2

Disenlightenment

Consider the following hypothetical scenario on social media. A friend makes an angry post on Facebook that begins with something like "Listen up [all members of some group]," or "I don't know who needs to hear this, but . . . ," or "Unpopular opinion here: I think . . . ," or "I'm sick and tired of . . ." What follows is a long rant about some possibly important matter, but one that might best be handled with more patience and tact. Soon a few people begin clicking the "like" button, indicating their agreement with the post. Others click the orange angry-face emoji, indicating their disagreement. In the comments section, the bouncing ellipses appear, indicating that someone is typing a reply. Those three dots set passive lurkers on edge. A comment then appears. It's a pointed objection. For the most part, it's civil, but for its condescending tone. The bouncing ellipses appear once again. The OP (original poster) responds with a defensive and sarcastic reply. Both comments receive likes, hearts, and orange angry-face emojis. The post has become divisive. The friend then returns with a second comment, this time abandoning the veneer of civility. What follows is a lengthy and tedious back-and-forth between the OP and the friend. Each doubles down, repeating themselves long-windedly. With each comment, they become increasingly acerbic and uncivil. Then they post dueling memes and GIFs designed to outwit each other, to poke and jab at each other's weak spots, portraying each other as blind and stupid. They're now trolling each other. They then threaten to "unfriend" each other. After seventy-five comments, the OP ends the discussion by blocking the friend, only to post a new rant and a new meme about annoying Facebook friends who show up just to argue.

Exchanges like this have driven many social media users to deactivate their accounts or delete them altogether. The stress of being dragged into yet another social media flame war can be simply too much for self-respecting souls to bear. Even watching these arguments from the sidelines is enough to give passive observers full-blown anxiety. It's not uncommon for users turned off by the nonstop sewage pipeline of angry oratory and endless bickering to romanticize

Trolling Ourselves to Death. Jason Hannan, Oxford University Press. © Oxford University Press 2023.
DOI: 10.1093/oso/9780197557761.003.0003

life before social media—a supposedly more innocent time when we were more logical and respectful, when we could hold constructive disagreements without fighting like children. The assumption behind this nostalgia for the old days is that social media are singularly to blame for the argumentative cul-de-sacs, histrionic feces-slinging, and instinctive trolling that have become so commonplace online. But is this perception of life before social media correct?

In the opening pages of *After Virtue*, Alasdair MacIntyre describes the nature of contemporary moral disagreement as follows:

> The most striking feature of contemporary moral utterance is that so much of it is used to express disagreements; and the most striking feature of the debates in which these disagreements are expressed is their interminable character. I do not mean by this just that such debates go on and on and on—although they do—but also that they apparently can find no terminus. There seems to be no rational way of securing moral agreement in our culture.[1]

MacIntyre wrote these words in 1981, long before the advent of social media. Yet what he describes here strongly resembles the flame wars we routinely encounter online. He notes that public discourse had become "a matter of pure assertion and counter-assertion."[2] When we disagree, we risk becoming locked in an argumentative standoff. Backed into a corner, we feel shaken and unsettled. We become defensive, angry, and *loud*.

This reaction, MacIntyre argues, betrays a certain hollowness in our thinking. It indicates that we do not really stand on solid ground—something we know subconsciously but are unlikely to admit. "It is small wonder," he says, "if we become defensive and therefore shrill."[3] That MacIntyre could write these words long before the age of social media suggests that the breakdown of our public discourse lies not in our media of communication but rather in something older and deeper. This is not to say that social media are irrelevant. They certainly amplify our voices, intensify our disagreements, and exacerbate our mutual antipathy. But the platforms cannot be singled out as the root cause of our angry and defensive speech.

What, then, is the origin of that anger and defensiveness? The historical thesis of *After Virtue* is that the rage in our public discourse has its roots in the Enlightenment, the eighteenth-century philosophical movement that set the terms and conditions of the modern world as we know it today. The primary task of what MacIntyre calls "the Enlightenment project of moral philosophy" was to furnish a rational and secular foundation for morality, an alternative to the theocratic order of the premodern world.[4] Morality can be understood as a medium of human relationships, a common code by which we hold each other accountable and negotiate conflict and disagreement. MacIntyre argues that the

Enlightenment failed to produce such a code—a rational and secular foundation for morality. The ensuing void, he says, was filled instead by the morality of the marketplace—the logos and ethos of capitalist individualism. The defining feature of capitalist individualism is instrumental social relations: treating each other as a means to our personal ends. It is here, MacIntyre argues, that we can find the roots of our communicative chaos. It is here also, I will argue by extension, that we can locate the roots of political trolling. This claim might at first seem implausible. But MacIntyre's historical argument shows why it could hardly have been otherwise. In what follows, I retrace his historical analysis and connect it to the phenomenon of political trolling today.

Morality in the Premodern World

The most practical way to make sense of MacIntyre's historical thesis about our communicative chaos today is to contrast the Enlightenment with the older political order against which it was an intellectual rebellion.[5] That older order was composed of a centuries-long political alliance between the Crown and the Church.[6] The theory supporting this alliance was the divine right of kings. There was no greater defender of this archaic theory of power and authority than the political theorist Sir Robert Filmer. In his short and feisty book *Patriarcha: Or the Natural Power of Kings*, Filmer presents the classical statement of the theory of divine right.[7] In keeping with an ancient political belief, he advances a view of the body politic as one large family. This is very much a traditional family, in which the father is head and master of the household and therefore the sole manager of the family's affairs.[8] Likewise, the king is head and master of the state. The king rules over his subjects like a father over his children, the latter born into a natural state of helplessness and submission.[9] Divine right is not self-proclaimed. It is inherited through an ancestral line that runs back to Adam, the first and original king. The basis for Adam's primordial status as first king, and for the royal status of his male heirs, is none other than God himself. As the executor of God's will on earth, the king thus holds total and absolute authority over his subjects. He answers to no worldly body—to no parliament and no court. Obedience to the king is thus obedience to God, a political structure blessed and protected by the spiritual body of the Church.[10]

The Church did more than legitimate the power of the king. It was also the source and foundation of morality—of norms and values. As the official institution responsible for the interpretation of Scripture, the Church provided the people with a moral code.[11] This code classified certain types of conduct as right, good, permissible, virtuous, pious, and holy. It classified other types as wrong, bad, impermissible, sinful, blasphemous, and evil. The moral code was the basis of the law. It supplied the normative standards for determining the legal and the illegal, standards to which even the king—in principle, though not necessarily in practice—was bound. In this earthly life, the code was enforced on pain of censure and punishment. Its ultimate force, however, lay beyond this world in the prospect of divine judgment: the desire for an eternity in heaven and the dread of an eternity in hell. Fear of divine judgment set the moral backdrop of everyday life. It governed conscious and subconscious moments, explicit and implicit thoughts, tacit and direct actions. It determined hopes and fears, dreams and nightmares, desire and aversion, pleasure and disgust. It provided the narrative framework, the structure of feeling, and the normative background for living a meaningful and purposeful life. The Church, in sum, was the foundation of both political legitimacy and moral objectivity.

The Enlightenment was, at its most basic, a revolt against this moral and political order. It celebrated freethinking, skepticism, reason, liberty, and tolerance. It therefore regarded the Church, and its alliance with the Crown, as the greatest enemy of reason, the source of pitiful ignorance and superstition, a mortal threat to liberty, and the cause of so much conflict, violence, and bloodshed.[12] For this reason, the Enlightenment actively sought to replace the old political and moral order with a rational and secular one. This project consisted of two separate and distinct tasks.

The first was to formulate a secular alternative to the divine right of kings. Without question, the most forceful critic of the theory of divine right, and the most influential exponent of a secular theory of government, was John Locke. In the first volume of his *Two Treatises of Government*, Locke mercilessly eviscerates Filmer, documenting his many factual and logical absurdities. How, as Locke notes, is a self-proclaimed king to trace his lineage convincingly back to the first man? If all men are heirs of Adam, how can we possibly decide between competing claims to being the one true king? Locke dismisses *Patriarcha* as the work of an idiot. As he says in the preface, if Filmer's words were stripped of their veneer, then any reader could see that "there was never so much glib nonsense put together in well-sounding English."[13] In place of the theory of divine right, Locke takes inspiration from Hugo Grotius and Thomas Hobbes to advance a theory of the social contract.[14]

Locke's alternative theory consists of three starting premises. The first premise is that everyone, by virtue of being a person, is the bearer of some set of natural rights. According to Locke, these are the rights of "life, liberty, and estate."[15] The second premise is that political legitimacy lies not in some preposterous and unverifiable claim to divine right but rather in the agreement and consent of the people.[16] Anything else amounts to unjustified power and coercion—in a word, tyranny.[17] The third premise is that individual citizens voluntarily relinquish some of their freedom and liberty in exchange for becoming a member of organized society.[18]

Locke's theory of the social contract was a powerful influence on the U.S. Declaration of Independence and the U.S. Constitution.[19] Along with Emmanuel-Joseph Sieyès's *What Is the Third Estate?* and Jean-Jacques Rousseau's *The Social Contract*, Locke's political theory also fed the intellectual milieu that produced the French Declaration of the Rights of Man and of the Citizen.[20] It is not an exaggeration to say that social contract theory effectively transformed political thought and practice in the Western world and beyond. Modern democracies are the institutional embodiments of social contract theory, a testament to the extraordinary success of the Enlightenment in effectively replacing the divine right of kings with a secular model of government and political legitimacy.

The second task of the Enlightenment was to replace the old order's religious foundation of morality with a secular alternative. This task proved to be far more challenging. It involved nothing less than the formulation of a new theory of morality. A successful theory would have to produce a new moral code, a new system of norms and values. It would have to yield a new vocabulary for moral argument. It would have to provide new categories for differentiating right from wrong. Most importantly, it would have to produce a new framework for making moral judgments. This new moral framework would have to carry the same force as its religious counterpart, command a comparable level of social consensus, achieve a comparable level of moral objectivity, and create a new moral backdrop for everyday life, shaping how people think, feel, speak, and act, all without recourse to scripture or the prospect of heaven and threat of hell. The goal, in short, was morality without God. This is what MacIntyre calls "the Enlightenment project of justifying morality."[21] This is what he contends was a failure.

Two Moral Paradigms

Where, then, to turn for an objective foundation for morality? If not to God, then to what? As MacIntyre observes, the Enlightenment was split between two competing approaches to this problem. The first approach turned to *nature*. The idea of nature plays a big part in Enlightenment thinking.[22] Nature is the realm of the empirically verifiable. We can study nature at a distance through a telescope or up close through a magnifying glass. We can measure it through different instruments. We can quantify, record, and preserve it. We can carve it up and classify it. We can subject it to experiments, using a variety of empirical methods. We can reach conclusive results and generate new theories and hypotheses. We can discover new laws and principles. Nature is a neutral court of appeal. It favors no culture, no religion, and no denomination. To a secular sensibility, nature is a powerful authority, even the secular counterpart to God. What better foundation for morality, then, than nature? This move, however, raises the nagging question of where, exactly, in nature to turn for this foundation.

One school of thinking turned to *human* nature. The cohort of Enlightenment philosophers who signed onto this approach is broad. Among them were Denis Diderot, Claude Adrien Helvétius, Anthony Ashley-Cooper, Francis Hutcheson, Adam Smith, and, most notably, David Hume. Their general view was that every one of us has natural desires, passions, and instincts. We have natural moral dispositions. Human nature does not vary from person to person. There is but one human nature, which cuts across the whole of humanity. As Hume puts it in *An Enquiry Concerning Human Understanding*, "Mankind are so much the same, in all times and places, that history informs us of nothing new or strange in this particular. Its chief use is only to discover the constant and universal principles of human nature."[23] Culture and custom, religion and tradition, folklore and ritual may reinforce our natural moral instincts. But those instincts originate from within us. Our natural desires, passions, and instincts equip us to tell good from evil, right from wrong, and virtue from vice. We just *know* that murder, theft, and rape are wrong because we have a natural, visceral revulsion toward these actions. Likewise, we know that honesty, kindness, and charity are good because we have a natural desire to enact these values.

According to Hume, the voice of moral authority speaks from within our hearts, if only we would listen to it. Human nature enables us to tell right from wrong without the external aid of scripture. It motivates us to do good and avoid evil without the otherworldly carrots and sticks of a divine overseer. For Hume, the beauty of human nature is that it spares us the trouble of having to infer moral injunctions from empirical descriptions of the natural world, that is, from having to derive an "ought" from an "is."[24] We need not bother reasoning our way to moral conclusions like "We ought not to steal" and "We ought not to murder." Human nature already inclines us against both theft and murder. The role of reason is purely technical: to assist us in achieving what we naturally regard as good and avoiding what we naturally regard as evil. For this school of Enlightenment thought, the answer to the riddle of morality without God could not be simpler, more obvious, or more conclusive.

A second answer to the riddle of morality without God was *reason*. Like nature, reason understandably occupies a big place in the Enlightenment imagination. Reason is distinct from *reasons*. The latter are arguments, mere propositions. Reason, by contrast, is the exalted faculty that produces such arguments and propositions. Reason belongs to the mind, not the heart. It is what makes us rational beings, what elevates us over the beasts in the wild. Reason is transcendent and ideal. It belongs to a higher dimension. It stands above the mundane world of human imperfection. We aspire to reason. We seek to tap into its sublimity. Reason is impartial, for it betrays no bias and no preference. It is universal, belonging to no culture or civilization. It is pure and clean, untainted by the soil of common, everyday fallacy. It is formal and impersonal, uncompromised by intoxicating feelings, emotions, desires, and impulses. Reason is precise and coherent, admitting of no fuzziness or ambiguity. Most importantly, reason is final and authoritative. It gives us the concrete ground of absolute certainty we so desperately crave.

The one name we invariably associate with this school of thought is Immanuel Kant, the singular giant of the German Enlightenment. Kant's view of morality can be understood as a devaluing of feeling, emotion, and desire, and an admonition against whim and caprice.[25] For Kant, morality is cold and dispassionate. It consists of an abstract system of formal rules and principles. Like a soldier following orders on the battlefield, Kant's ideal reasoning subject follows the rules and principles of morality, not out of pleasure but out of duty. The sole criterion for telling right from wrong is the will. Acting on good will, on the right intentions, is all that matters. So long as we follow valid moral principles out of duty and obligation, we are in the right and have acted properly, regardless of the outcome. The true measure of acting on good intentions is not joy but rather pain and difficulty. When we act *against* our natural inclinations, when we follow moral principles *in spite* of our natural feelings and desires, then we know we have acted on sound intentions. Put simply, duty is discomfort.

The formula at the heart of Kant's austere approach to morality is the categorical imperative. Like an algorithm that churns out quasi-divine commandments at the push of a button, the categorical imperative is a rule generator, the rule of all rules. Through this universal formula, we can supposedly discover the rules of morality. In principle, this formula is accessible to all rational people. Anyone can apply it to discover a true moral principle, what Kant calls a universal maxim. The categorical imperative reads: "Act only in accordance with that maxim through which you can at the same time will that it become a universal law."[26] In other words, a moral principle is valid only if we can imagine a community of rational people collectively following it. Thus, "Always tell the truth" is valid and universal, but "Lie if you must" is not. Under no circumstances is lying ever permissible, for once we open the door to opportunistic lying, the moral order risks collapsing into corruption and chaos.[27]

Kant recognizes that his formula has one major flaw. We can imagine a rational community whose inhabitants follow the maxim "Always act out of self-interest." This maxim runs against the spirit of always acting out of duty. Also, like opportunistic lying, acting out of self-interest would lead to the corruption and breakdown of society. Hence, Kant introduces a second imperative: "So act that you use humanity, whether in your own person or in the person of any other, always at the same time as an end, never merely as a means."[28] Everyone is thus to be respected as an autonomous person, not used like a tool. In Kant's ideal kingdom of ends, all human beings have an intrinsic value, which no amount of money can buy. All human beings must therefore be treated as rational and autonomous, as ends in themselves, not as instruments for personal gain. Kant is confident that, taken together, these two imperatives—the universalizability principle and the humanity principle—provide objective and universal foundations for morality.

To summarize, the Enlightenment sought to replace the religious foundation of morality with a rational and secular one. But it produced not one but two mutually exclusive moral paradigms, each premised on axiomatic assumptions fundamentally at odds with the other. The first can be abbreviated as *desire without reason*; the second, *reason without desire*. Both paradigms have been enormously influential in the modern study of ethics. Each has its formidable latter-day heirs. But this influence is limited to the highly specialized domain of academic moral philosophy. Neither succeeded in playing the public role once occupied by the Church. According to MacIntyre, this should not have been a surprise.

MacIntyre's Critique of the Enlightenment Project

As a historian of ethics with a critical eye for the way in which ideas, concepts, and theories evolve over time, MacIntyre offers a unique insight into the nature and structure of morality. This insight concerns the *form* of morality, not the *content* of any morality in particular. MacIntyre says that when we speak of "morality" and "ethics," and when we use terms like "good," "bad," "right," and "wrong," we unwittingly make use of concepts that originally had their home within a teleological paradigm.[29] The classical statement of this paradigm, MacIntyre reminds us, is Aristotle's *Nicomachean Ethics*.[30] The key to understanding the *Ethics* is the concept of a *telos*. According to Aristotle, everything has a *telos*—a purpose, a function, a goal, an ultimate aim. In the light of that *telos*, we can make straightforward, matter-of-fact judgments of "good," "bad," "right," "wrong," and the like. Simple objects from everyday life illustrate this well. A clock, for example, has a purpose: to tell time. A child can tell us that a good clock tells time accurately and that a bad clock does not. That same child can tell us that the purpose of a lightbulb is to emit light. If it does not do this well or at all, it is, plainly, a bad bulb.

The teleological paradigm views human beings much the same way. To modern ears, this will sound odd, if not absurd. We are not like clocks and lightbulbs, it will be said. We are creatures of rationality, will, and autonomy. But the apparent oddness and absurdity of this idea can be tempered by considering certain familiar social roles. We know that doctors, for example, have a purpose: to heal their patients. A doctor with a long record of successfully treating their patients can be confidently judged a good doctor. But a doctor who makes inaccurate diagnoses, prescribes the wrong medications, and violates doctor-patient confidentiality is, plainly, a bad doctor. Likewise, teachers have a purpose: to teach. The role of a teacher is to convey and elucidate ideas. Teachers nurture and cultivate understanding. They shape and mold their students. They train, mentor, and guide them. As much as teachers might dislike it, they are judged on their performance each time their students fill out their teaching evaluations. They may object that they have been judged unfairly. But they would not object in principle to being held accountable according to practice-based standards of excellence (*aretê*) in teaching. Assuming that doctors and teachers are evaluated in good faith, we can see how judgments of "good" and "bad" can be a straightforward and uncontroversial affair.

The teleological paradigm extends this logic by viewing all people, regardless of their individual occupational roles, as having a general *telos*. Like a seed genetically programmed to develop into a tree, Aristotle says, our natural end is *eudaimonia*.[31] This is sometimes translated as "happiness," though a more accurate translation is "flourishing." Our purpose in life, says Aristotle, is to flourish, to thrive, to live well. Behavioral traits and qualities that contribute to the aim of living well are virtues. Those that obstruct the aim of living well are vices. A "good" person is one who embodies the virtues of living well. A "bad" person is one who embodies the vices that obstruct the aim of living well. For Aristotle, the purpose of ethics is not to speculate about the meaning of life or to debate abstract ethical puzzles, but rather to educate young and old alike in the art (*tekhnê*) of living well. Ethics is an eminently practical affair, as opposed to a matter of idle speculation. It seeks to cultivate the practical wisdom (*phronêsis*) necessary for living well. To summarize, then, the teleological paradigm consists of the following elements: (1) the human agent in a state of unrealized natural potential, (2) the *telos* of human flourishing, (3) a technical vocabulary for distinguishing good from bad, and virtue from vice, (4) a practical basis for making judgments about human conduct and character, and (5) a practical education for the art of living well.[32]

The morality of *The Nicomachian Ethics* can be practiced on secular terms. It need not require belief in a higher power or adherence to a religious text. However, it can take a religious form. As MacIntyre points out, the Christian morality against which the Enlightenment rebelled is a theistic variation of the teleological paradigm.[33] It, too, is a purpose-driven, goal-based morality. The purpose is to obey the commandments of God, to seek God's pleasure, and to avoid incurring God's wrath. Instead of flourishing in this life, the goal is eternal happiness in the next. Moral concepts like piety and sinfulness are merely religious counterparts to virtue and vice. Although this theistic variation includes the elements of scripture, the interpretive institution of the Church, and the judicial role of God, the overall structure is nonetheless distinctly teleological.

According to MacIntyre, the reason the Enlightenment project failed is that it tinkered with this basic teleological structure of morality.[34] It divorced the very idea of morality, as well as basic moral terminology, categories, and distinctions, from the practical, goal-oriented framework in which these elements originally had their place. Once divorced from that framework, "morality" becomes an abstraction. "Good," "bad," "right," and "wrong" become intrinsic properties, as opposed to extrinsic qualities judged in the light of a human *telos*. In the absence of God, "permissible" and "impermissible" become free-floating injunctions unmoored to any conscious authority that grants or withholds permission. In the absence of God, quasi-divine commandments like "Always tell the truth" and "Never steal" become faceless admonitions, a stern moralizing voice without a moralizing command-giver. Uprooted from its practical context, moral terminology thus loses its normative power, like hitting a tennis ball into an open grassy field and declaring victory in the absence of a court or a game. Without a *telos*, it becomes a great philosophical mystery as to how moral judgments can possibly be grounded and how moral arguments are capable of possessing any normative power at all. The most glaring feature of the appeals to human nature and reason is just how patently unconvincing and utterly subjective they can be.

The Rise of Market Morality

Toward the end of *After Virtue*, MacIntyre describes how the moral void left by the failure of the Enlightenment project came to be filled by a new paradigm: the culture, values, and ethos of the marketplace.[35] The primary driver of this cultural transformation was not philosophy but the Industrial Revolution: the rapid proliferation of factories and their eventual dominance over early modern society. MacIntyre vividly describes the corrosive effects of factories upon social life, upending and uprooting human communities and undermining social bonds. Prior to the age of factories, he reminds us, production was based in the home. Work was linked to communal life. It formed an integral part of a meaningful and coherent, if far from ideal, social existence. But that model of work changed with the growth of factories, which forced production out of the household and onto the factory floor.[36]

The institution of the factory reduced complex human beings to mere workers, one-dimensional creatures whose entire existence was now devoted to survival. Instead of living for the goods of communal life, workers lived for personal acquisition. They exchanged their labor for low wages, paltry sums on which they could barely feed and clothe their families. Factory work was neither unlimited nor guaranteed. Workers were forced by necessity and desperation into a vicious competition for jobs, like starving wolves fighting over scraps of meat. The deliberate creation of a culture of vicious competition, says MacIntyre, is what led to the vice of *pleonexia*, or acquisitiveness, being elevated to the status of a modern-day virtue. As MacIntyre puts it:

> As, and to the extent that, work moves outside the household and is put to the service of impersonal capital, the realm of work tends to become separated from everything but the service of biological survival and the reproduction of the labor force, on the one hand, and that of institutionalized acquisitiveness, on the other. Pleonexia, a vice in the Aristotelian scheme, is now the driving force of modern productive work. The means-end relationships embodied for the most part in such work—on a production line, for example—are necessarily external to the goods which those who work seek; such work too has consequently been expelled from the realm of practices with goods internal to themselves.[37]

In an amoral world of unprincipled competition, greed becomes a virtue, because greed is necessary for survival. The cold-blooded and pitiless nature of the labor market forced workers to internalize the competitive ethos of the marketplace. Private capital succeeded in recreating human beings in its avaricious image.

The capitalist paradigm envisioned a social world of competition, in which workers and bosses alike were driven by self-interest and the pursuit of private wealth. Society, according to this paradigm, is one giant marketplace, and everyone in it a merchant, a tradesperson, a wheeler-dealer of some kind or another. The morality implicit in this economic social structure is given explicit content in Locke's political philosophy. The moral centerpiece is the idea of the individual. In his *Second Treatise of Government*, Locke conceives of the individual as absolute master, lord, and sovereign of his own person.[38] The individual is a free man—liberated not just from the shackles of Crown and Church but also from history, tradition, culture, community, and even language.[39] Against John Donne, who wrote, "No man is an island, entire of itself, every man is a piece of the continent, a part of the main," Locke defined the individual as an autonomous entity, free of the oppressive burdens of social bonds. For Locke, society is not Donne's interconnected continent but rather an amorphous collection of disconnected and atomized individuals. Locke's conception of rights, in which everyone, by virtue of being an individual, possesses a natural and inviolable right to "life, liberty, and estate," is the morality of commerce.[40] MacIntyre argues that the doctrine of the individual is the ideological root of the breakdown of public discourse today.[41]

Moral Instrumentalism

Locke's political philosophy gives primacy to the freedom of the individual. Typically, the doctrine of liberal individualism is expressed along the following lines: everyone is free to pursue their individual idea of the moral life, so long as they do not interfere with the freedom of others to do the same. If individuals are sovereign, then they decide for themselves what counts as the good and the right. Morality, like religion, becomes a private affair.[42] On this view, you may object to pornography, polyamory, cloning, and Cardi B's "WAP," so long as you let others do what they want with their lives. But in a social universe composed of sovereign individuals not bound by a shared moral framework, what becomes of human relationships? On what basis do so many sovereigns, lords, and masters relate to one another? On what terms do they speak and deliberate?

A liberal society, as MacIntyre shrewdly observes, is the opposite of Kant's kingdom of ends. It is a kingdom of means, in which the pursuit of personal desire reigns supreme. The premise of a society composed exclusively of sovereigns, lords, and masters is "the obliteration of any genuine distinction between manipulative and non-manipulative social relations."[43] Instead of regarding others as rational and autonomous agents, capable of independent thought and judgment, a liberal society encourages us to regard each other as gullible and manipulable. Instead of seeking to persuade each other by appeal to impersonal standards of morality, we are inclined to resort to manipulation. That is, we are inclined to practice what Edward Bernays called the "engineering of consent."[44] We are tempted to employ whatever rhetorical devices, tricks, and gimmicks will be most effective in bending others to our individual will. In a word, the prevailing form of rhetoric in a liberal society is sophistry. In the kingdom of means, social life is but a contest for sophistic manipulation. In our private and individual capacities, we think like the executives of *Mad Men*. We become architects of deception, seeking to persuade, influence, convince, control, shape, mold, deceive, and manipulate each other for the realization of private and individual gain.

MacIntyre points out a curious consequence of instrumental social relations for moral rhetoric. If morality is a private matter, then it is not morality in any sense of the term. In a liberal society in which morality is a personal affair, impersonal concepts like "good," "bad," "right," and "wrong" are emptied of normative content. They become expressions of personal will, desire, and preference.[45] This is what, in the philosophy of language, is called emotivism.[46] A moral assertion like "Guns are good" just comes to mean "I like guns." By contrast, "Guns are evil" just comes to mean "I really, really dislike guns." In a battle between "I like *x*" and "I dislike *x*," there can be no rational resolution.[47] What this means is that public reasoning is not a rational practice. Our moral disagreements are not disagreements at all but rather a clash of personal wills, desires, and preferences. When will battles will, desire battles desire, and preference battles preference, it should come as no surprise that we become loud, angry, defensive, and repetitive. In a battle of wills, the louder and angrier we are, and the more defensive and repetitive we become, the more likely we are to prevail. The nonrational nature of moral conflict and the instrumental character of social relationships inevitably encourage ever more extreme forms of political speech in the public sphere.

Consequences of Instrumentalism

MacIntyre points out three material consequences of this culture of moral instrumentalism. The first is the act of unmasking the covert will and desire of the enemy. In the humanities, we are accustomed to thinking of unmasking as a radical mode of cultural critique. We have long used the critical methods of Marxism, psychoanalysis, feminism, and postcolonialism to unmask and expose the subtle and hidden machinations of social and institutional power. We seek to uncover the artifice of capitalist reason, the force of unconscious desire, the tenacity of patriarchal will, and the lasting forms of colonial power and domination. We have formalized these methods of critique, employing them in our scholarly work. We teach them in the classroom, educating and training our students in these methods. We encourage our students to use them outside of class to think critically about the world in which we live. We take the subversive nature of these critical methods for granted.

But the act of unmasking the true motives of the enemy cuts both ways. Reactionary conservatives have appropriated the practice of cultural criticism to "expose" the true motives of the left-liberal-Marxist-socialist-communist-homosexual-Islamic enemy. To take one vivid example, in a 2006 interview with television personality Donny Deutsch, commentator Ann Coulter argued, incredibly, that former president Bill Clinton's unbridled womanizing was evidence of his "latent homosexuality":

COULTER: I think that sort of rampant promiscuity does show some level of latent homosexuality. . . . I think anyone with that level of promiscuity where, you know, you—I mean, he didn't know Monica's name until their sixth sexual encounter. There is something that is—that is of the bathhouse about that.

. . .

DEUTSCH: But where's the—but where's the homosexual part of that? I'm—once again, I'm speechless here.

COULTER: It's reminiscent of a bathhouse. It's just this obsession with your own—with your own essence.
DEUTSCH: But why is that homosexual? You could say narcissistic.

...

COULTER: Well, there is something narcissistic about homosexuality. Right? Because you're in love with someone who looks like you. I'm not breaking new territory here, why are you looking at me like that?[48]

This strange attempt at psychoanalytic critique is representative of Coulter's rhetoric. She has long recognized the futility of moral argument. She therefore specializes in the reactionary politics of unmasking the enemy, even if it amounts to a comical performance. There is a long history of conservative figures who have built their careers on the reckless practice of purportedly unmasking and exposing the enemy, a topic explored in more detail in Chapter 3. If academic cultural critics belong to what Paul Ricoeur called "l'école du soupçon," then their reactionary counterparts may rightly be said to belong to "l'école de la paranoïa."[49] In their desperate attempt to dig deeper into the minds, hearts, and lives of the enemy, conservative critics are wont to expose imaginary demons. This in part explains the epidemic of conspiracy theory in conservative social media bubbles, a topic explored in more detail in Chapter 5.

A second consequence of the culture of moral instrumentalism is the prevalence of protesting as a dominant form of moral rhetoric. As with unmasking, we are in the habit of thinking of protesting as an inherently subversive practice. When we think of protest movements, we think of the civil rights movement, the women's movement, the antiwar movement, and the environmental movement. But MacIntyre reminds us that protest movements have no inherent political orientation. Protests are a type of speech act. They express moral opposition and outrage. Protests can just as easily express a reactionary will as they can a radical and progressive one. While protest movements have been vital for challenging unjustified power, undoing social hierarchy, and expanding the scope of equality, they have also become effective instruments of defending and restoring power and privilege. As MacIntyre puts it, "It is easy also to understand why *protest* becomes a distinctive moral feature of the modern age and why *indignation* is a predominant modern emotion." Although protest originated as an act of bearing witness in favor of something, it is now "almost entirely that negative phenomenon which characteristically occurs as a reaction to the alleged invasion of someone's *rights* in the name of someone else's *utility*."[50] As will be discussed in the next chapter, conservatism specializes in appropriating the political styles of the left, including the act of public protest for reactionary ends.

A third consequence is the invocation of individual rights for antisocial purposes. There are numerous contemporary examples of claims to antisocial rights: Second Amendment fundamentalists who claim a natural, God-given right to carry a semiautomatic rifle into shopping malls, churches, and university campuses; anti-maskers who claim an inviolable right not to wear a mask in public indoor spaces, despite putting others at risk of infection, serious illness, and death; trophy hunters who claim a natural right to kill endangered animals; neighbors who claim a natural right to fly flags bearing swastikas; diesel truck drivers who claim the individual right to practice "coal-rolling," the sociopathic act of pumping dark plumes of black, sooty exhaust into the air, especially in front of a Prius or a Tesla, *just* to make a statement.[51]

Rights are a mixed blessing. They have aided the most important social movements in modern history. But they have also become the rhetorical weapons of choice for those who oppose those very same movements. The reactionary turn to antisocial rights serves to entrench power, protect privilege, and dig one's heels deeper into the ground to oppose and resist social change. Following Marx, MacIntyre views the instrument of individual rights as reinforcing the social division at the heart of liberal societies.[52] As he puts it:

> The arrival upon the scene of conceptions of right, attaching to and exercised by individuals, as a fundamental moral quasilegal concept . . . always signals some measure of loss of or repudiation of some previous social solidarity. Rights are claimed *against* some other person; they are invoked when and insofar as those others appear as threats.[53]

We can extend MacIntyre's analysis to see how the three consequences just discussed—unmasking, protesting, and the invocation of antisocial rights—bleed into a fourth consequence: the speech act of trolling. Trolling can be seen as one more symptom of the instrumental nature of social relations and the abandonment of even the pretense of moral argument. When journalist Naomi Klein asked environmental activist Greta Thunberg how she can be supported in dealing with incessant trolls, Thunberg offered the following reflection: "Sometimes I have a competition with myself to find the most absurd conspiracy theory. Because they go after things like my personality and how I am, how I look, how I behave. That is just a sign . . . that they don't have any more arguments to go after you."[54] Thunberg here succinctly captures the fourth consequence of our emotivist culture: the impulse to turn disagreements into personal attacks.

Trolling is one more way of compensating for the failure of moral argument. It is now a popular tactic among those who have given up on the idea of public reasoning and the common good.[55] Trolling is the habit of those who have succumbed to cynicism, distrust, and paranoia, who have taken social division and enemyship as their moral starting point. It is the proud and defiant embrace of malice, childishness, boorishness, nastiness, and sheer viciousness, the celebration of chaos and mayhem. Trolling is the felicitous abandonment of even the pretense of logic, integrity, and principle, the dismissal of any concept of shame. Trolls, we might say, are paragons of disenlightenment.

While political liberalism created the epistemic conditions for interminable disagreement and consequently for rampant trolling, political conservatism crystallized an entire moral attitude of contempt and antipathy toward the underprivileged: the poor, women, and racial minorities. Political conservatism easily slides from contempt and antipathy into the unreason and physical violence of far-right trolls. This is the subject of the next chapter.

3

Unreason

William F. Buckley is widely regarded as the father of modern American conservatism. He was born in New York, raised in Paris and London, and educated by private tutors. He attended Yale University, where he studied political science, history, and economics, became chairman of the *Yale Daily News*, and earned a campus-wide reputation as a masterful orator and debater. In the 1950s, Buckley began writing a series of influential books that established his reputation as a leading conservative intellectual. These include *God and Man at Yale*, *McCarthy and His Enemies*, and *Up from Liberalism*.[1] In 1955, he founded the *National Review*, which fast became the official periodical of the American conservative movement. An extremely prolific writer, Buckley published over fifty books and over five thousand articles. His collected papers, all preserved at Yale, reportedly weigh seven tons.[2] He was also the host of *Firing Line*, a long-running current affairs program in which he debated numerous left-wing intellectuals, including James Baldwin, Huey Newton, Betty Friedan, Harriet Pilpel, and Noam Chomsky. Through his impassioned oratory, his cogent and prolific writings, and his distinct, if rather affected, patrician personality, Buckley built a formidable following in America and even abroad. He was without question the preeminent leader of the American conservative movement right up until his death in 2008.[3]

What, then, might Buckley, American conservatism's grand old man of ideas, have thought of Donald Trump, a vulgarian who lacks ideas, who speaks like a fourth grader, who famously despises reading, who watched a staggering eight hours of television per day during his presidency, and whose independent literary output consists of semiliterate and paranoid tweets?[4] What might Buckley have made of Trump's authoritarian demagoguery, his rage-filled, chest-thumping campaign rallies, his inability to debate ideas with his critics, his penchant for harassing and bullying people online, his habit of name-calling, his use of doctored videos, or his promotion of conspiracy theory?[5] In short, what would Buckley have made of a troll as the new de facto leader of the American conservative movement?

Trolling Ourselves to Death. Jason Hannan, Oxford University Press. © Oxford University Press 2023.
DOI: 10.1093/oso/9780197557761.003.0004

Buckley's son, Christopher Buckley, says the question is moot, since it presumes that Trump is a bona fide conservative. The younger Buckley insists that Trump is no conservative at all; indeed, that "it's difficult to discern any identifiable ideology, philosophy, or politics behind his curtain," and that what lurks beneath is "an insistent, clamant narcissism."[6] Buckley the younger suggests that his deceased father would have roundly rejected Trump as a wolf in conservative clothing. He would not have been alone.

Numerous conservative public figures have insisted that Trump cannot seriously be regarded as a conservative. George Will, another prolific writer and one of Buckley's most prominent intellectual heirs, has called Trump's presidency "one giant act of trolling," a relentless assault upon the American psyche.[7] David Frum, a former speechwriter for George W. Bush, regards Trump's embrace of trolls as part of the corruption of the American republic.[8] Rick Wilson, a longtime political strategist who has worked for George H. W. Bush, Dick Cheney, and Rudy Giuliani, has called Trump and his followers "the Troll Party."[9] In 2020, a large number of conservatives united in opposition to Trump's reelection on the grounds that he was never a true conservative, that his incessant lying, hateful behavior, and incurable incivility clashed with the spirit of the conservative tradition.[10]

But is there any merit to this argument? On what basis can these self-appointed guardians of the conservative tradition assert that Trump is not a true conservative? This chapter explores the historical and ideological link between conservatism as a political tradition and the contemporary phenomenon of political trolling. In what follows, I show why Frum, Will, Wilson, and other moderate conservatives are wrong to insist that Trump and his band of trolls are some sort of deviation from conservatism. Revisiting some of the key ideas and themes in the history of the conservative tradition, I argue that conservatism at its core is inherently oriented toward political unreason.[11] What has long been central to conservatism as a political tradition is precisely what animates conservative political trolling today. I then look at the examples of Rush Limbaugh and Ann Coulter, two of the most toxic media personalities of our time. Limbaugh and Coulter can rightly be described as ur-trolls—political shock artists who pioneered the art of scandalizing the liberal enemy.

What Is Conservatism?

Making sense of conservatism is a difficult task. The problem of defining conservatism can be illustrated by the vast gulf between conservatism in theory and practice. We are inclined to think of conservatism as a principled defense of the free market, limited government, fiscal responsibility, family values, law and order, free speech, and individual liberty. This popular view of conservatism reflects the familiar talking points of conservative intellectuals, organizations, and political parties. But these talking points routinely clash with conservative policies. Government bailouts of private businesses, for example, contravene the very idea of a free market.[12] Bloated military budgets and the suppression of reproductive rights are not forms of limited government.[13] Tearing migrant children away from their parents and imprisoning them in cages without basic necessities like beds, blankets, showers, and toothbrushes are not a defense of family values.[14] Criminalizing Black Lives Matter demonstrations and banning critical race theory are not defenses of free speech.[15] Tax breaks for the rich and steep cuts to social spending do not demonstrate fiscal responsibility.[16] The racial profiling of Arab and Muslim people constitutes an egregious assault upon individual liberties.[17] The list of such contradictions can be extended nearly without end. The massive disjuncture between conservative principle and practice is difficult to deny. This, then, raises the question of how we can account for the consistency of conservative practice, if not by appeal to explicit principle.

Another way of making sense of conservatism is to look at its historical roots and origins, the conditions and circumstances under which it was conceived, the social and political events to which it was a local and contingent response, and the thought of the early figures who defined its terms and set its course for later generations. A historical approach helps us to uncover conservatism's enduring ideological core, the wood beneath the veneer, the normative substance behind the superficial talking points and official party platforms that have become a tiresomely familiar part of conservative political rhetoric today.

Edmund Burke and the Reaction Against Equality

Historians tend to identify Edmund Burke as conservatism's founding figure and Burke's *Reflections on the Revolution in France* as its founding text.[18] Burke's political philosophy can be best understood as a negative reaction to the fight for equality. His primary target is political revolution. For Burke, the revolutionary fervor for equality is a threat to social stability, historical continuity, and the natural order of things. Against the intoxicating clamor of political revolution, Burke insisted upon the necessity of what he called "tradition."[19] Not to be confused with a blanket nostalgia for the past, tradition for Burke is the slow, gentle, and methodical evolution of society over time. Tradition respects the past. It draws from the wisdom of antiquity to navigate its way through the novelty of the present. As Burke puts it:

> I set out with a perfect distrust of my own abilities; a total renunciation of every speculation of my own . . . I was resolved not to be guilty

of tampering: the odious vice of restless and unstable minds. I put my foot in the tracks of our forefathers, where I can neither wander nor stumble.[20]

This does not mean a generic hostility to change. Burke can at least appreciate that change is inevitable. But he distinguishes between good change and bad. Societies grow and develop best not through abrupt fits and starts, not through violent breaks and ruptures, but rather through mild "reform," Burke's technical term for benign, healthy, and desirable change. Revolution, by contrast, is a form of "innovation," a dirty word for Burke denoting a radical departure from the past.[21] Innovation is anarchic. It discards the time-tested wisdom of the ages and puts untested ideas into practice. Once we discard the past, we necessarily veer into ruin. Warning against such folly, Burke expresses full confidence that "the people of England will not ape the fashions they have never tried."[22]

If tradition were little more than a continuity with the past, it might seem harmless enough. But there is another facet to Burke's concept of tradition. Burke was concerned about the potency of reason to spark insatiable demands for wholesale, radical change. Reason is a poison mistaken by naive agitators as a cure. When used for social critique, when wielded for political change, reason contaminates, corrupts, and destroys. "It is always to be lamented," says Burke in one of his parliamentary speeches, "when men are driven to search into the foundations of the commonwealth."[23] In a letter to his friend Richard Champion, a Quaker industrialist, Burke writes, "A party which depended upon rational principles must perish the moment reason is withdrawn from it."[24] If reason attacks the present, if it demands a new social order, then how do defenders of the existing social order respond? If not by appeal to reason, then to what?

Burke's answer to this question is to celebrate "prejudice." In his *Reflections on the Revolution in France*, Burke refers to "our church establishment" as "the first of our prejudices." This is not "a prejudice destitute of reason, but involving in it profound and extensive wisdom."[25] Prejudice for Burke is composed of the religious customs, the cultural habits, the social biases, and ingrained dispositions we inherit from the past. Prejudice is distinct from reason. If reason is abstract, then prejudice is concrete. If reason is impersonal fantasy, then prejudice is personal reality. Prejudice cannot, by definition, counter reason on its own terms. But prejudice is what keeps us grounded. It gives our lives meaning, substance, and direction. Without it, we would be adrift, like the debris of a shipwreck floating aimlessly at sea. Rather than look upon prejudice as some sort of moral or philosophical liability, Burke encourages his fellow countrymen to celebrate the prejudices and the obstinacy that make up the English character. As he puts it, "Thanks to our sullen resistance to innovation, thanks to the cold sluggishness of our national character, we still bear the stamp of our forefathers."[26] "In this enlightened age," he says,

> I am bold enough to confess, that we are generally men of untaught feelings; that instead of casting away all our old prejudices, we cherish them to a very considerable degree, and to take more shame to ourselves, we cherish them because they are prejudices; and the longer they have lasted, and the more generally they have prevailed, the more we cherish them.[27]

If the answer to reason is the celebration of prejudice, then it is a short step from here to the celebration of ignorance. In a letter to his friend Richard Champion, Burke writes, "What a firm dependence is to be had upon ignorance and prejudices!"[28] During the period leading up to the French Revolution, Burke writes approvingly of ignorance. He commends the power of a "well-wrought veil" to induce political passivity.[29] He worries that "all the pleasing illusions which made power gentle and obedience liberal" risk being "dissolved by this new conquering empire of light and reason."[30] Veils and illusions are the "decent drapery of life," which reason threatens to have "rudely torn off."[31] For Burke, the core elements of tradition, then, are prejudice, obstinacy, ignorance, veils, and illusions.[32] But to whom do these core elements apply?

Surely not to Burke and those like him—members of the English elite who can recognize prejudice, obstinacy, ignorance, veils, and illusions. No, these components of tradition apply to "the poor and the lower orders."[33] Burke and his fellow members of the English elite drew a crucial distinction between citizens and subjects, between those entitled to the franchise and participation in government and those whose political role is limited to unquestioning obedience and deference to "the true natural aristocracy."[34] England's elites were horrified to learn of the poor French masses claiming the titles *citoyen* and *citoyenne* following the French Revolution.[35] They were likewise horrified to see similar rhetoric on English soil. The greeting "Britain! Fellow citizens!" struck them as an abomination, a contradiction in terms.[36] Mere subjects had no business talking like citizens. They therefore had to be put in their place.

Dr. Johnson, a close friend of Burke and a fellow Tory, argued that it was the duty of elites, those "who have leisure for enquiry," to "lead back the people to their honest labour; to tell them that submission is the duty of the ignorant, and content the virtue of the poor; that they have no skill in the art of government."[37] Bishop Samuel Horsley, the reactionary Anglican divine who debated Joseph Priestley over the theological validity of the doctrine of the Trinity, believed that political activity on the part of the lower orders should be limited to petitioning.

A fierce defender of the monarchy, Horsley confessed that he "did not know what the mass of the people in any country had to do with the laws but to obey them."[38]

The belief that citizenship belonged to the few and obedience and passivity to the many betrayed one of the distinctive elements of conservatism as an emerging political philosophy: a view of social order as hierarchy. Because "subordination," as Johnson put it,

> is very necessary for society, and contentions for superiority very dangerous, mankind, that is to say, all civilized nations, have settled it upon a plan invariable in principle. A man is born to hereditary rank; or his being appointed to certain offices, gives him a certain rank. Subordination tends greatly to human happiness. Were we all upon an equality, we should have no other enjoyment than mere animal pleasure.[39]

Johnson was genuinely heartbroken by the steady dismantling of hierarchy and subordination. As he wrote, "Subordination is sadly broken down in this age. No man, now, has the same authority which his father had. . . . No master has it over his servants: it is diminished in our colleges; nay, in our grammar schools."[40]

In a polemic against Thomas Paine's *The Rights of Man*, the barrister John Bowles remarked that "nothing can be more different from a pure and generous spirit of real patriotism . . . than that course and illiberal disposition which delights in abuse and invective against all persons with power and authority."[41] Bowles regarded egalitarianism as an assault upon "the higher powers" and "the dignity of superiors."[42] The barrister, Whig politician, and evangelical poet William Cowper, speaking of what he saw as the characteristic extremism of the French in times both old and new, was genuinely scandalized and heartbroken to see "princes and peers . . . reduced to a plain gentlemanship," and "gentles reduced to a level with their own lackeys." "Difference of rank and subordination," Cowper affirmed, are "of God's appointment and consequently essential to the well being of society."[43]

Not surprisingly, Burke rejects the liberal theory of the social contract, with its unnatural and corrosive egalitarianism. Against the worldly and collective contract, Burke affirms "the great primeval contract of eternal society, linking the lower with the higher natures, connecting the visible and the invisible world, according to a fixed compact sanctioned by the inviolable oath which holds all physical and all moral natures each in their appointed place."[44] A common rhetorical theme in early conservative thought was to use the metaphors of the head and feet to distinguish between the higher and lower orders. To encourage the feet to act like the head is to throw the whole of society into chaos. In his "Essay on Man," Alexander Pope writes:

> What if the foot ordain'd the dust to tread,
> Or hand to toil, aspir'd to be the head?
> What if the head, the eye, or ear repin'd
> To serve mere engines to the ruling mind?
> Just as absurd for any part to claim
> To be another, in this gen'ral frame:
> Just as absurd, to mourn the tasks or pains,
> The great directing Mind of All ordains.[45]

The conservative view of social order as hierarchy was not framed in arbitrary and self-serving terms. Rather, it was taken as a self-evident feature of nature, like the rising of the sun and the moon or the regularity of the tides. In this light, political revolution was seen as an attack on nature itself.

As Arthur Lovejoy has shown, the view of social order as hierarchy had been known since antiquity as the Great Chain of Being.[46] At the top of the chain is God. The subsequent links in the chain consist of, in descending order, angels, humans, animals, plants, and, finally, rocks and soil. Humanity itself is divided into a natural hierarchy, with the aristocracy and the clergy at the top and the poor and the uneducated at the bottom. Lovejoy notes that belief in a natural hierarchy reached its zenith in eighteenth-century Europe.[47] It formed a critical part of the moral and intellectual backdrop in which conservatism was conceived. It is therefore not surprising that the idea of the Great Chain of Being should form a constitutive component of the conservative worldview.[48]

However much contemporary conservatism might wish to portray itself as a grassroots movement against liberal elites, there is no getting away from the striking condescension of conservatism's founding figure toward the so-called lower orders. In one of the most memorable passages of *Reflections on the Revolution in France*, Burke affirms the role of "ancient opinions and rules of life" as the indispensable moral compass of society. Without that compass, he says, Europe would be lost. This "European world of ours," says Burke, has "depended for ages upon two principles." These are "the spirit of the gentleman and the spirit of the religion."[49] The nobility and the clergy have preserved and transmitted classical wisdom through the ages, in the midst of both peace and conflict, through the funding of education. But when education expands beyond the upper crust of society, it threatens to subvert the natural order. The very thought provokes Burke's ire: "Happy if they had all continued to know their indissoluble union and their proper place! Happy if learning, not debauched by ambition, had been satisfied to continue the instructor, and not aspired to be the master!" Burke continues, "Along with its natural protectors and guardians, learning will be cast into the mire and trodden down under the hoofs of a swinish multitude."[50] Likening the poor to a drove of pigs captures conservatism's quintessential antipathy and disdain for the underclasses.

From Hierarchy to Paranoia

How does a political ideology conceived in defense of ruling elites inspire conduct that clashes so strikingly with the social norms of royalty, the refined manners of the aristocracy, the codes of the gentleman and the lady, and the stern discipline and sobriety of the clergy? Conservatism's war on revolutionary movements for social justice and equality can be said to license irrational thinking and behavior that contrast with the proprieties of conservatism's founding figures. This is not a total irrationality. It is a calculated unreasonableness, irrationality with a purpose, strategic madness. In his reading of the conservative tradition, Corey Robin reveals conservatism's surprising admiration for the revolutionary enemy. As Robin notes, Burke, in his *Letters on a Regicide Peace*, plots a clever strategy against Jacobin-style revolutionary movements. Deploring England's strange production of music in response to the French Revolution, Burke sternly warns that "to destroy the enemy, by some means or other, the force opposed to it should be made to bear some analogy and resemblance to the force and spirit which that system exerts."[51]

If revolution thrives on popular dreams, hopes, agitation, and anger, then the conservative counterrevolution must feed on the same popular sentiments. Conservatives, Robin observes, "often are the left's best students."[52] They carefully study left-wing movements, mimicking their revolutionary style and rhetoric, putting them to counterrevolutionary ends. Conservatives may harbor a contempt for the poor. But what they learn from the revolutionary enemy is "the power of political agency and the potency of the mass."[53] They specialize in the art of stirring the people into a frenzy, fomenting agitation over some exaggerated or imaginary demon, while ensuring that the people will never get a taste of power. Conservatives target a sense of loss—economic deprivation, growing numbers of immigrants, a changing culture—and exploit that loss for cynical purposes. They specialize in what Robin calls an "upside down populism," inciting rage against "elites."[54]

The conservative strategy of brewing upside-down populism includes feeding paranoia, delusion, and wild conspiracy theories. In his classic work *The Paranoid Style in American Politics*, the intellectual historian Richard Hofstadter observes that delusional paranoia has been part of the fabric of American culture from its very inception.[55] As far back as 1797, the geographer and pastor

Jedidiah Morse sparked public unrest after delivering wild sermons about the Bavarian Illuminati. Morse claimed the Illuminati had orchestrated the French Revolution and that they were plotting similar subversive activities in America. Paranoia about the Illuminati and campfire tales of Masonic activity have remained a part of popular American lore ever since.[56] In 1835, Samuel Morse, son of Jedidiah Morse and inventor of the telegraph, published *Foreign Conspiracy Against the Liberties of the United States*, in which he alleged that Jesuit priests were infiltrating America and plotting to subvert American values.[57] That same year, Lyman Beecher, father of Harriet Beecher Stowe, published *A Plea for the West*, in which he stoked fear about Catholic immigrants outnumbering Protestant Christians and preparing for a hostile takeover of America.[58] This nativist panic often culminated in violence against Catholics, especially when they sought to exercise their right to vote. When Senator Eugene McCarthy conducted his infamous public hearings to expose alleged Communists within the United States military, he drew upon a long cultural history of hostility and paranoia toward the Other. In the case of McCarthy's hearings, it was the Communist rather than the Catholic who embodied some congenital anti-American and anti-Christian essence.

Hofstadter observes that while the paranoid style has a long history tied to religious animosity, it has taken on a unique character in American conservatism. Unlike paranoia about the Illuminati or Catholics, American conservatism is premised on an acute sense of dispossession in the here and now, the fear that "America has been largely taken away from them and their kind, though they are determined to try to repossess it and to prevent the final destructive act of subversion."[59] He identifies three main elements in the peculiar paranoia of American conservatism: the belief that New Deal social programs are a threat to freedom, the belief that American government officials covertly serve sinister foreign interests, and the belief that universities, the news media, and the entertainment industry are working in concert to indoctrinate and corrupt ordinary Americans. This is a virtual template that Republicans have followed ever since to stoke distrust and paranoia among the American public. After the presidency of Donald Trump, in which the world was bombarded with absurd conspiracy theories for four straight years, it is easy to forget that conspiracy theory has long been a part of American conservatism's paranoid style.

The paranoid style reinforces, and is reinforced by, what many scholars have called "the politics of resentment."[60] This is a purely negative, antisocial politics, which does not so much say what it stands for as highlight what it stands against. The politics of resentment is premised on distrust, suspicion, paranoia, and hostility toward the Other. The Other is taken to be at once mysterious and transparently evil. The Other is perpetually scheming and conniving, seeking to undermine "our" interests. The Other is not one of "us." The Other does not share our national aspirations or national pride. The Other is a domestic threat. The Other is irredeemable. The Other is, in a word, the enemy. Like a devil in disguise, the enemy takes many forms. The enemy is the liberal, who wants to raise our taxes; the socialist, who wants public healthcare; the feminist, who attacks the rights of men; gay people, who undermine traditional marriage; trans people, who prey on children; Hollywood, which propagates liberal values; the university, which teaches students dangerous ideas; and the Muslim, who wants to implement Shari'ah law and take away our freedoms. In short, the enemy is everywhere.

The politics of resentment is not an agonistic politics, in which political rivals are mere competitors in a fair contest for power. Fairness does not factor into the political equation. Because the Other is the enemy, ordinary rules of politics do not apply. Principle is irrelevant, even naive. Following principle in a war against the enemy would be like playing chess on a real battlefield. It would be the wrong game. For this reason, the politics of resentment is deeply corrosive to a democratic culture. It undermines the very ideas of fairness and principle. What matters for the politics of resentment is not fairness but stratagem—routing the enemy by any means necessary, thereby thwarting the enemy's political designs. In the politics of resentment, the sole purpose of voting is to secure political victory, principles be damned. After the embarrassing revelations in the fall of 2022 that Republican Senate candidate and vocal abortion opponent Herschel Walker had paid multiple women to have abortions, right-wing radio host Dana Loesch remarked, "Does this change anything? Not a damned thing. How many times have I said four very important words. These four words: Winning. Is. A. Virtue." Loesch went on to say, "I don't care if Herschel Walker paid to abort endangered baby eagles. I want control of the Senate."[61]

In the politics of resentment, even active voter manipulation, obstruction, and intimidation are justified means of achieving political victory. Voter intimidation notably soared in the 2020 U.S. general election, due to Trump supporters. In late October 2020, Kristen Clarke, president and executive director of the National Lawyers' Committee for Civil Rights Under Law, reported that her organization's election protection hotline received over a hundred thousand calls since July 1 of that year.[62] Just days later, a group of armed Trump supporters, determined to ensure Trump's political victory, swarmed Joe Biden's campaign bus in an attempt to run it off the highway. The Biden campaign was forced to cancel their event out of concern for public safety.[63] Trump later defended his supporters, saying, "These patriots did nothing wrong."[64]

The Politics of Fear

In the family of toxic human emotions, fear is a close cousin of resentment. Fear is yet another emotion that political conservatism eagerly seeks to exploit. In the *Rhetoric*, Aristotle defines fear as "a painful or troubled feeling caused by the impression of an imminent evil that causes destruction or pain."[65] Fear is a reaction not to distant evils but rather to evils that appear "near at hand."[66] Fear is the unsettling anticipation that "we are going to suffer some fatal misfortune."[67] Because fear is so easy to manipulate, it is a natural political weapon. Fear is the tool of the tyrant and the autocrat, who subdue and pacify restless populations with mass injections of fear. But fear is also a dominant emotion in free societies. In liberal democracies composed of sovereign individuals, fear is one of the few foundations for social cohesion. Fear brings otherwise solitary and atomized individuals together. As Corey Robin puts it in his historical study on fear, "Convinced that we lack moral or political principles to bind us together, we savor the experience of being afraid . . . for only fear, we believe, can turn us from isolated men and women into a united people."[68] Conservatism thrives on fear. It turns fear into a comprehensive worldview, a lens for making sense of social and political reality.

As David Altheide says, "Fear has become a dominant perspective. Fear begins with things we fear, but over time, with enough repetition and expanded use, it becomes a way of looking at life."[69] The linguist Ruth Wodak describes the right-wing "politics of fear" as consisting of multiple specific fears: fear of cultural change, fear of losing one's job, fear of strangers, fear of globalization, fear of surrendering national sovereignty, fear of a disappearing heritage, and fear of eroding morals and values.[70] According to Wodak, the politics of fear inevitably divides the world into "us" and "them."[71] It appeals to exclusionary identities. It rests on a denial of historical injustice against minority groups. It leaves the public more susceptible to the false appeals of charismatic demagogues. Wodak finds that the politics of fear inevitably relies upon the power and appeal of patriarchy.[72]

The Rise of Ur-Trolls

It is not difficult to see how the many ideological components of conservatism— the celebration of prejudice, obstinacy, ignorance, veils, and illusions; conservatism's upside-down populism; the elevation of paranoia to the status of a political metaphysics; the pathological belief in conspiracy theory; the cultivation of fear as a systematic worldview; and the belligerent politics of resentment—are the basic ingredients for political trolling. Two of America's most notorious conservative personalities, Rush Limbaugh and Ann Coulter, were pioneers in elevating trolling into a political art form. They helped establish trolling as the defining ethos of American conservatism.

Limbaugh revolutionized talk radio in the 1980s. Through a syndicated show broadcast on hundreds of stations across America, Limbaugh combined the petty prejudice, defiant ignorance, and blue-collar aesthetics of Archie Bunker with a perverted delight in aggressively pushing the boundaries of public decency to a breaking point. He successfully converted talk radio from a tame and polite format into a viral outrage machine. His radio show was premised on the politics of resentment. He pushed a view of America as embroiled in a historic battle, an end-of-days culture war between "us" and "them."[73] Limbaugh did not bother with even the slightest pretense of civil discourse. He proudly adopted the standpoint of a militant engaged in ideological combat. Talk radio for Limbaugh was guerilla warfare through the airwaves.[74]

One of Limbaugh's most influential contributions to American political culture was to introduce childish name-calling into conservative rhetoric. An insatiable misogynist bitterly opposed to feminism, he coined the term "feminazis," insisting that women who advocate for gender equality "can't get a man" and that "their rage is one long PMS attack." He blasted Black political leaders as latter-day slaves working on a "liberal plantation." He disparaged those who campaigned for the homeless as "compassion fascists." He framed environmentalists as "extremist wacko-nut cases" and "a bunch of socialists who want bigger government and poorer people." He blasted animal rights activists, claiming they wanted no less than "the extermination of the human race."[75]

In 1990, during the height of the AIDS crisis in America, Limbaugh displayed a horrifying lack of basic human decency and feeling in a segment called "AIDS Update," in which he mocked those who had died of AIDS to the tune of Steam's "Na Na Hey Hey Kiss Him Goodbye." Even as the death toll from AIDS reached a staggering 100,000 victims, he had the temerity to say, "Gays deserved their fate."[76] When Michael J. Fox endorsed Claire McCaskill in her Senate race because of her backing of stem cell research, Limbaugh accused Fox of faking the symptoms of his Parkinson's disease, even going so far as to impersonate Fox's tremors and convulsions.[77] In 2012, when Georgetown University student Sandra Fluke testified before Congress to support coverage for contraceptives under the Affordable Care Act, Limbaugh subjected Fluke to one of the most vicious tirades of his career, calling her a "slut" and a "prostitute" who "wants to be paid to have sex." Claiming to speak for taxpayers subsidizing her sex life, he tastelessly demanded to see videotapes of Fluke in the act.[78] *The Atlantic* summarized Limbaugh's abuse of Fluke succinctly: "Rush Limbaugh Is Trolling Us."[79]

Though Limbaugh was forced to apologize for some of his most shocking and offensive antics on air, he never renounced his vicious misogyny, racism, and homophobia. Had his sponsors not threatened to abandon him following his worst outbursts, he likely would never have apologized at all. Bigotry was very much baked into his persona and message. His defiance was part of his rhetorical style. For this reason, he became a role model for conservatives seeking a meaningful path in an ostensibly liberal world. He inspired generations of reactionary talking heads on both television and radio. As Sean Hannity put it, "There is no talk radio as we know it without Rush Limbaugh; it just doesn't exist." Had it not been for Limbaugh, Hannity added, "there's no Fox News."[80]

Whereas Limbaugh limited himself mostly to talk radio, Coulter took to every media format possible to deliver her incendiary anti-liberal message. Coulter began her career as a professional troll in the 1990s during the Clinton years. Educated at Cornell University and University of Michigan Law School, Coulter applied her aptitude for words to conservative punditry.[81] Like all political pundits, she created a unique shtick designed to set her apart from the competition, which then was still largely male and stodgy. Coulter found her niche as America's most extreme political shock artist. Like Limbaugh, she abandoned all pretense of decorum, every norm of civil discourse. She, too, positioned herself as liberalism's ultimate nemesis. In effect, she became the Marilyn Manson of the American right. She reveled in being a monster, the grisly embodiment of liberal fears and nightmares. Coulter acquired a masterful understanding of the liberal mind, preying on its sensitivities, weaknesses, and vulnerabilities. She honed the skill of cutting and wounding the liberal enemy where they were most likely to bleed and suffer. Like Limbaugh, Coulter helped turn hatred of liberals into an all-American blood sport.

Coulter's books, speeches, columns, interviews, and tweets are a multimedia gallery of political trolling. She has expressed her inveterate nativism, racism, xenophobia, homophobia, and misogyny through a third-rate stand-up comedy routine. She has said, for example, that women should never have been given the right to vote,[82] that the United States should disregard civilian casualties and drop a nuclear bomb on North Korea,[83] that the U.S. government should spy on all Arabs and engage in "torture as a televised spectator sport,"[84] that liberals are "driven by Satan,"[85] and that the Bible commands us to "go forth, be fruitful, multiply, and rape the planet."[86] Unlike traditional conservatives, Coulter does not hide her racist contempt for non-European peoples. In an interview with Fusion TV's Jorge Ramos before a live studio audience, Coulter flatly declared Mexico to have an inferior culture.[87] When a member of the audience, an undocumented immigrant, asked Coulter for a hug as a sign of their mutual humanity, Coulter refused. When confronted by an Arab Muslim Canadian about her remark that Muslims should travel on "flying carpets" instead of airplanes, Coulter dismissively said, "Take a camel."[88]

Coulter's provocations are so extreme that it can be hard to tell whether she actually believes her own words. There is nothing factual or logical in any of her outrageous remarks. Liberals exasperated over her flagrant disregard for truth, reason, and basic human decency are torn over what to make of her. Chris Sosa, a managing editor at AlterNet, has argued that Coulter is a masterful satirist, laughing at liberals who take her too seriously. According to Sosa, recognizing Coulter as a mere comedy act would deprive her of the power to shock and offend.[89] Amanda Marcotte, writing for *Slate*, insists that Coulter is not a satirist but a charlatan specializing in scandalous speech merely to sell books and appear on television. Marcotte sees Coulter as a genuine conservative, albeit a shameless and opportunistic one who has "figured out how to bilk the rubes while also organizing the rubes for political gain." Marcotte regards Coulter as a political genius, insisting that we should "respect her work for what it actually is."[90]

We might say something similar about Limbaugh. He, too, was a showman, whose sincerity is open to question. But seeking to make sense of Coulter and Limbaugh as either satirists or charlatans misses something far more crucial about them: their role in revolutionizing conservative speech. As ur-trolls, they helped lay the foundations for the mainstreaming of political trolling. If earlier conservative icons like William F. Buckley worked hard to make conservatism intellectually respectable, then Limbaugh, Coulter, and kindred ur-trolls worked hard to remove from conservatism any semblance of a moral conscience. They fought to inoculate conservatives against guilt and remorse for cruel, obnoxious, and antisocial speech. They taught conservatives to enjoy their cruelty and to delight in provocation for its own sake. In short, they turned American conservatism into a vast community of political trolls, paving the way for Milo Yiannopoulos, Steven Crowder, Alex Jones, Lauren Southern, and Ben Shapiro. They helped set the conditions for the rise of the alt-right, the Boogaloo Bois, the Proud Boys, and Turning Point USA. When the guardians of an older conservatism like David Frum, George Will, and Rick Wilson deny that Trump and his supporters are conservative, or when they lament the downward spiral of the Republican Party into the gutter of rabid trolling, they are defending a mythical moral and intellectual integrity against conservatism's inherent unreason. If conservatism has been taken over by trolls, it is merely realizing its *telos*.

4

Shame

Natalie Wynn is an anomaly on social media. A transgender socialist fluent in cultural and political theory, Wynn has built a formidable reputation for taking on the far right on YouTube. Through slickly produced videos set against elegant Gothic backdrops, Wynn performs entrancing monologues in glamorous attire, glittery makeup, and extravagantly long nails. She often intersperses her comments with sips from a goblet or a champagne flute. She also throws in a bit of trailer park chic into her videos, just to underscore the ironic nature of her performances. Wynn's videos offer unusually insightful, entertaining, and provocative commentary on gender, sexuality, culture, class, and politics. She has educated literally hundreds of thousands of viewers about what it means to be transgender: the idea, the experience, the struggle, the suffering. Her social media presence earned her widespread praise, both online and offline, making her one of the most sought-after guests on podcasts, radio shows, and university campuses.[1] That is, until she got canceled.

Wynn's story is a case study in a kind of liberal excess: when the ostensible commitment to uphold equality and justice devolves into disproportionate punishment and the purging of the enemy from social space. In September 2019, Wynn posted a series of tweets expressing her disaffection over cisgender people going out of their way to share their pronouns in her company. For Wynn, this new form of social etiquette, despite its well-intended aim of creating a welcoming and inclusive space for trans people, had the opposite effect. It made her feel otherized and alienated. As she tweeted, "There's this paradox where I can go to a sports bar in North Carolina and be miss/ma'am'd all night no question, but in self-consciously trans-inclusive spaces I have to explain my pronouns & watch woke people awkwardly correct themselves every time they say 'you guys.'" Wynn then followed up by tweeting, "I guess it's good for people who use they/them only and want only gender-neutral language. But it comes at the minor expense of semi-passable transes like me and that's super fucking hard for us."[2]

Trolling Ourselves to Death. Jason Hannan, Oxford University Press. © Oxford University Press 2023.
DOI: 10.1093/oso/9780197557761.003.0005

For many of Wynn's followers, this last tweet crossed a line, since it appeared to minimize the struggle of nonbinary people for recognition and trivialize their plea to be addressed through gender-neutral pronouns. Wynn was therefore castigated for being insensitive toward nonbinary people. The criticism grew so severe that Wynn deactivated her Twitter account. This move only served as ammunition for her right-wing adversaries, who used it as an excuse to indulge in transphobic bigotry. Disheartened that her departure from Twitter was being exploited by right-wing trolls for cynical and manipulative purposes, Wynn returned to Twitter to make a heartfelt apology. She acknowledged the insensitivity of her words and, following a now-familiar form of online apology, vowed to "do better."[3]

But this controversy was soon overshadowed by one far more grave and tragic. In the fall of 2019, Wynn posted a video entitled "Opulence," in which she used a class lens to examine the ostentatious displays of style and glamour of the rich and powerful.[4] The video features several quotes from prominent figures read by guest voice actors. One of those voice actors was Buck Angel, a long-time transgender rights activist and pornographic film star. Angel has become a controversial figure in the LGBTQ community on account of his outdated use of terms like "transsexual" and his unapologetic transmedicalism, the view that transgender identities are contingent upon experiencing gender dysmorphia or undergoing gender-affirming medical treatment. To Wynn's critics, the inclusion of Angel in the "Opulence" video, even as a voice actor, not only crossed another line, but also seemed to confirm a pattern of insensitivity and bigotry. Although Wynn posted a statement rejecting transmedicalism, her critics found it insincere. In their eyes, her pattern of mistakes had become unforgivable. A large segment of her followers reacted with fury, demanding that she be canceled—the term du jour for bringing someone's career to an end.[5]

But the judgment on Twitter was not limited to Wynn. Her close friends and collaborators, including prominent YouTube video essayists like Kat Blaque, Harris Brewis, Lindsay Ellis, and Abigail Thorn, also came under fire. Some of Wynn's critics demanded that these friends issue a statement condemning her actions. Others insisted that they disavow her friendship. Still others subjected Wynn's friends to a torrent of trolling. Thorn, who runs Philosophy Tube, posted a statement in support of nonbinary people, but also revealed that she had been subjected to vicious abuse for her friendship with Wynn:

> Sadly, I've also been harassed, threatened, doxxed, had my private life speculated on and my loved ones insulted . . . [I]n recognizing the feelings of those who kindly raised their concerns in a polite way, I do not wish to legitimize the great many people who use their hurt as a cover for unacceptable toxic and abusive behavior.[6]

After posting this statement, Thorn was subjected to further abuse. Even those with no relationship to Wynn, such as YouTube personality Mia Mulder, were harassed and placed on "the list," merely for leaving a heart in response to Thorn's statement. The uproar revealed the reality and severity of guilt by association. As Wynn put it, "We're only missing a couple of degrees of separation before every living person on the planet Earth is canceled."[7]

Natalie Wynn's story is by no means unique. It is merely one of countless stories, most of which we never read about. These stories reveal the shifting terms and evolving ethics of moral accountability in the age of social media. Despite its being a new cultural concept, we are already tired of hearing about cancel culture. It has become an emotionally exhausting topic in part because we cannot seem to agree on how to make sense of it or what to do about it. There are both conservative and liberal takes on cancel culture. Conservatives have effectively created a moral panic about it. Indeed, the very idea of "cancel culture" is a conservative invention.[8] To invoke the concept is already to be implicated in a reactionary logic. Conservatives see cancel culture as only the latest iteration of the eternal tyranny of political correctness.[9] By contrast, liberal defenders of cancel culture insist that canceling the guilty is a necessary and justified tool for holding people in power accountable. Liberals regard the critique of cancel culture and its close sibling call-out culture as a transparent attempt to evade moral accountability.[10] Then, there are people in between. Loretta Ross, a leading Black feminist and pioneer of reproductive justice, has become a notable critic of cancel culture and call-out culture.[11] Ross argues for calling *in* rather than calling out. She encourages having difficult conversations and holding each other accountable with love and compassion. The irony, however, is that Ross herself has been called out for calling out call-out culture.[12]

How, then should we make sense of this tiresome yet widespread practice in digital spaces? This chapter moves beyond the moral panic over cancel culture, a common obsession among conservatives, liberals, and leftists alike. This moral panic fixates too heavily on free speech and the tyranny of social justice warriors at the cost of understanding how social media set users against each other and also profit from their strife. I therefore explore the nexus of debt, guilt, and capital on social media. Drawing from Friedrich Nietzsche's analysis of morality and the forgotten relationship between debt and guilt, I show that by joining a social network, we become indebted to each other for our digital existence. This indebtedness is intimately bound up with the possibility of judgment and punishment. To be indebted is to be at the mercy of others. Online shaming, I will argue, functions as a social mechanism for the communal reclamation of debt and the practice of punishment, a means to teach the guilty a lesson about breaching social norms.

Nietzsche on Debt and Guilt

The Genealogy of Morals is Friedrich Nietzsche's most provocative and influential work. It can be read as a penetrating diagnosis of an underlying cultural disease in the modern Western world. The *Genealogy* is Nietzsche's attempt to lift the veil from contemporary morality, whose true nature and origins, he argues, have been buried and forgotten beneath the sediments of history. By revealing the vast difference between morality's origins and its contemporary self-image, Nietzsche hopes to carve out a different mode of being in the world, a new consciousness unimprisoned within the guilt cult of modern morality. To do this, he brings the techniques of philological analysis to bear upon the language of morality—its terms, concepts, phrases, categories, and distinctions. In the first of the three essays of the *Genealogy*, Nietzsche argues that the original meanings of the concepts of "good" and "bad" corresponded to class positions. "Good" simply referred to the values and the ethos of the ruling classes in ancient Rome, and "bad" to the lives of the poor and plebeian. "Good" and "bad," he contends, were originally elite concepts, invented by the powerful to distinguish themselves from the lower orders. Nietzsche takes issue with certain unnamed historians of morality, who argue that the original meaning of "good" was altruism and that the original meaning of "bad" was selfishness. These historians, Nietzsche contends, are profoundly mistaken in anachronistically projecting contemporary meanings onto the past. When we conduct a philological analysis of moral terms, we can uncover historical clues as to their true origins.[13]

Nietzsche applies this approach to the concept of "guilt" in the second essay of the *Genealogy*.[14] In our contemporary moral parlance, "guilt" is either the legal status of having violated some law or the feeling of remorse over having committed some moral offense. But Nietzsche argues that "guilt" originally had nothing to do with what we today call morality. He points to the double meaning of the German word *Schuld*, which denotes both debt and guilt.[15] He tells us that the origins of guilt, both as a status and as a psychological state, lie in economic relationships of exchange: buying, selling, and trading. This is the relationship of the creditor to the debtor. On the original meaning of *schuld*, to be guilty was to be in debt, a state of financial obligation. Commerce, Nietzsche says, is what first conditioned us to become creatures of responsibility. Unlike nonhuman animals, we humans developed the capacity to be responsible for our actions. This capacity comes through an expansive sense of time. We navigate our way not just through the physical world but also through time, that is, with an awareness of the past, present, and future. Our ability to plan for the future implies that our desired outcomes are not inevitable. We may well forget to act on our intentions. We therefore require a psychological mechanism for keeping ourselves in check.

Nietzsche argues that our conscience arose for this purpose. Our conscience is our system of moral checks and balances, our internal bookkeeping of our promises and commitments. It helps us keep track of our responsibilities and obligations. But our conscience could not have arisen spontaneously. It had to be conditioned through repetition, much like the dogs in Ivan Pavlov's experiments, who were trained to salivate at the ringing of a bell. The birth of consciousness therefore required techniques of memory, or *mnemotechnics*.[16] Nietzsche contends that the cultivation of memory could not have been achieved through pleasure and comfort. He cites an old adage: "If something is to stay in the memory, it must be burned in: only that which never ceases to *hurt* stays in the memory."[17] Our ability to be responsible, to make oaths, promises, pledges, and pacts, is the legacy of some primeval violence. At some point, the argument goes, we discovered that pain was the most effective means of cultivating memory. As Nietzsche puts it:

> Man could never do without blood, torture, and sacrifices when he felt the need to create a memory for himself; the most dreadful sacrifices and pledges (sacrifices of the first-born among them), the most repulsive mutilations (castration, for example), the cruelest rites of all the religious cults (and all religions are at the deepest level systems of cruelties)—all this has its origins in the instinct that realized that pain is the most powerful aid to mnemonics.[18]

Nietzsche argues that the weaker the memory, the more severe the pain necessary to build that memory, in order to leave lasting impressions upon the mind and thereby cultivate our conscience. He lists some of the extreme forms of cruelty among the ancient Germans for building memory: stoning, the breaking wheel, piercing the body with stakes, being pulled apart or trampled by horses, being boiled alive, being flayed alive, cutting out chunks of flesh, and being covered with honey and left out in the heat to be swarmed by insects.[19] It was only through such extreme acts of cruelty, inflicted over and over again through public spectacle, that we learned the meaning of "do" and "don't," that we acquired a sense of responsibility, and that we learned what promises are and the consequences of breaking them.

Financial obligations were the original form of promise-making. To take a loan was to enter a state of financial obligation, of debt or guilt, until the loan was paid.[20] Contrary to our contemporary understanding of moral accountability, guilt originally had no connection to intention. The punishment of the guilty was not contingent upon judgments of criminal intent or determinations of wrongdoing. Nietzsche insists that any such theory about the origins of punishment necessarily places the cart before the horse. In the historical chain of events, punishment was originally conceived as a form of financial compensation, an option for settling one's debts. Punishment was written into the contract between creditors and debtors, who together decided that the *financial* injury of the creditor could be paid in full through the *physical* injury of the debtor.

To enter into a financial contract was thus to make a promise, one that required that an indelible memory be seared into the mind. Promises were kept on threat of pain. Debtors guaranteed their ability to repay their loans by offering as collateral their possessions, their wives, their bodies, even their lives. The contractual relationship stipulated the precise equivalence between loans and specific forms of physical injury. In the event that debtors defaulted on their loans, creditors were entitled to "inflict every kind of indignity and torture" upon the bodies of debtors.[21] Payment collection was therefore an occasion of spectacular pain and cruelty. The act of punishing the debtor was carried out not with anger but rather with pleasure. As Nietzsche puts it:

> Let us be clear as to the logic of this form of compensation: it is strange enough. An equivalence is provided by the creditor's receiving, in place of literal compensation for an injury (thus in place of money, land, possessions of any kind), a recompense in the form of a kind of *pleasure*— the pleasure of being allowed to vent his power freely upon the one who is powerless, the voluptuous pleasure "*de faire le mal pour le plaisir de le faire*," the enjoyment of violation.[22]

Nietzsche notes the inverse relationship between status and pleasure: the lower the creditor's rank in the social hierarchy, the greater the pleasure in punishing the debtor. By meting out punishment, the creditor enjoyed, if only for a moment, the coveted "right of the masters," the thrill of wielding power over an inferior. For creditors of a lower social rank, exercising their "title to cruelty" brought greater pleasure than mere monetary compensation.[23] Acts of cruelty were carnivals of sadistic pleasure, for in punishment, as Nietzsche puts it, "there is so much that is *festive*."[24]

Nietzsche describes the relationship between creditors and debtors as basic to humanity. There is something universal and everlasting about it. It defines so many forms of social life, especially life in a community.[25] To dwell with others is to reap the rewards of communal life. Communities provide security and protection from injury. They confer benefits and privileges unattainable to outsiders living on their own. (Nietzsche highlights the double meaning of the German word *Elend*, which denotes both exile and misery.)[26] The benefits of communal life are not unconditional. Membership in a community takes the form of a promise, the pledge to conform to the community's rules. To violate those rules, to break the pledge, is to enter a state of guilt with respect to the community—the grand creditor. Nietzsche notes that the precise damage caused by violating the community's rules is of less significance than the fact of having violated them. To violate the rules is to injure the dignity of the community. Violations qualitatively transform members into debtors. At that point, the community is entitled to teach the offending members an unforgettable lesson about communal life, to remind them "what these benefits are really worth."[27] This lesson is taught by stripping offenders of their communal rights and privileges, reducing them to outsiders, treating them as reviled enemies, as prisoners of war, who are to be subjected to spectacular acts of cruelty and punished without mercy, as if to celebrate victory in battle. Nietzsche notes that as with social rank, so, too, with communal power. The less powerful a community, the more cruel and extreme the punishment, for the exercise of cruelty offers a rare and exquisite taste of power.

Nietzsche does not see this thirst for cruelty as either immoral or unnatural. Rather, he sees it as part of our primal natures. Just as a lion craves the taste of flesh and blood, we human animals crave the thrill of inflicting cruelty. But, he says, this natural craving has been suppressed ever since the rise and dominance of Christian morality. Christian morality redefines "good" and "bad" in cosmic and metaphysical terms, as eternal standards that reside outside of time and history. According to this new system of morality, all human conduct is measured against these timeless standards by an imaginary judge, who ensures that ultimate justice will be delivered in the afterlife. This judge is the personification of the feelings of rancor and resentment, the fantasy of those who envy the powerful. Religious morality thrives on fear. It appeals to its vengeful and vindictive phantasm of a deity for psychologically coercing its members into submitting to its conceptions of good and bad, which are now redefined in metaphysical terms as good and evil.

Christian morality alters the creditor-debtor dynamic once again. Because of Christ's self-sacrifice on the cross, Christians are forever indebted to their lord and savior—the ultimate creditor. This sacrifice, rather than being a source of universal liberation, leaves the believer trapped in a state of permanent guilt. Now the instincts for cruelty and violence turn inward. Rather than directing our appetite for violence exclusively toward others, we internalize it, unleashing it upon ourselves. This, argues Nietzsche, marks the birth of the "soul."[28] When the instincts for violence and cruelty turn inward, we experience what Nietzsche calls "bad conscience," the *feeling* of guilt. Bad conscience is the psychological anguish and torture of being scolded by the voice of a silent judge in our minds, the voice of God. Believers consumed by guilt "lacerate," "persecute," "assault," and "maltreat" themselves.[29] They behave like a caged animal, "rubb[ing] itself raw against the bars of its cage as one tries to 'tame' it."[30] The more intense the internalized instincts for cruelty, the more severe the self-torture and punishment. Believers subject themselves to psychological and even physical flagellation to pay back a debt that can never be settled. This endless pain, this pointless suffering, this act of "man's suffering *of man, of himself*," is the degenerative cultural disease from which Nietzsche had hoped to provide a way out.[31]

What are we to make of Nietzsche's argument about debt and guilt? When Nietzsche says the feeling of guilt "had its origins ... in the oldest and most primitive personal relationship, that between buyer and seller, creditor and debtor," is he right?[32] The *Genealogy* is unusual among Nietzsche's writings. It was composed as long-form essays, as opposed to the collections of acidic aphorisms for which he is better known. Presumably, because of the complexity of the subject matter, Nietzsche thought it necessary to rely upon a more formal genre of writing. Yet Nietzsche's bald assertions about the origins of guilt and morality lack evidence. Other than interesting philological insights, he provides no empirical evidence, no historical research and scholarship, to support his claims. Even as he resorted to a formal mode of argument, he resisted the formal empirical methods of historiography.

Even to ask these questions, however, is already to have misunderstood Nietzsche's aim. As David Graeber points out in his anthropological study on debt, "to ask for evidence would be to miss the point. We are dealing here not with a real historical argument, *but with a purely imaginative exercise*."[33] Graeber points out that Nietzsche's argument makes sense and becomes terrifyingly plausible if we accept the premise that "the most primitive personal relationship" is indeed that between buyer and seller, between creditor and debtor. "The problem," says Graeber, "is that the premise is insane." And so Graeber writes:

> There is also every reason to believe that Nietzsche knew the premise was insane; in fact, that this was the entire point. What Nietzsche is doing here is starting out from the standard, common-sense assumption about the nature of human beings prevalent in his day (and to a large extent, still prevalent)—that we are rational calculating machines, that commercial self-interest comes before society, that "society" itself is just a way of putting a kind of temporary lid on the resulting conflict. That is, he is starting out from ordinary bourgeois assumptions *and driving them to a place where they can only shock a bourgeois audience.*[34]

As Graeber suggests, Nietzsche's argument is indeed powerful and illuminating if we accept his starting premise that human relationships are best understood in terms of the marketplace—that we humans are buyers and sellers by nature. If we begin with this assumption, then the world does indeed appear as Nietzsche describes it, a world plagued by debt and guilt, and fated to merciless cruelty. However, if we take the *Genealogy* to be an abstract philosophical exercise rather than an empirical historical argument, then how might we make sense of the link between debt and guilt under the regime of digital capitalism in which we all participate today? To this question, the Frankfurt School philosopher and literary critic Walter Benjamin offered the clues for an answer.

Benjamin on the Cult of Capitalism

If *The Genealogy of Morals* is a provocative thought experiment about religious society conceived in bourgeois terms, then Walter Benjamin's 1921 essay "Capitalism as Religion" is an ominous account of bourgeois society conceived in religious terms.[35] "Capitalism as Religion" is a fragmentary reflection about modern society that was never intended for publication. It appeared in print only in 1985, more than four decades after Benjamin's tragic death. The actual text of the essay is a mere two pages long, written in Benjamin's characteristically dense, cryptic, and evocative prose style. Yet it is rich with profound insights that can illuminate both the nature of capitalism in general and life in the age of social media in particular.

Benjamin opens his essay with a rather bold and direct assertion: "A religion may be discerned in capitalism—that is to say, capitalism serves essentially to allay the same anxieties, torments, and disturbances to which the so-called religions offer answers."[36] What Benjamin sets out to analyze here is the concealed religious structure of capitalism, or what we might call our "economic theology."[37] Benjamin seeks to go much further than Max Weber in *The Protestant Ethic and the Spirit of Capitalism*, where Weber argues that Calvinist theology had laid the moral foundations and set the social terms in which capitalism could take root. On Weber's historical reading, the religious gave way to the secular. While the one may have shaped the other, there was nonetheless a decisive break. But according to Benjamin, this is a serious misunderstanding of modernity that overlooks the theological continuity between Christianity and capitalism. Capitalism is very much a religion, and a dogmatic one at that, replete with devotional rituals and fanatical observance. Benjamin acknowledges that his claim "would still lead even today to the folly of an endless universal polemic."[38] If that was true in 1921, it would be even more true today.[39]

Benjamin identifies four features of the religious structure of capitalism. First, he says, capitalism is a "purely cultic religion, perhaps the most extreme that ever existed."[40] What makes capitalism a cultic, as opposed to non-cultic, religion is that, unlike the "so-called religions," it lacks an explicit theology. Under capitalism, everything has its meaning only in its "relationship to the cult."[41] Here, "the cult" is a reference to capital, the forms of wealth that grow through circulation as money and commodities within the market system. Benjamin regards capital as a hidden god, the tacit object of our desires. When seen through this lens, he says, even "utilitarianism acquires its religious overtones."[42] That is, the impersonal and hypercalculative practices of capitalism—investment, speculation, buying, selling, and trading—can be understood as the dogmatic rituals of a bona fide cult. Another sign of capitalism's cultic nature, Benjamin suggests, is that its practitioners are incapable of recognizing that they belong to a religion. Their fanatical devotion becomes a barrier to self-awareness.

The second feature of capitalism is what Benjamin calls "the permanence of the cult." By this, he means that capitalism is the never-ending, round-the-clock "celebration of a cult *sans rêve et sans merci.*" Under capitalism, there are no distinctions between weekdays and weekends, between workdays and holidays, between work and home life. Each day is a "feast day." Each day requires extravagant displays of "sacred pomp." "Each day," therefore, "commands the utter fealty of each worshipper."[43] Benjamin here describes capitalism's all-encompassing power, in which every aspect and every moment of our existence is lived in devotion to the cult. As Michael Löwy puts it in his commentary on Benjamin's essay, "Capitalist practices do not know any pause, they rule over the life of individuals from morning to night, from spring to winter, from the cradle to the grave."[44] Capitalism is a totalitarian system, "an iron destiny from which no one seems able to escape."[45]

The third feature of capitalism is that, like Christianity, it produces guilt. As Benjamin puts it, "the cult makes guilt pervasive." Endless devotion and endless guilt are two sides of the same religious coin. But unlike Christianity, capitalism "creates guilt, not atonement."[46] This is the most intriguing element of Benjamin's account of capitalism. Whereas Christianity at least offers the self-conscious believer the *promise* of atonement, even if it can never be fully achieved in practice, capitalism does not even offer this much to its dutiful followers. It creates guilt without end. Because it lacks an explicit theology, its followers labor and toil without any self-awareness of their sin and guilt, which remain forever implicit and subconscious. Benjamin here is worth quoting in full:

> In this respect, this religious system is caught up in the headlong rush of a larger movement. A vast sense of guilt that is unable to find relief seizes on the cult, not to atone for this guilt, but to make it universal, to hammer it into the conscious mind, so as once and for all to include God in the system of guilt and thereby awaken in Him an interest in the process of atonement.[47]

As a German literary critic, Benjamin is also attuned to the dual meaning of *Schuld.* He draws our attention to "the demonic ambiguity of this word."[48] Like Nietzsche, he recognizes that the psychological torture of bad conscience is intimately bound up with a sense of indebtedness to a deity. But unlike Nietzsche,

Benjamin sees capital as the true god and real ultimate creditor of the modern world. Under capitalism, a sense of guilt becomes pervasive because we feel a personal obligation toward the hidden and tacit god of wealth in all its multifarious forms: money, property, commodities, investments. We neurotically devote ourselves to working tirelessly before the altar of capital, even during our personal time in the privacy of our homes.

This devotion is very much in keeping with the Protestant ethic. As Weber says in his discussion of the possibilities and limits of pleasure in Puritan theology, "Man is only a trustee of the goods which have come to him through God's grace." Man is therefore obligated to "give an account of every penny entrusted to him." To those pious believers who wish to remain within these good graces, Weber observes, it is risky to "spend any of it for a purpose which does not serve the glory of God but only one's own enjoyment." This responsibility, "man's duty towards his possessions," "bears with chilling weight on his life." The "greater his possessions," the greater "the feeling of responsibility" for preserving them "undiminished for the glory of God." While Weber sees this weighty sense of personal responsibility as merely a cultural influence of the Protestant ethic upon the spirit of capitalism, Benjamin sees it as central to capitalism's cultic nature. Everyone, rich and poor alike, is indebted to capital. Everyone feels the "chilling weight" of that responsibility upon their lives. Everyone, then, is consumed by guilt. For many, that guilt soon devolves into despair. Benjamin's short, rich, and powerful essay offers insights into the guilt cult of capitalism and social media.[49]

The Guilt Cult of Social Media

Given Benjamin's description of capitalism, we can see how life on social media can be understood in terms of a guilt cult. The media scholar Alice Marwick has shown how social media platforms like Facebook, Twitter, and YouTube have created a culture of competition for status online.[50] Marwick examines numerous design features of social media platforms that reproduce the logic and social relationships of the marketplace. At their most basic, social media platforms fundamentally reconceive the self in terms of a private business. Users internalize the worldview, values, mission, and bureaucratic psychology of a profit-driven corporation. Social media platforms foster an ethos of individualism and entrepreneurialism. By design, they feed an online culture of avaricious competition. The object of this competition is status. The title of Marwick's book, *Status Update*, is a play on words. "Status" can mean a user's current state or condition. But it can also mean a user's rank in a social hierarchy, a virtual caste system in which some users, by virtue of their popularity, occupy a higher social rank than others. Online, as offline, status is power. Social media platforms initiate users into a contest—rarely benign, often vicious—for popularity. This popularity contest turns each social media user into a one-person marketing team obsessively devoted to narcissistic self-promotion.

Marwick identifies three common marketing techniques for boosting one's status online. The first is "lifestreaming," the public broadcasting of one's personal life.[51] This includes showcasing attention-worthy personal details, including everything from major achievements and vacation photos to daily meals and random thoughts about everyday minutiae. Life on social media is a round-the-clock reality television program. Social media are designed for users to broadcast their lives according to the unique design of each platform. In this respect, as Marwick notes, lifestreaming is the digital equivalent of a daily diary.[52] It offers one's followers a window onto an idealized life. If the aim of social media is to boost one's status, there can be no end to lifestreaming, no arc and no conclusion to one's life narrative online. It is not enough to have told one's story. The story must be literally endless.

The second technique is self-branding, the reduction of the self to a commodity. Once transmogrified, the self is promoted like any other product. Digital selves and personas are intensely curated. They are carefully crafted, edited, monitored, and protected. If life on social media is a market competition for status and popularity, then self-branding becomes a necessary mechanism, a technology of the self, to rise above the competition.[53] The point of self-branding is to confer upon one's online persona an appealing and marketable uniqueness.

The third technique is the cultivation of what Marwick terms "microcelebrity."[54] Social media create the conditions under which alternative forms of celebrity become possible. To be popular on social media, to attract a large following and achieve vast social influence, is to carry a kind of star power. Such star power becomes the object of intense envy on the part of those lower down on the digital social ladder. Social media encourage users to think of themselves as celebrities. It transforms the relationships between "friends" into that between celebrities and fans. On Twitter, Instagram, and TikTok, users have "followers," not friends. From the standpoint of the individual user, the relationship to other users is thus inherently asymmetrical. Celebrities, by definition, look down upon, not up to, their fan base. An online social universe in which self-styled celebrities aggressively compete for status, something that by nature cannot be shared equally, is an obvious recipe for social strife and volatility.

In short, what Silicon Valley has effectively created is a virtual economy in its own image, a moral universe whose ultimate values are not democracy or community or social solidarity but rather wealth, fame, success, and power. These entrepreneurial values govern social relationships online. They determine the micropolitics of individual encounters. Each time we post, like, heart, react, comment, reply, and share, we participate in a contest for status, a game whose rules were written for us by Silicon Valley engineers. Posting, commenting, and sharing are the social media equivalents of investing, buying, and selling. They are the devotional market rituals of digital life. Because competition for status is encoded into the design of social media platforms, there is no way to circumvent it. To play the social media game is necessarily to compete for status—constantly. To resist the game is to be condemned to irrelevance.

Compared to other forms of capital, like property, status is highly unstable. For microcelebrities on social media, status is not the sort of thing that can be preserved for very long. Status has a short shelf life. If lifestreaming, self-branding, and the cultivation of microcelebrity are necessary to achieve status, then these marketing techniques are also necessary to preserve it, too. To go silent, to remain inactive for prolonged periods of time, is to let one's star power rapidly evaporate. Social media therefore demand that we perpetually devote ourselves to the pursuit of status. It keeps us in a state of perpetual obligation, even when we are offline, even especially when we are offline. Put differently, social media leave us in a state of permanent guilt. This much is sometimes admitted in rare moments of honesty by social media gurus themselves.

In an astonishing essay on the online publishing platform Medium, Tim Denning, a self-help writer for aspiring social media influencers, offers a revealing, if unintentional, look at the guilt cult of social media. Denning's essay, "The Crippling Guilt of Being Away from Social Media," is intended as a self-help guide for those seeking to maintain their online "momentum."[55] Denning opens by saying, "If you have invested a lot of time into social media like I have over the years, you may have experienced the guilt of being away from it on holidays." Denning says he has been in the habit of posting multiple times a day for the last several years on LinkedIn, his social media platform of choice. He says he noticed that when he does not post for several days, his audience starts wondering what happened to him, leading him to become consumed by guilt. As he puts it:

> When you have spent so much time building an audience online, being away from it can cause all sorts of weird thoughts like "Could it all go away while I'm gone?" or "How much momentum am I losing while on holiday?" . . . *I believe it's normal to feel guilty* about being away from social media when you've spent considerable time working on your craft.[56]

Denning offers his readers a "simple cure" to rationalize their "time off." His advice consists of several one-line affirmations, the type to be read out loud in front of a bathroom mirror. These affirmations are designed to convince his readers that pulling away from social media temporarily ultimately enhances their social media productivity. Denning admits to reciting these affirmations "every time the social media gods were calling my name and creating that horrible fear of missing out feeling." His unironic use of the term "cure" is an inadvertent admission of an addiction. His use of the phrase "time off" reveals that social media labor is nothing less than a full-time job, which for the vast majority of users is unpaid. Lastly, his reference to "the social media gods," though possibly intended as humor, is a disturbing testament to the religious and devotional nature of life online. Despite these frank admissions, Denning appears not to have the slightest intimation that what he is describing is an outright cult, one that comes with a steep price for membership.

Recognition as Debt

Reconceiving social media as a guilt cult is a necessary step toward understanding public shaming and humiliation in digital spaces. The heart of this antisocial dynamic, its economic core, is the creditor-debtor relationship. On the platforms, status is recognition. As media scholar Richard MacKinnon observed about Usenet forums in the early 1990s, existence online rests on recognition from other users. Descartes's *cogito* cannot explain the nature of existence and subjectivity in digital spaces. Only a recognitive model holds explanatory power. As MacKinnon puts it, "Whereas 'I think, therefore I am' is insufficient for this purpose, so too is 'I write, therefore I am.' . . . A further modification to the premise results in 'I am perceived, therefore I am.' "[57] If this formula holds true for existence and subjectivity on Usenet forums, it holds doubly true for status on social media. Status on social media can only be achieved through recognition from other users. To become a microcelebrity is to be dependent upon one's social network for status and power. On the platforms, *recognition is debt*. The formula might therefore be modified as "I am recognized; therefore, I am indebted." If status is indebted to social recognition, then the social network is necessarily the de facto creditor.

Everyone on social media, then, is beholden to their social network. Just as the community confers status upon an individual user through collective recognition, it can deprive that same user of status by revoking their recognition. Hence, the volatility of status on social media. Online status is subject to the law of the market. The same market forces that enable some users to rise rapidly through the ranks to achieve a high social status also leave them vulnerable to losing their status just as rapidly. Recognition can instantly switch from positive to negative, from praise to censure. While the microcelebrity might enjoy power and influence within a social network, the network ultimately holds decisive power over the individual, including the power to destroy the individual's life, both online and offline. As the de facto creditor, the community can move—quickly, decisively, and mercilessly—to punish those who violate its idiosyncratic social norms. Like a bank foreclosing on property, the community can foreclose on the primary asset of microcelebrities: their status. Unbound by humanitarian principles, online communities have revived the premodern torture rituals that Michel Foucault describes in extraordinary detail.

Public Punishment: Our Forgotten Past

Foucault opens *Discipline and Punish: The Birth of the Prison* with a vivid account of public torture from a forgotten era:

> Damiens had been condemned, on March 2, 1757, "to make honorable amends before the main door of the Church of Paris," where he was to be "brought on a cart, naked but for a shirt, holding a torch of burning wax weighing two pounds"; then, "in said cart taken to the Place de Greve, where, on a scaffold that will be erected there, the flesh will be torn from his breasts, arms, thighs, and calves with red-hot pincers, his right hand, holding the knife with which he committed the said [regicide], burned with sulphur, and, on those places where the flesh will be torn away, poured molten lead, boiling oil, burning resin, wax and sulphur melted together and then his body drawn and quartered by four horses and his limbs and body consumed by fire, reduced to ashes and his ashes thrown to the wind."[58]

Why such a harrowing description of torture? *Discipline and Punish* charts the historical transition from a penal system centered upon public torture to one centered upon imprisonment. Of the many ways we might demarcate the modern from the premodern, Foucault makes the unusual move of pointing to penal reform as one of the critical moments of historical transformation. The key difference between the two systems, he argues, is that torture was conceived as a punishment of the *body*, whereas prison was conceived as a punishment of the *soul*. This is not the literal soul of Christian theology. Rather, Foucault invokes the concept of the soul as a metaphor for the modern conscience, a moral sensibility "born ... out of the methods of punishment, supervision, and constraint."[59] The soul, in this sense, is the subject of modern disciplinary power. Foucault argues that the birth of the prison, far from humanizing punishment, only strengthened and expanded state power and control, introducing new forms of cruelty and violence.

For our purposes, what is most useful about Foucault's historical analysis is the vivid and elaborate descriptions of public punishment in the premodern era. In making sense—historical, conceptual, institutional, and cultural—of the modern penal system, Foucault describes in disturbing detail the brutal and sadistic public spectacles of punishment and pain that preceded the birth of the modern prison. He situates these spectacles within a despotic system of power. Under this system, crime was taken to be a grave moral offense against "the rectitude of those who abide by the law."[60] Crime was a personal and physical attack upon the sovereign. It therefore demanded redress "for the injury that has been done to his kingdom."[61] Hence the need for the sovereign to respond to crime with great force. Only through a dramatic ceremony of violent and public retribution might "the momentarily injured" king or prince restore his name and honor.[62]

This punishment was not meted out willy-nilly. The accused first had to confess their guilt. This confession was, as a matter of standard procedure, extracted through torture. Torture played two functions. It was a method of judicial procedure for determining guilt. It was also the punishment that followed judgments of guilt. Torture was thus the sovereign's twofold "technology of power."[63] The aim of judicial torture was to produce judicial truth—the truth that the accused was guilty. A confession of guilt, even if extracted through torture, *especially* if extracted through torture, was incontrovertible evidence of manifest guilt. It was also the moral justification for the sovereign's principled "exercise of 'terror.' "[64]

Foucault identifies three features of punishment under the despotic penal system. First, punishment had to produce pain—pain of a certain kind, severity, and duration as befitting the nature of the crime. Second, public punishment was fully ritualized. As a matter of ceremonial ritual practice, the truth of the criminal's guilt was branded upon his body. Third, public torture was a spectacle, a carnival of pain. In this "theatre of cruelty," the public was invited to laugh, jeer, hector, and verbally and even physically abuse the guilty. Foucault takes great care to emphasize the role of public ceremonies of pain in the production of truth. By being tortured in public, the criminal was the "herald of his own condemnation." The great pomp of public execution was "the moment of truth." The slow and protracted process of torture was a preview of the afterlife, a "theatre of hell" signaling that the "eternal game has already begun."[65]

The Rebirth of Public Punishment

If *Discipline and Punish* documents the transition from a premodern to a modern penal system, then the rise of social media marks the emergence of a virtual penal system centered upon the punishment of what we might call the "digital soul." Following Foucault, we might argue that the digital soul, the new selves we have fashioned online, is born of the guilt cult of social media. Online shaming can be understood as a brutal and unforgettable lesson about the dos and don'ts of a community. The more cruel and merciless the punishment, the stronger the public memory. The purpose of online shaming is not so much to ensure that the accused will never forget. Rather, it is to ensure that everyone observing will never forget. The punishment must be so severe and unusual as to burn a memory into the collective psyche. The accused thereby becomes a public monument to guilt, like a dead body rotting on a cross, a reminder about what happens to those who violate communal norms.

Online shaming marks the expansion not of the powers of the state but rather of private capital over our lives. Online, we are subject to the justice of the algorithm. Algorithmic justice has introduced both new forms of crime and new forms of cruelty and violence. Offensive tweets from ten years ago are taken to be a grave moral offense against, to borrow from Foucault, "the rectitude of those who abide by the law."[66] These offenses are treated as an attack upon the social network. As the ultimate authority, the network must bring about redress through public ceremonies of violent retribution.

Justice on social media reflects the technological rationality of the platform.[67] Confessions are not necessary. There is no jousting, no play of power between a sovereign and the accused to extract a confession of guilt. The digital judicial process skips straight to judgment and punishment. Truth and guilt are determined by popular opinion. In social media communities, there are no constitutional standards, no legal principles, no formal or deliberative procedures for determining guilt. There is no presumption of innocence until the accused is proven guilty. Rather, truth is whatever is trending. If judgments of guilt are trending because of the market logic of the algorithm, then the accused is, for all intents and purposes, guilty. Nor is there a distinction between judgment and punishment. The two meld into one. Online shaming is mass public judgment, marking the switch from the positive recognition on which a user's digital life had hitherto depended to the negative recognition on which a user's digital life is effectively destroyed. The harsh judgment of observers and onlookers is often severe enough to ensure a painful and decisive digital death.

As with public punishment in the premodern world, punishment on social media has three core features. First, online punishment must produce pain and torment in the form of shame. Second, online shaming takes a ritual form. As with physical torture, online shaming marks the accused with the truth of their guilt. Third, online shaming is a public spectacle, a virtual theatre of cruelty, in which witnesses are encouraged to laugh, jeer, hector, and abuse the guilty. This is the joy of the righteous in the face of the guilt of the damned. In the first essay of the *Genealogy*, Nietzsche seizes upon a striking passage from Thomas Aquinas in his *Summa Theologica*: "The blessed in the kingdom of heaven will see the punishments of the damned, *in order that their bliss be more delightful for them*."[68] These revealing words perfectly capture the sadistic psychology of self-righteous digital spectators who delight in watching hapless souls tortured online.

Instead of inflicting violence upon the physical body, online shaming inflicts violence upon the user's digital soul. It amounts to watching a life go up in flames. This is a straightforward act of power. The historian Ute Frevert finds a striking continuity in public shaming over the last three hundred years, drawing a direct parallel between public acts of physical torture in the past and online shaming today.[69] At bottom, Frevert notes, public shaming is about not justice but rather the display of power. As she puts it, "By bringing people to their knees in front of others, social actors emphatically assert their superior, more powerful position."[70] Noting that shame has long been recognized as a tool for social control, Frevert observes that the "presence and witness of others is a crucial aspect."

Shame is a social emotion. To shame someone is to subject them to "the power of the public gaze, a gaze that cannot be avoided, that gets beneath our skin and marks the body of the humiliated."[71] Public shaming is "the play of power and powerlessness, shame and disgrace, perpetrator and victim." Public shaming involves two types of aggressors. First, there are the perpetrators, those who initially name and condemn those they judge to be in violation of some inviolable social norm. Second, there are witnesses, both "real and imaginary."[72] As Frevert puts it, witnesses "can approve of acts of shaming and intensify them." We know how this works on social media. By liking, hearting, and sharing comments and tweets that name and shame some offender, witnesses on the sidelines contribute to public acts of humiliation.[73]

What is termed "call-out culture" is driven by the sadistic pleasure of witnessing public spectacles of shame and humiliation. If the accused is guilty, then witnesses need not feel guilty about watching them suffer. The Michael Jackson popcorn-eating GIF, so often posted in response to public call-outs, expresses a lurker's delight, the pleasure from the sidelines of watching someone get publicly eviscerated.[74] Witnesses are thus integral players in acts of public shaming. But they need not remain entirely passive. Unlike actual trials, social media trials do not require observers to remain quiet and passive on the sidelines. Anyone can switch from observer to judge to executioner, adding to the chorus of self-righteous condemnation. On social media, everyone is a debtor. Everyone is also a creditor. Every negative comment or tweet aimed at the accused is the act of a creditor claiming their rightful pound of flesh, intensifying the torture and suffering of the guilty, through what, following Foucault, we might call the digital microphysics of power. A call-out is a digital death by a thousand tweets.

It is difficult to overstate the violence of online shaming. Martha Nussbaum argues against the recent revival of public shaming as a form of punishment in American law.[75] Drawing from both clinical literature and philosophical meditations on shame, Nussbaum offers five reasons public shaming should not be revived as a form of punishment under the law. First, public shaming is a form of mob justice not unlike the public pillories, forced head shavings, and walks of shame of the past. Second, public shaming is an excessively cruel punishment disproportionate to the crime. Third, it is unlikely to be an effective deterrent against future crimes. Fourth, it runs the risk of being abused by the state and becoming a medium of social control. Fifth, public shaming is an obvious and grotesque violation of human dignity, depriving the offending party of the ability to retain any self-respect.

As Nussbaum argues, acts of public shaming express "the intent to degrade and humiliate."[76] Nussbaum draws a distinction between punishments that focus on specific *acts* and those that focus on the *person*. Penalties such as fines, community service, or probation focus on specific acts. Such penalties convey that these acts are violations of the law. By serving a penalty, wrongdoers will have redeemed themselves. But public shaming and humiliation "are ways of marking a person, often for life, with a degraded identity."[77] To shame someone publicly is to brand them a defective person. Historically, such methods of shaming as branding, shaving, and tattooing were used to mark a certain class of people as social deviants. To mark someone was to "announce that spoiled identity to the world."[78] Thus when we shame someone online, we are scorning not a specific action but the whole person. Nussbaum also points out that the act of shaming implies a social hierarchy between those who shame and those who are shamed. Those who shame presume a sense of superiority. They presume that they are free of whatever incurable moral blemish they condemn in the accused. They take themselves to belong to the class of the unblemished.

Public shaming therefore creates a division between the virtuous, the honorable, and the righteous and the corrupt, the depraved, and the wicked. This is not a lateral division but rather a hierarchy, in which the virtuous wield power over the damned. Nor does public shaming treat this hierarchy as contingent and fluctuating. Moral character is taken to be fixed and immutable. To be shamed is to be exposed as inherently, congenitally, essentially corrupt. Accordingly, once guilty, always guilty. There is nothing one can say or do to escape this guilt, no possibility of paying off one's debt, no hope of atonement. The condemned are left to a state of permanent despair, just as Benjamin had described.

As media scholar Elisha Lim has argued, online shaming replicates one of the most notorious features of Calvinist theology.[79] In *The Protestant Ethic*, Weber highlights a critical link between Calvinism and capitalism. In the sixteenth century, Calvinism introduced the doctrine of predestination, according to which

God decides in advance who is destined for an eternity in heaven and who, an eternity in hell. In this earthly life, we walk among the saved and the damned. How to tell which is which? In response to the desperate need among dutiful believers for signs of salvation, Calvinism introduced the ancillary doctrine that worldly and material success is a sign of divine grace and selection. The rich are rich because they are among the elect. The poor are poor because they have been condemned from birth to suffer in this life and the next. This belief created a rigid social hierarchy, in which the elect stood over the damned. As Weber puts it, "by founding its ethic in the doctrine of predestination," Calvinism gave rise to a "spiritual aristocracy of the predestined saints of God within the world."[80] This new aristocracy was sharply separated from "the eternally damned remainder of humanity."[81] The hierarchy "penetrated all social relations with its sharp brutality." Weber goes on to say:

> This consciousness of divine grace of the elect and holy was accompanied by an attitude toward the sin of one's neighbour, not of sympathetic understanding based on consciousness of one's own weakness, but of hatred and contempt for him as an enemy of God bearing the signs of eternal damnation.[82]

Online shaming mimics the uncompromising and puritanical fanaticism of Calvinist theology. It feeds a climate of extreme paranoia online, driving a frantic and obsessive search for signs and clues of moral character, some indication of whether a user belongs to the saved or the damned. This explains the mad drive to dig up old tweets, which are taken to be proof of some permanent moral corruption. Second, by demarcating the boundaries between the pure and the impure, between the virtuous and the damned, online shaming is an opportunity for those insecure about their moral standing to feel virtuous. Condemnation feeds a personal sense of moral security, the reassurance of being among the elect. Online shaming and Calvinist theology reflect the same existential fears and anxieties. Those who subject others to public shame and humiliation are, according to Nussbaum, "very often not expressing virtuous motives or high ideals, but rather shrinking from their own human weakness." At bottom, the act of shaming others is motivated by a "fragile narcissism," a desire that can only be "satisfied by humiliation." This desire explains the brutality and sadism of the new torture rituals on social media.[83]

Debt Is Guilt Is Shame Is Money

In 2015, the British journalist Jon Ronson published a collection of stories of online shaming and humiliation.[84] Ronson draws our attention to the rapid transformation of social media from an unrestricted and carefree space, in which we once freely disclosed salacious personal stories and indulged in forbidden humor, to a space of collective invigilation, in which we police each other for moral infractions, major and minor. Ronson shares the stories of an especially unlucky group of people whose lives were destroyed by online shaming. The group includes Jonah Lehrer, the disgraced journalist who was exposed for plagiarism, fabrication, and misrepresentation. It includes Adria Richards, the Black female programmer who called out two white male colleagues on Twitter for sexually suggestive jokes at a tech conference. After they were fired, Richards was herself subjected to public shaming and subsequently fired. There is also the story of Justine Sacco, the public relations executive who attempted to satirize American cultural ignorance by tweeting, "Going to Africa. Hope I don't get AIDS. Just kidding. I'm white!" Sacco, too, was promptly fired. Then there is Lindsey Stone, the charity worker who was photographed displaying her middle finger and pretending to shout at Arlington National Cemetery, her sad attempt at being irreverent. Following a public outcry, Stone was also fired from her job.

Although Ronson's book might seem dated by internet time, it does a remarkable job of describing a very contemporary phenomenon. In fact, the book is arguably more relevant today than it was when Ronson first published it. It also provides a perspective that tends to get lost in the moral panic over cancel culture and free speech. What we learn from his collection of stories is just how cruel, pitiless, and incredibly sadistic public shaming can be. Ronson documents the perverse public exhilaration in watching the life of some unfortunate victim unravel in real time. That exhilaration can quickly turn into violent fantasy. Justine Sacco was subjected not just to childish and vicious name-calling but also to graphic rape and death threats. During an online shaming campaign, when the accused are deemed irredeemably corrupt, threats of violence and death suddenly become acceptable.

We also learn from Ronson that this cruelty cuts across the ideological spectrum. Contrary to the disingenuous conservative framing of cancel culture as a liberal or left-wing phenomenon, conservatives have their own penchant for public shaming, as the case of Lindsey Stone amply demonstrates. Although Ronson does not address it, the undying conservative hostility to left-wing academics offers the most salient examples of the conservative enthusiasm for subjecting dissident intellectuals to the public pillory.[85]

Ronson does not deny that public shaming can be used to hold the rich and powerful accountable. His concern is for those who are neither rich nor powerful, and who are also not guilty of some heinous and unconscionable crime. Justine Sacco's inept tweet and Lindsey Stone's public display of irreverence, while both tasteless in their own ways, were hardly a justification for their lives being destroyed. Ronson shows us how the penchant to cancel the guilty can be reckless and irresponsible. There is no accountability for this instrument of accountability. Online shaming, even if well intentioned, can all too easily devolve into outright abuse, leaving its targets traumatized, depressed, anxious, and suicidal, on top of being unemployed.

Who, then, benefits from this destructive behavior? Ronson posed this question to some internet economists. He asked them specifically about Google and whether it had profited from the public shaming and annihilation of Justine Sacco. Based on Google's business model, which generates ad revenue through search queries, these economists estimated that Google made somewhere between $120,000 and $450,000 from the 1.2 million Google searches for Justine Sacco during her ordeal.[86] Although a paltry sum for Google, it is still obscene. Digital platforms do not deliberately profit from public shaming. Rather, that profit is entirely incidental to their amoral business model.

To summarize, the phenomenon of online shaming is best understood as a feature of the guilt cult of social media capitalism. Social media have turned us into status fiends. By creating a fierce competition for status and an insatiable hunger for recognition, social media platforms create a creditor-debtor relationship between social media users—between the individual who seeks recognition and the social network that offers it. This relationship leaves the community in a position to judge and punish moral offenders who violate social norms. The very design of the platforms renders them ideal sites for public shaming. What allows us to connect with each other also allows us to eviscerate each other. Platform design encourages a new theatre of cruelty. Although Nietzsche brilliantly describes the logic and psychology behind this cruelty, it is imperative to resist his cynicism about human nature. That cynicism only encourages the problem of trolling. Chapter 6 will explore an alternative medium for building a different kind of culture, one that defies both the economic logic of the platforms and Nietzsche's cynical view of humanity. But first, it is necessary to examine the personal and political cost of the breakdown of trust.

5

Conspiracy

Dr. Nili Kaplan-Myrth is a family physician in Ottawa. In the spring of 2021, Dr. Kaplan-Myrth organized "Jabapalooza," a public campaign featuring outdoor vaccination clinics in residential neighborhoods. Designed to encourage the public to get vaccinated, the campaign had the unintended effect of attracting anti-vaccine trolls. At first the trolling was limited to online harassment. Soon, however, Kaplan-Myrth began receiving death threats in the mail. "It's one thing when it's a troll on Twitter who tells us that we're horrible people for immunizing. We can just block that kind of vitriol," she said. "But when it comes to somebody actually sending a letter saying that I should be killed, that's a line that can't be crossed." Kaplan-Myrth decided that she could no longer hold her outdoor clinics out of fear for her safety. As she remarked, "I'm literally afraid now to walk outside of my office, even in broad daylight because somebody has said they're going to kill me." Kaplan-Myrth publicly called on Prime Minister Justin Trudeau to take active measures to protect healthcare workers from harassment and violence.[1]

The trolling of healthcare workers is just one small episode in a much larger and ongoing saga about COVID-19 conspiracy theories. Other episodes include the early belief that 5G networks cause COVID-19, which led to many 5G towers being set on fire.[2] It includes the claim that face masks are dangerous because "you're breathing in all the stuff you breathe out."[3] The anti-vaccine movement has vigorously promoted hydroxychloroquine and ivermectin, the latter an antiparasitic drug typically used in veterinary medicine, as safe and reliable remedies for COVID-19. One conservative journalist warned on Twitter that the Moderna vaccine contains a tracking agent named after the devil.[4] In the spring of 2021, users on TikTok, YouTube, Instagram, Twitter, and Facebook posted videos of themselves sticking spoons to their bodies, claiming the vaccines had rendered them magnetic.[5] Even social and political theory fell prey to this paranoia. The Italian philosopher Giorgio Agamben, famed for his analyses of biopolitical power, scandalized the academic world by denying the very

Trolling Ourselves to Death. Jason Hannan, Oxford University Press. © Oxford University Press 2023.
DOI: 10.1093/oso/9780197557761.003.0006

existence of the pandemic and vocally opposing public safety measures, calling them "techno-medical despotism."[6] In Canada and the United States, many conspiracy theorists have insisted that the coronavirus is a hoax and have refused to get vaccinated, even as they take their last gasps on their hospital deathbeds. Anything, apparently—even dying—to troll the libs.[7]

The global proliferation of coronavirus conspiracy theories presents public health officials, scientists, and media scholars with two urgent tasks. The first is to determine how best to combat the spread of medical disinformation. The two most common strategies for this task are practicing more effective science communication and deplatforming conspiracy theorists from social media.[8] The premise behind these two strategies is the belief that the popularity of false ideas reflects widespread public ignorance. On this view, merely removing false information and providing hard, cold, objective facts will effectively counter the menace of disinformation.[9] Under pressure from public health officials to address the spread of COVID-19 disinformation, Facebook, YouTube, and Twitter (pre–Elon Musk) adopted these two strategies, removing accounts that spread coronavirus conspiracy theories and offering resources for accurate information about COVID-19.[10] Their efforts, however, have had a negligible effect.[11] The glaring failure even to make a dent in the massive and growing culture of conspiracy theory suggests that the problem is far more complex than mere public ignorance of science.

The second task, related to the first, is to understand the underlying reasons behind coronavirus disinformation. If public ignorance of science is not the underlying problem, then what is? This chapter sets out to answer that question. Unlike the two counterdisinformation strategies discussed above, this chapter does not treat the premise about public ignorance as a given. Rather, it puts that premise into question. In what follows, I argue that the proliferation of COVID-19 conspiracy theories is rooted not in ignorance but in the loss of social trust. That is, the popularity of conspiracy theory reflects mass isolation, atomization, loneliness, distrust, cynicism, suspicion, and paranoia—in short, the antisocial effects of life in a free market, individualist society. The term for this phenomenon in Marxist social theory is alienation. For different historical reasons, alienation theory has long since fallen out of academic fashion.[12] However, it is arguably more relevant now than at any time before.

In what follows, I first provide a basic picture of the causal relationship between capitalism and alienation, describing how a society premised on competition necessarily leads to isolation and loneliness. I then describe one of the most damaging effects of prolonged isolation and loneliness: the fragmentation of the self into bits and pieces of disconnected subjectivity—when the parts of the self become alienated from one another. Following Alasdair MacIntyre, I argue that this fragmentation amounts to the loss of narrative continuity, the inability to make sense of one's life from one key moment to the next through an overarching story. It is precisely because of this painful breakdown of personal narrative that conspiracy theories are so powerful and seductive. What they offer the alienated and fragmented subject is a restoration of personal meaning, intelligibility, and purpose, but at the cost of reality.

The Idea of Alienation

Whenever we speak about alienation in the modern world, some elaboration is always necessary. The idea of alienation has a long and complicated history that undermines any facile presumption of a single definition. In *The Phenomenology of Spirit*, Hegel writes at length about "the world of self-alienated Spirit." Alienation is an "unhappy consciousness" deriving from a certain misguided Christian longing for a divine realm of spiritual perfection that lies beyond the moral debasement of the material world.[13] In Hegel's view, alienation can only be overcome in the material world itself, when Spirit achieves complete self-awareness by recognizing itself in external objects. Hegel later proposed a more historical theory of alienation in his *Lectures on the Philosophy of World History* and *Lectures on the Philosophy of Religion*. There he argued that the modern world had separated us from the historical and cultural roots of our identities, erasing what makes each of us who we are by subsuming us within an artificial universality. This condition, Hegel argued, must be overcome through a reconception of social life that honors our individual histories and particularities.[14]

Hegel's excessive focus upon mind, consciousness, and recognition to the neglect of the economic foundations of society led Marx to propose a radically different concept of alienation. In his *Economic and Philosophic Manuscripts of 1844*, Marx writes in elaborate detail about alienation, clearly impressed by the idea but determined to provide a less mysterious and more practical theory of modern alienated subjects.[15] Marx describes not one but four distinct types of alienation, all resulting from the capitalist mode of production:

1. *The estrangement of workers from the products of their labor.* Despite investing so much of their time and effort into the production of commodities, workers have no ownership over and no connection to what they produce. The products of their labor get appropriated by the capitalist, who sells them for profit. Hence, workers are necessarily alienated from the products of their own labor.

2. *The estrangement of workers from their labor itself.* Workers in a capitalist economy are not free and autonomous. They work not out of choice but rather out

of the need to survive. When they sell their labor to the capitalist, they sell a part of themselves, thus becoming alienated from it.

3. *The estrangement of workers from their human nature.* What separates humans from animals is that humans can live for more than mere biological survival and reproduction. Humans can, under the right conditions, pursue poetry, literature, music, philosophy, science, and art. That is, humans can rise above the realm of nature into that of culture. But the perpetual servitude of workers ensures that they will never live more than a mere animal existence— competing, like animals, for survival.[16]

4. *The gulf that separates "man from man."* In a market system in which the capitalist exploits the worker, and in which workers compete for the opportunity to be exploited, the relationship between workers becomes instrumentalized. Competition is division, leaving the population of workers, the mass of society, alienated from each other.

This chapter builds upon Marx's fourth type of alienation. As Marx puts it, "An immediate consequence of the fact that man is estranged from the product of his labour, from his life activity, from his species-being is the estrangement of man from man." Marx goes on to say, "The estrangement of man, and in fact every relationship in which man [stands] to himself, is realized and expressed only in the relationship in which a man stands to other men."[17] That relationship is one of separation, not solidarity.

Perhaps the most vivid depiction of this fourth type of alienation is Hwang Dong-hyuk's television series *Squid Game*. Set in contemporary South Korea, *Squid Game* is a nightmarish story about a class of all-powerful, ultrawealthy, and indescribably sadistic elites, who derive a morbid pleasure from pitting members of a wretched and desperate debtor class against each other. These elites devise an elaborate contest consisting of a series of increasingly violent and deadly versions of classic children's games. The ultimate prize is a giant pot of cash. Each time a contestant dies, the prize grows larger. The central theme of *Squid Game* is the erosion of trust and solidarity. Friend betrays friend, brother betrays brother, lover betrays lover, young betrays old, citizen betrays foreigner. In the end, the sole survivor, Seong Gi-hun, wins the pot of cash but as a result loses his soul. He is not only estranged from his fellow contestants, all of whom are now dead; he is also a walking ghost of his former self. *Squid Game* is a dramatic illustration of how desperation coupled with vicious competition results in a severe deformation of the human soul, culminating in "the estrangement of man from man."

What Marx presents as a needless social tragedy and a distortion of human nature, early modern political thinkers such as Thomas Hobbes and John Locke famously present as a necessary element of human societies. In the writings of Hobbes and Locke, the estrangement of man from man is an inescapable fact

of the human condition and therefore the moral starting point for an unsenti-
mental picture of a just social order. What Marx treats as the structural effect of
a deeply unnatural and violent economic system, Hobbes and Locke elevate to
the status of a normative worldview. As I argue below, that worldview is the one
we inhabit today. It forms the moral and cultural background in which the proliferation of conspiracy theory and the rise of political trolling is best understood.

Alienation as Political Atomism

The political form of "the estrangement of man from man" is also known as
political atomism. Charles Taylor describes political atomism as a view of society composed of a collection of isolated and disconnected individuals, each of
whom pursues private and individual ends.[18] In an atomized society, there is no
overarching social telos other than the preservation of the economy. Political
atomism prioritizes the rights of the individual over the whole of society. It takes
a strictly instrumental view of human relationships, in which sovereign individuals interact with one another not on social or moral terms but rather on legal and
contractual terms. The governing principle of political atomism is the exercise of
individual liberty and the pursuit of self-interest—to the very limits of the law.
The isolated and disconnected individual has no need to dwell with others, no
need to work with others, no need for the goods of social life. Rather, the individual is perfectly independent and self-sufficient, even in total isolation.

As Taylor notes, political atomism arose in the seventeenth century, its
two most influential proponents being Hobbes and Locke. In *Leviathan*,
Hobbes paints a famously grim and depressing picture of humanity. Although
he acknowledges that "nature hath made men so equal in the faculties of the
body and the mind" that no one can claim any natural superiority over another,
Hobbes nonetheless regards individual prudence and self-interest as the crucial
factors that differentiate the members of humanity. Each of us seeks to increase
our personal fortunes. Thus, our "equality of ability" and "equality of hope" leave
us in perpetual competition with each other. If two individuals desire something
that cannot be shared, "they become enemies" and "endeavour to destroy or subdue one another." Should an individual "plant, sow, build, or possess" something
widely desirable, others may "come prepared with forces united" to take it by
forceful means, including murder.[19]

We thus live in perpetual "diffidence," a Middle English term denoting distrust. According to Hobbes, the basic and inescapable reasons for social division and conflict are three: competition, diffidence, and vainglory.[20] The state of
nature for Hobbes is not one of social trust and cooperation but rather "the war
of all against all." Without a powerful sovereign to impose law and order, Hobbes

contends, there would be no industry, no agriculture, no trade, no commerce, no economy. And without an economy, there would be no higher cultural pursuits, "no account of time, no arts, no letters, no society." Instead, we would confront "continual fear and danger of violent death." Hence, "the life of man" is necessarily "solitary, poor, nasty, brutish, and short."[21] As will be shown below, the Hobbesian worldview is a very good description of the paranoid and combative mindset of contemporary conspiracy theorists, who inhabit a modern-day war of all against all.

As noted in Chapter 2, Locke's view of the state of nature is similarly grim and depressing. Instead of a powerful sovereign who preserves social order, Locke regards private property as the foundation of human society. Like Hobbes, Locke assumes a basic and universal human equality. In Book II of his *Two Treatises of Government*, Locke says humanity possesses a natural and God-given right to "their preservation, and consequently to meat and drink, and such other things as nature affords for their subsistence"[22] God made the world for "the children of men" and endowed them with reason "to make use of it to the best advantage of life and convenience."[23] Yet this indiscriminate divine generosity poses a problem for the entrepreneurial individual: how can private property ever be justified? Locke takes great pains to show how, despite a basic and universal human equality, "men might come to have a property in . . . that which God gave to mankind in common." Locke's theory of private property is premised on two assumptions: that every individual's body is their private property and that the products of their individual labor are therefore their private property, too. From these premises, Locke advances a theory of the individual's natural right to unlimited private property, "which another had no title to, nor could without injury take from him."[24] As Locke would have it, land that remains untilled is ripe for the taking. Working the land, sowing seeds, growing crops, and farming animals are investments of personal labor, which transforms unworked land into private property. Locke treats the institution of private property as sacred, something that must be protected at all costs. Private property for Locke is a basic feature of human life. To be properly human is thus in some fundamental sense to exclude the rest of humanity.

Political atomism is more than a mere doctrine of seventeenth-century political philosophy. It is also more than the antisocial effects of capitalist modes and relations of production. As Taylor argues, political atomism has come to be embodied in the dominant institutions of modern secular societies.[25] This marks a decisive historical shift in our social and political order, from the *Gemeinschaften* of the past, in which the members of society related to one another through shared traditions and ancient codes, to the *Gesellschaften* of the present, in which the members of society relate to one another through the impersonal contracts and transactions of the marketplace.[26] Political atomism, that is to say, is not a mere seventeenth-century philosophical abstraction. It is our social reality today. What was once just an idea in the bleak minds of Hobbes, Locke, and other protomodern political philosophers has, through a series of structural revolutions—economic, political, and legal—become the ideological foundation of modern political orders. Taylor admittedly departs from a strictly materialist view of history, which sees economic change as the driver of political change. Instead, he contends that international political rivalry was the principal catalyst for the growth of industrial production and the eventual rise and dominance of the mercantile class. The effect, however, was same: the rapid ascent of the economic sphere to the center of society.

This historical shift in social and political order, Taylor shows, brought about a profound transformation in how we make sense of who we are. Rather than conceiving of society as a *people* bound by a common tradition, we now see society as an *economy*, a system of production, exchange, and consumption that operates according to its own natural and eternal laws. The marketplace becomes the principal frame through which we interpret the world and ourselves. Our entire society has become the structural expression of an atomistic worldview, in which the principles of competition and possessive individualism are the defining features of the prevailing social ethos.[27] Political atomism, that is to say, has become naturalized. It has blended into our moral background, what Taylor calls the liberal social imaginary.[28] We now take political atomism for granted, much like the ground on which we walk and the air that we breathe, such that we no longer take notice of it. So much of everyday life, including childhood, school, work, friendship, love, marriage, divorce, retirement, and death, is experienced through an atomistic frame. Contemporary social life, no matter how personal and intimate, would have been quite bizarre and alien to a premodern sensibility.

Alienation and Loneliness

If the "estrangement of man from man" is not just one of the tragic effects of capitalist relations of production, but rather the underlying moral fabric of modern political orders, then it is little wonder that alienation should become such a widespread, even generalized, social condition. Little wonder, too, that loneliness should become one of the most common, if silent and taboo, emotions of the modern era. We notably hold two glaringly contradictory views about loneliness. On the one hand, we often view widespread loneliness as only a very recent phenomenon. Bookstores today feature entire shelves of self-help literature devoted to alleviating loneliness. Cultural commentators are wont to attribute widespread loneliness to smartphones and social media.[29] Medical journals like *The Lancet* have raised alarms about the epidemic of loneliness.[30] Britain, known as "the loneliness capital of Europe," once even appointed a Minister of Loneliness.[31] On the other hand, we also tend to view loneliness as a timeless feature of the human condition, a universal malaise from which we are inevitably prone to suffer. Neither of these views of loneliness is accurate. As the cultural historian Fay Bound Alberti has shown, a careful reading of Western cultural history reveals that loneliness, like the individual, is a modern invention.[32]

Alberti goes to great lengths to show that loneliness was not a widespread social problem or even a clear and substantive concept until the nineteenth century. Before 1800, loneliness was "oneliness," a synonym for solitude.[33] In *A Dictionary of the English Language* (1755), Samuel Johnson defined "lonely" as the state of being physically alone.[34] In Johnson's eighteenth-century milieu, loneliness was not yet a social or psychological concept, let alone a condition carrying intense stigma. In fact, solitude was considered a virtue, a means of building moral character, strengthening the mind, and healing body and soul. Although premodern medical writers warned of the dangers of prolonged solitude, these were largely physiological in nature.[35] Daniel Defoe's *The Life and Adventures of Robinson Crusoe* depicts a castaway who spends twenty-eight years in solitude on a desolate island. Yet at no point does Robinson Crusoe ever suffer from loneliness. As Alberti argues, the term "loneliness" was almost never mentioned in books and articles prior to the nineteenth century. It was only at this late stage that the meaning of "loneliness" underwent a critical mutation from being an infrequently used synonym for an idealized physical state of social solitude to the primary term for the dreaded emotional state of social deprivation. Shortly after 1800, "loneliness" appeared in a rapidly growing number of publications, reaching its peak at the end of the twentieth century.[36]

Alberti observes that the modern preoccupation with loneliness coincides with four critical transformations in Western societies: the invention of the individual, the rise of market economies, the emergence of secular society, and the development of the new sciences of the mind.[37] She emphasizes that these were interdependent transformations, not distinct and unrelated ones. The invention of the individual marked an inward turn, in which modern subjects began to look within themselves, rather than toward community and tradition, for a sense of self.[38] The myth of the individual was in turn both a necessary philosophical premise and the inevitable psychological effect of a new social order that revolved around relationships of individual exchange.

The ascent of the economic sphere to the center of society notably filled the void left by the fall of the Church. In the premodern world, the Church dominated public life, bolstering the collective sense that God was omnipresent. As Alberti asks, "And how could one be emotionally lonely when He was always there?"[39] Following the withdrawal of the Church from public life, the feeling of walking in the eternal presence of the divine begins to wane, leaving behind a haunting sense of cosmic emptiness.

Perhaps most importantly, the early sciences of the mind, the disciplines of psychiatry and psychology, regarded the mind as an independent entity separate from the body.[40] Mental illness came to be treated through mind-specific interventions, which sought to excavate the mind's mysterious depths and crevices for the sources of emotional anguish, as well as for their remedies. This, as Alberti indicates, is the signature clinical approach of psychoanalysis, which focuses on the internal dynamics of the mind, the interplay of the conscious and the unconscious, as the therapeutic method par excellence for treating mental illness.[41]

As evidence of the sudden and dramatic interest in loneliness, Alberti points to notable examples of nineteenth-century literature depicting lonely protagonists in search of meaning, purpose, and human connection in a cold and impersonal world, with such stories often set against the backdrop of modern industrial society. The new social preoccupation with loneliness coincided with the historical emergence of the novel, the preeminent bourgeois literary form that catered to a new leisure class possessing both the time and the literacy to consume elaborate tales of personal discovery. Very often, the lonely protagonists in these stories were women who, despite their well-to-do economic status, lacked social agency. Some of the most familiar examples of novels about loneliness include Jane Austen's *Emma* (1815), Charlotte Brontë's *Jane Eyre* and *Villette* (1853), Anne Brontë's *Tenant of Wildfell Hall* (1848), George Eliot's *The Mill on the Floss* (1860), Thomas Hardy's *Tess of the d'Urbervilles* (1892), and Florence Marryat's *The Blood of the Vampire* (1897). Joseph Conrad's *An Outcast of the Islands* (1896) and *Lord Jim* (1900) portray lonely male protagonists. Charles Dickens tells the stories of lonely child protagonists in *Oliver Twist* (1838) and *Great Expectations* (1861). Without question, the most extraordinary meditation on loneliness in all of nineteenth-century literature is Mary Shelley's *Frankenstein* (1818). Victor Frankenstein's monster, born of modern science and technology, is a disquieting parable about loneliness in the industrial age. "I am alone and miserable," says the monster, for "man will not associate with me."[42]

If the individual quest to overcome loneliness is a salient theme in nineteenth-century literature, then we might say that twentieth-century literature is notable for its resignation in the face of loneliness. Loneliness becomes less an obstacle to be overcome than a fateful aspect of the human condition. In *A Cocktail Party*, T. S. Eliot's controversial play about loneliness in marriage, the character of Celia Coplestone discloses her fear that "everyone's alone," unable even to communicate with each other:

> They make noises, and think they are talking to each other;
> They make faces, and think they understand each other.
> And I'm sure that they don't. Is that a delusion?[43]

Here, Coplestone expresses the nightmare of solipsism, a fear that logically follows from thinking of communication, as Locke originally conceived it, in terms of the transmission of content from one private mind to another. Coplestone articulates the familiar existential nightmare that each of us is hermetically sealed and trapped within our own minds.[44]

Similarly, in *Mrs. Dalloway*, Virginia Woolf tells a story about the modern dread of loneliness and incommunicability. Even in the crowded and bustling intersection of Piccadilly Circus, the heart of downtown London, Clarissa Dalloway suffers from incurable loneliness. As Woolf writes, "She had a perpetual sense, as she watched the taxi cabs, of being out, out, far out to sea and alone; she always had the feeling that it was very, very dangerous to live even one day."[45] In her diary, Woolf describes her own repeated descent into loneliness when writing *A Room of One's Own*, her cultural commentary on the social and financial challenges faced by women writers. "Often down here I have entered into a sanctuary; a nunnery; had a religious retreat; of great agony once; and always some terror: so afraid one is of loneliness: of seeing to the bottom of the vessel."[46] For Woolf, the experience of loneliness was a necessary precondition for being able to see clearly, for reaching "a consciousness of what I call 'reality.' "[47]

Loneliness as an inescapable fact of the human condition is also a theme in the work of numerous nineteenth- and twentieth-century artists. Edvard Munch, for example, expressed in visual form the austere and chilly mood that Kierkegaard had earlier developed into an entirely new style of philosophy.[48] Munch is of course best known for *The Scream* (1893), a meditation on the isolation and anxiety of modern life. Its ghostlike central figure cries out in pain, frantically hoping to escape from some inner torment. The wavy lines in the orange sky indicate the frightful experience of personal chaos and breakdown. Yet despite this scene of psychological torture, the passersby in the background are completely oblivious, exacerbating the subject's sense of excruciating loneliness in the moment.

Like Munch, Picasso offered his own commentary on what it means to be human in the modern world. During his infamous Blue Period, brought on by the suicide of a friend, Picasso captured the feeling of loneliness and despondency in a series of portraits. Fashioned from a palette of blue and gray, these portraits tell the story of lonely people in the aftermath of some undisclosed and desensitizing personal event. The subjects appear lifeless, expressionless, dispirited, and abandoned, like empty vessels of their former selves, silently awaiting their own deaths.[49]

Similarly, the work of the American realist painter Edward Hopper captures the crushing spirit of loneliness in modern American life. Hopper seized upon familiar moments of loneliness at home, at work, in hotels, in restaurants, and on trains, moments alone and moments between couples, friends, and strangers, in which time appears to have slowed to a perfect standstill and all the meaninglessness and emptiness of modern life have been compressed into a singular moment of melancholic self-reflection. Like Munch and Picasso, Hopper's paintings leave the impression that beneath the gloss of everyday American life, something ominous is about to unfold.[50]

The theme of loneliness in modern literature and art has multiple dimensions, from the loneliness of the rich in F. Scott Fitzgerald's *The Great Gatsby* (1925) to the loneliness of the poor in John Steinbeck's *The Grapes of Wrath* (1939), from the loneliness of the queer experience in Radclyffe Hall's *The Well of Loneliness* (1928) to the loneliness of the Black experience in Ralph Ellison's *Invisible Man* (1952), and from the loneliness of mental illness in Gustave Courbet's *The Desperate Man* (1845) and Sylvia Plath's *The Bell Jar* (1963) to the loneliness of old age in van Gogh's *At Eternity's Gate* (1890). One arresting feature that cuts across these diverse portrayals of loneliness is the menacing feeling, again, that danger is just on the horizon, that individual or social breakdown is imminent. If one of the functions of literature and art is to capture the implicit mood of the age, then one of the functions of political theory is to articulate that mood in explicit terms. The one political theorist who most perceptively grasped the political dangers of mass alienation and loneliness in modern society was Hannah Arendt, whose personal experience of, and subsequent investigations into, militarized German society under the Third Reich enabled her to work out the disturbing implications of loneliness for the political realm.

The Danger of Loneliness

Published in 1951, *The Origins of Totalitarianism* remains the most original, searching, and illuminating account of totalitarian societies that we possess. It explores the history and politics of modern antisemitism and imperialism, from which Arendt was able to extract several key features of totalitarian societies. These features include the relationship of the masses to the elite, the techniques of totalitarian propaganda, the structure of totalitarian government, the methods of totalitarian rule, and the will to absolute domination. In 1966, Arendt added a chapter entitled "Ideology and Terror: A Novel Form of Government." In it she sets out to identify the ideological and emotional core of the two paradigmatic forms of totalitarianism in the twentieth century: Nazism and Stalinism. Arendt reminds us that totalitarian government is distinct from other, more familiar forms of oppressive rule. Unlike despotism, tyranny, and dictatorship, which thrive on brute force, totalitarianism is animated by an ultimate and all-encompassing *idea*.[51]

In totalitarian societies, Arendt argues, this ultimate and all-encompassing idea holds a status more basic, fundamental, and authoritative than any doctrine, tradition, custom, or institution. The ultimate idea carries greater moral power and authority than even positive law. Anything that deviates from or contradicts it is necessarily in the wrong. Under Hitler, the ultimate idea was Nature, according to which the Aryan race was biologically destined to rule over the rest of humanity. Under Stalin, it was History, according to which a classless society was destined to emerge through economic forces beyond the control of human agency. In totalitarian societies, Arendt explains, the ultimate idea is more than a formal concept to be logically grasped by the human mind. Rather, the ultimate idea is taken to be a suprahuman, quasi-divine power. Like a train moving forcefully through the continuum of time, the ultimate idea is the driving mechanism by which historical events unfold. It plows forward with a brutal disregard for human casualty, rendering individual and collective will powerless before its overwhelming momentum. Humanity, on this view, does not write history. Rather, humanity is the vehicle through which the ultimate idea exercises its cold and impersonal will. To a totalitarian ruler, the ultimate idea is the greatest gift, the perfect excuse for every act of brutality and every crime against humanity.[52]

One of the central concepts in Arendt's theory of totalitarianism is ideology. Arendt defines ideology as a belief system that rests on an ultimate idea. She identifies three recurring components of ideological thinking: (1) the pretension to "total explanation," a single analytical key by which to unlock every mystery, to decipher every event, to make sense of the totality of human experience across past, present, and future, (2) its complete detachment from reality and its imperviousness to the jagged dissonance of practical experience, and (3) its uncritical, uncompromising, and absolutist logic.[53] Because ideology is so far removed from reality, it inevitably imposes meanings, patterns, and significance upon the surrounding environment, seeing concerted plotting and malicious intent where none necessarily exist. Every event, no matter how minuscule, no matter how trivial, is imbued with covert political purpose. Hence, why "the concept of enmity is replaced with that of conspiracy," for ideology is a degeneration from specific political hostilities into wholesale paranoia and delusion about some amorphous, omnipresent, and universal evil.[54] What drives the individual to this kind of thinking? What makes the individual so open to such wild belief? What social condition, what state of mind, leaves the individual so prone to paranoia and delusion? The answer, says Arendt, is isolation and loneliness.[55]

Arendt takes care to distinguish isolation from loneliness. Isolation, she observes, is a ubiquitous feature of modern life. Labor is almost always isolating. It is impossible to produce most goods and services without some degree of isolation. Yet this state of isolation does not automatically entail loneliness.

Even in isolation, we can still be social creatures through what George Herbert Mead calls a social self.[56] Our sense of self derives from our social history. Our private thoughts are an internal dialogue. To think to oneself is a distinctly social phenomenon, made possible by our mental impressions of talking to others. But this connection to the social world, Arendt argues, is lost when labor is no longer an end in itself but rather a means to mere survival. When forced to compete in the labor market just to make ends meet, the dignity of *homo faber* is lost to the degradation of *animal laborans*, a creature that modern society regards not with admiration but with contempt. At this point, says Arendt, "isolation becomes loneliness."[57]

Loneliness, as Arendt describes it, is essentially the loss of the social self. Loneliness is the absence of our internal dialogue, the disappearance of our silent interlocutors. Without the lasting and reassuring voices of significant others lingering in our memory, the isolated individual is liable to lose all sense of identity. Arendt defines loneliness as "uprootedness" and "superfluousness," the feeling of not belonging anywhere, of not having a recognized and valued role in society.[58] Loneliness is the distinct impression that you could disappear and that it would not make the slightest difference to the world. The decisive breaking point in the personal deterioration into loneliness is the loss of trust, not just in others but also in oneself. When we lose trust in ourselves, we no longer possess "that elementary confidence in the world which is necessary to make experiences at all. Self and world, the capacity for thought and experience, are lost at the same time."[59] Without the ability to trust others or oneself, the lonely individual is prone to paranoia, for paranoia is nothing if not the loss of trust in the world. The loss of trust, Arendt suggests, is why totalitarianism is so appealing to lonely individuals, for it confirms their worst suspicions about others and about the world around them. Totalitarianism feeds on loneliness, filling the lonely individual's inner emptiness with the rock-solid certainties of ideology, conspiracy theory, uncompromising logic, and some grand and intoxicating ultimate idea.

Arendt provides an invaluable insight into the appeal of conspiracy theory and the disturbing implications of loneliness for the political realm. For our purposes, however, her brief remarks about loneliness and the loss of trust take us only so far. While totalitarianism certainly relies upon conspiracy theory for its seductive power, conspiracy theory is not always coterminous with totalitarianism. Conspiracy theory, after all, thrives in nontotalitarian societies. We also still need to account for the link between loneliness, conspiracy theory, and digital media, something that Arendt, for all her social insight, could never have foreseen. Filling this gap requires delving deeper into the loss of the self. It requires that we describe in meaningful terms an experience that marks a descent into meaninglessness, formlessness, and inner chaos.

Narrative Life, Narrative Breakdown

Missing from Arendt's account of loneliness is an appreciation of the narrative structure of a human life. In *After Virtue*, MacIntyre presents a now-familiar picture of the human subject as a storytelling and story-living creature.[60] According to this picture, we *homo narrans* make sense of our lives through stories. Our grasp of everyday life—our memory of the past, our experience in the present, our expectations for the future—is organized in narrative terms. Characteristically, narratives are composed of a beginning, a middle, and an end. They feature protagonists and antagonists. They feature main and secondary characters. They revolve around plots, subplots, arcs, tensions, climaxes, and denouements. Their dramatic moments are made up of friendships, alliances, rivalries, feuds, victories, and defeats. Our everyday lives, MacIntyre argues, are composed of these same elements. Each of us is the protagonist in our personal story, itself embedded within a web of other such stories. Social life is nothing if not the ongoing historical development of this complex web.

That human life takes the form of a dramatic narrative does not mean that we are fated to live according to a prewritten script. Rather, we play an authorial role in our personal stories. By thinking, speaking, and acting in the present moment, by making decisions about the here and now, and by planning for the future, we write the unfolding story of our lives in real time. What makes this experience meaningful is the possibility of choice, of acting with purpose and intention. We make sense of our lives in light of the reasons for which we act in both the long and short term. If we act for no discernible reason, then our actions are, by definition, pointless. Acting for reasons, living our lives according to purpose and intention, is what allows us to tell an intelligible story about ourselves *to* ourselves.

This act of self-narration is an ongoing task, a constant balancing act to maintain personal coherence and intelligibility. Our daily encounter with unpredictable events, the practical need to confront an endless stream of surprises, plot twists, and digressions, demands that we continually order and reorder the bits and pieces of our lives into an intelligible pattern. That pattern necessarily takes a teleological form. As MacIntyre puts it, "There is no present which is not informed by some image of the future and an image of the future which always presents itself in the form of a *telos*—or a variety of ends or goals—towards which we are moving or failing to move in the present."[61] This is not to say that the ends of our lives are fixed or preordained. Rather, it is merely to say that without ends and goals, our lives are, in a very real sense, pointless. Our *telos* is the contingent anchor that enables us to order the data of practical experience into coherent form.

Not everyone can maintain this ongoing task of self-narration. Those hopelessly unable to tell a coherent story about their lives to themselves and others, to connect the past to the present to the future, are liable to plunge into personal meaninglessness, formlessness, and inner chaos. "The larger project," as the phenomenologist David Carr puts it, "has disintegrated for us, has lost its wholeness, completeness, or coherence."[62] In these darkest moments, nothing seems to make sense. We find ourselves trapped in "radical incoherence, whereby the elements of life become detached from each other and fail to add up to a whole." At this point, the self becomes "fragmented, distracted, dispersed, disconnected."[63] Lived experience becomes a meaningless sequence, like the endless ticking of a clock, without any overarching end or purpose. We might know what we are doing in the immediate moment, but we struggle to say why. Properly speaking, radical incoherence is not so much experience per se but rather "the dark and looming outer limit of experience, the chaos which stands opposed to order."[64] To pass over to the other side of experience, to flounder beyond the limits of narrative intelligibility, is to lose our grasp of the world and ourselves. "Mere sequence," Carr says, "is one of our ways of representing madness."[65]

Alienation is thus more than the separation of "man from man" and the loss of trust. In its most extreme form, alienation is also the loss of the narrative self, the decomposition of the teleological character of a human life. In the absence of a meaningful personal story, the prospect of death might well seem preferable to the torture of remaining alive. As MacIntyre writes:

> When someone complains—as do some of those who attempt or commit suicide—that his or her life is meaningless, he or she is often and perhaps characteristically complaining that the narrative of their life has become unintelligible to them, that it lacks any point, any movement towards a climax or a *telos*. Hence the point of doing any one thing rather than another at crucial junctures in their lives seems to such a person to have been lost.[66]

This is precisely where and why social media become so relevant. On social media platforms, we find interfaces optimized for personal meaninglessness. Social media are ideal vehicles for disseminating conspiracy theories perfectly suited for the lonely, isolated, and fragmented subject.

A World of Mere Sequence

If, as Carr argues, mere sequence is "one of our ways of representing madness," then it is quite telling that the core experience of social media is precisely that of mere sequence. Scrolling is the primary mode of navigating through the literally bottomless stream of visual, aural, and semantic content on social media. Like walking through an endless shopping aisle, surrounded on both sides by one eye-catching product after another, scrolling has become both a mode of navigation and a form of reading. Scrolling through Facebook, Twitter, Instagram, and TikTok is very different from the kind of careful, methodical, and close reading demanded by a long and intricate book. Scrolling belongs to a new mode of cognition for the digital age that James Sosnoski calls "hyper-reading" and that N. Katherine Hayles calls "hyperattention."[67] To navigate the infinite sequence of status updates, tweets, links, pictures, and videos demands an attention span conditioned to mere sequence. Instead of close, patient, and scrupulous reading, scrolling encourages browsing, scanning, skimming, glancing, and peeking.

Unlike a narrative, social media feeds are endless. Properly speaking, there is no beginning, middle, or end, no narrative arc or structure to provide a sense of time. Hence, why hours of continuous scrolling—going down the rabbit hole—can feel like an instant. Without the temporal guideposts of a beginning, middle, and end, we become lost in the abyss of the present. It is no secret that social media feeds were designed to mimic slot machines.[68] Both types of interface tantalize the user with the promise of some jackpot that never comes. Social media users scroll and scroll and scroll and scroll, chasing after an elusive prize forever beyond their grasp. In the process, they risk losing their sense of self and the means-end structure of deliberate and purposive reasoning. To scroll for hours on end is to watch an endless sequence of content with no overarching purpose, pattern, or order. The experience of passively gliding past one item of glossy content after another is literally meaningless. It is not just that a social media feed is pointless. By scrolling daily for hours on end, our lives are liable to feel pointless, too. Habitual scrolling reflects a loss of narrative structure. Little wonder, then, that constant scrolling is correlated with addiction and depression.[69]

Pathological scrolling risks a gradual slide into radical incoherence, an empty, formless, and structureless void, what Fredric Jameson, following Jacques Lacan, calls schizophrenia.[70] Under this extreme condition, the "series of signifiers" that links one thought to the next has disintegrated. Plagued by "linguistic malfunction," we wander aimlessly through "a rubble of distinct and unrelated signifiers."[71] Like an insentient organism that predictably jumps and reacts in the face of environmental stimuli, the experience of the schizophrenic individual is loosely strung together through "a series of pure and unrelated presents in time."[72] The most significant units of experience are sporadic moments of "heightened intensity."[73]

Although Jameson has in mind the mental life of a television society, we can see how his observations pertain to the mental life of a social media society. Because lived experience on social media lacks any overarching meaning, the individual stimuli that prod us in this and that direction acquire a magnified potency. The individual stimulus, the "signifier in isolation," exerts a powerful grip upon our consciousness.[74] It sparks an entire world of sensation unto itself, taking hold of us with "indescribable vividness," leaving us breathless and overawed.[75] A standalone status update, tweet, meme, or reel can become a self-contained universe of experience, the entire structure of our thinking and consciousness—at least until it loses its novelty, after which we scroll on in search of the next self-contained signifier that can deliver the same sensation.

Jameson likens an encounter with the isolated signifier to the experience of the sublime—the feeling of awe, wonder, and fear before the mysterious, the ineffable, the transcendent. When Edmund Burke and Immanuel Kant theorized about the nature of the sublime, they had in mind such objects of veneration as music, art, and God.[76] But in our schizophrenic condition, we experience what Jameson calls the "hysterical sublime," that is, acute feeling without cognitive content.[77] The hysterical sublime can take the form of sharp anxiety, of dark and foreboding gloom. It can also take the form of extreme exhilaration and euphoria. In the absence of a larger framework of meaning, we are liable to chase after these euphoric intensities, much like an addict chasing after a high.

Trapped in the cognitive prison of mere sequence, where repetition without difference risks a descent into madness, a chance encounter with a clear, reductive, and inspiring story about the world can offer the promise of salvation. As Carr puts it, "The fragmentation of existence can be overcome by the assumption of a rigidly laid-out social role."[78] The appeal of conspiracy theory is precisely that it provides this kind of clear and stable social role. It offers those suffering from radical incoherence and agonizing emptiness, those who float about like particles in the air, the comforting and empowering illusion of solid ground.

Conspiracy Theory: Amphetamine of the Alienated

The popularity of conspiracy theory, I want to suggest, lies not in its explanatory appeal to the stupid and the uneducated but rather in its narrative appeal to the lonely, the paranoid, the fragile, the desperate. Conspiracy theory fills an existential void. It overcompensates for this void by imposing a forceful and exacting sense of structure, meaning, and purpose. It furnishes a spatial and temporal architecture by which to regain one's geographical bearings in the world and a chronological sense of past, present, and future. It offers the promise of reenchantment in a disenchanted world. Most importantly, it invites lonely and alienated subjects to participate in a captivating social drama, in which they, too, can finally enjoy a sense of belonging and membership in a community of elective affinity. Conspiracy theory makes the world less lonely.

Conspiracy theories are commonly thought of as elaborate, complicated, and confusing explanations of some facet of the social world. We typically visualize conspiracy theories as wild and convoluted patchworks of newspaper clippings, maps, pictures, and notecards on a corkboard, all tied together with pins and string running every which way. Given their characteristic messiness, it can be difficult to see how anyone could find conspiracy theories intelligible, let alone believable. Beneath the superficial appearance of messiness, however, invariably lies a simple and enchanting story.

At their core, conspiracy theories are straightforward morality tales of absolute good and evil. They feature exaggerated heroes, exaggerated villains, and exaggerated victims, all bound together in a plot of cartoonish simplicity.[79] Their narrative structure lacks nuance and subtlety. Instead, their logic is necessarily austere and uncompromising. Even the slightest admission of ambiguity would threaten to unravel the entire edifice. Because conspiracy theories rest on distrust, they necessarily have a self-radicalizing logic. None but the select are to be trusted. The world is a theatre of evil. Common sense and conventional wisdom are the temptations of the devil. Reality is necessarily counterintuitive. Truth is stranger than fiction. To a conspiracy theorist, absurdity is a mark of excellence. The more absurd and far-fetched a story about the world, the more plausible and believable.

It is instructive in this regard to consider the case of QAnon, one of the most persistent sources of COVID-19 disinformation and the inspiration behind so much online harassment and abuse of healthcare workers and scientists.[80] Like all conspiracy theories, QAnon offers a simple picture of reality. It reduces the complexity of the social world to a thrilling adventure story. It promises a sense of absolute certainty and the illusion of authoritative knowledge. It provides a universal key to unlock the mysteries of the world and finally overcome doubt and confusion. In this respect, QAnon is deeply empowering. But it does more than merely offer answers. It also provides a social script, a triumphalist plot in which believers can play a powerful role in making history. QAnon tells its followers not just what to think but also what to do. It adds a program of action to mere explanation, making it doubly empowering.

The QAnon universe is a pulp thriller. Donald Trump is the hero of the saga, a champion of freedom and liberty who has valiantly devoted his life to fighting evil. The villains are many: Democrats, the media, and Hollywood. Together, the villains carry out the most unspeakable evils, including child sex trafficking and child sacrifice. The mysterious figure of Q serves as an oracle, posting "Q-drops" on 4Chan and 8Chan. The base of the movement is the global community of believers, an army of digital soldiers, who have joined the epic battle of good versus evil. QAnon is a choose-your-own-adventure story, in which believers are real-life characters. The story synthesizes spy novel fiction with elements of apocalyptic Christianity.[81] Trump is very much a messianic figure, and Q, a seer and diviner who prophesies about the future. Q-drops have become the movement's scripture, spawning an entire priestly cast of commentators who decoded Q's enigmatic words for the faithful.

Because of their mortal need to believe the overarching story at all costs, believers flatly disregard Q's many contradictions and failed prophecies, happily explaining them away as the result of faulty interpretation.[82] They look upon the media much as they would Satan, a wily tempter constantly seeking to deceive the believers and lead them astray, forcing them to remain ever vigilant against the devil's seductive charms. Believers even attend weekly sermons and meet for regular study in a kind of Sunday school. Ultimately, QAnon's battle narrative strongly resembled holy war.[83] Hence, the movement's propensity toward violence and political trolling.

Since the humiliating defeat of Donald Trump in the 2020 general election and the failed uprising at the U.S. Capitol on January 6, 2021, QAnon has mutated and morphed into different beasts. In Canada, it merged with the anti-5G movement to form the notorious Freedom Convoy of early 2022, which occupied downtown Ottawa and other major cities across Canada in an attempt to force the federal government to lift pandemic safety measures.[84] To the Canadian arm of the global QAnon movement, Justin Trudeau became the primary enemy.[85] The elements of the story changed, but the apocalyptic battle between cosmic good and evil, between freedom fighters and oppressive tyrants, has remained the same. Healthcare workers notably came to be regarded as part of the system of tyranny and therefore became a target of trolling and harassment. The abuse was so extreme that British Columbia was forced to introduce "bubble zones" to protect healthcare workers from convoy demonstrators.[86] Although anti-vaccine trolls jeered, taunted, and provoked their victims, their underlying motives were anything but playful.

For a QAnon troll, the lulz are but a thin veil for inner pain and turmoil. In the United States, QAnon followers have confessed to suffering from a wide range of mental health problems, including bipolar disorder, depression, anxiety, and addiction. Almost 70 percent of QAnon members convicted of crimes before and after the January 6, 2021, uprising at the U.S. Capitol have been diagnosed with mental health problems, including post-traumatic stress disorder, paranoid schizophrenia, bipolar disorder, and Munchausen syndrome by proxy.[87] Of the dozens of QAnon followers who committed crimes leading up to the January 6 uprising and after, more than 40 percent had undergone some form of trauma.[88] The pattern of trauma among QAnon followers helps explain their addiction to conspiracy theory.[89] The evidence of mental illness suggests that the QAnon community is but a symptom of a much deeper public health crisis. It suggests that conspiracy theory has become a kind of soothing elixir that alleviates acute existential anguish. It is tempting to propose therapy and counseling as the answer to this crisis.[90] This chapter, however, suggests something different. If the popularity of conspiracy theory is an expression of mass isolation, loneliness, distrust, and paranoia, then perhaps a more practical answer is to build a culture of trust, a topic that will be explored in the final chapter.

6

Trust

In the closing pages of *Amusing Ourselves to Death*, Postman issued a dire "Huxleyan warning." He foresaw a time in which "Big Brother does not watch us, by his choice. We watch him, by ours."[1] Postman warned that there would be no need for a Ministry of Truth to control what we see, hear, and think. Rather, we would be so absorbed by trivia, so hungry for visual stimulation, so determined to be entertained at all costs, that we would risk losing any semblance of a free and democratic society. Our pathological craving for amusement would be our submission. Postman acknowledged an obvious difficulty in painting so bleak a picture of our impending future. If the consequences of television for truth, reason, and public discourse were as severe as he made them out to be, then what hope could there possibly be for cultural resistance? As Postman saw it, the only hope lay in developing a widespread "media consciousness."[2] For this, he conceived of two possibilities. The first was to use television to critique television— that is, something very like what would eventually become *The Daily Show*. This idea Postman dismissed as "nonsensical."[3] Using a medium to critique that very medium, he believed, would only reinforce the power and authority of the medium. The second possibility was to turn to "the only mass medium of communication" in which we could realistically cultivate a critical understanding of television on a broad social scale: public schools.[4] What Postman envisioned here was something like a general curriculum in media studies through which to build mass television literacy.

Like Postman, MacIntyre issued a similarly dire warning in the final pages of *After Virtue*. After going to great lengths to show how and why moral language had degenerated into "a state of grave disorder," culminating in an increasingly acrimonious public discourse, he offered a similarly bleak prognosis of our impending future.[5] The corrosive effects of liberal individualism upon the language of morality were so all-consuming, he argued, that even left-wing revolutionary politics had been affected.[6] Where, then, to turn and what to do? MacIntyre called for "the construction of local forms of community," in which

Trolling Ourselves to Death. Jason Hannan, Oxford University Press. © Oxford University Press 2023.
DOI: 10.1093/oso/9780197557761.003.0007

reason and civility could be preserved in the face of "the coming ages of barbarism and darkness."[7] These local forms of community would help us resist the corrupting instincts, values, ideology, and rhetoric of the marketplace.

How might these twin pleas guide our response to the problem of political trolling today? This chapter revisits the main themes of this book—the various historical and contemporary elements that make up the culture of political trolling. It takes up the responsibility for answering the urgent question "What is to be done?" To that end, this chapter synthesizes Postman's call for turning to public schools and MacIntyre's plea for building local forms of community to propose a pedagogy of trust as our best hope for dismantling the culture of political trolling. The primary inspiration for this chapter is Robert Brandom's mammoth book *A Spirit of Trust*, one of the most original and productive readings of Hegel's *Phenomenology of Spirit* in recent years.[8] *A Spirit of Trust* is many things: a story of the modern world, a history of modern thought, an account of the malaises of modernity, a theory of alienation, a model of public reason, and a forceful case for building a spirit of trust. Because Brandom's argument is extremely technical and abstract, the precise relevance of *A Spirit of Trust* for something as tangible and dirty as trolling might at first blush seem like a bit of a stretch. In what follows, I therefore hope to capture the gist of this rich and difficult book to make its relevance for trolling explicit to the reader with no familiarity with Brandom's philosophical oeuvre. More importantly, I hope to translate his argument for building a spirit of trust into a practical response for grappling with the culture of political trolling. To that end, I propose a critical pedagogy that synthesizes Brandom's ideas with the thought and practice of Paulo Freire and bell hooks. The classroom, I will argue, is an ideal space in which to build a spirit of trust and launch a widescale resistance against a culture of mass distrust, cynicism, paranoia, and rampant political trolling.

A Semantic Theory with an Edifying Intent

How, then, to begin talking about *A Spirit of Trust*? Brandom's book is, among other things, an ambitious answer to basic human questions: What is truth? What is real? What is good? What is right? Who are "we" and what do "we" stand for? These questions lie at the heart of organized human life. They have long animated human practices like poetry, art, music, religion, and philosophy. We disagree about these questions vehemently, even to the point (especially when they turn political) of trolling ourselves to death. Modern philosophy is the attempt to answer these basic questions without appeal to faith or scripture— the search for some neutral and impartial ground, a common court of appeal, the alternative to the imposition of a purportedly divine will or some arbitrary and sectarian human authority. Modern philosophy has been divided over how best to approach these questions. Early in the modern era, the rationalist school put forth the view that pure reason is the only possible ground of genuine knowledge. Shortly thereafter, the empiricist school countered this view with the claim that the only possible ground for genuine knowledge is sensory perception. The tension between the appeal to pure and abstract reason and the appeal to sensory perception has formed much of the intellectual backdrop of modern thought.

The most influential school to arise in response to the conflict between rationalism and empiricism was that of German idealism. The idealist school sought to appreciate the insights of both rationalism and empiricism without falling back upon the reductive tendencies and unequivocal conclusions of either. The core insight of the idealist school was that we do not apprehend the world directly, that we do not have access to the essence of things. This elusive essence is what Kant famously called the *Ding an sich*, or thing-in-itself.[9] On the idealist understanding, the world comes to us not directly but *conceptualized*. That is, our minds impose some form or structure, some conceptual wrapping paper, upon reality. We may switch from one wrapping paper to another, but we have no ability to remove the wrapping paper altogether and apprehend reality through something like direct vision. To claim direct access to the essence of things, whether a physical entity like an atom or an abstract concept like justice, is on the idealist view an unjustified and authoritarian assertion, akin to claiming to know the mind and will of God.

For the idealist school, the key question concerns the nature of the basic concepts by which we acquire knowledge about the world. As indicated in Chapter 2, Kant took the view that all true knowledge—that is, knowledge about what the natural world empirically is and what the social world morally ought to be—ultimately rests on transcendental concepts.[10] Like numbers, these basic and foundational concepts belong to an abstract realm, waiting to be discovered. As such, they are fixed, timeless, ahistorical, and universal. Hegel, by contrast, took the view that our knowledge of the world, both empirical and moral, ultimately rests on concepts brought into being through discourse.[11] On Hegel's historicist view, the foundational concepts of human knowledge are not fixed for all eternity but rather are subject to change and evolution through the public practice of linguistic communication. *A Spirit of Trust* is a formidable expansion of Hegel's historicist view of concepts. It offers an original reading of Hegel's thought, demonstrating its explanatory power for diagnosing and treating the malaises of modernity. As Brandom puts it, *A Spirit of Trust* is a semantic theory "with an edifying intent."[12]

Why a semantic theory with an edifying intent? Of what relevance is such a theory to contemporary politics and a cultural problem like political trolling? We can answer this question by considering the meaning of a crucial political idea like justice. In a secular world, how do we decide the meaning of justice? If not by appeal to God, then to what? Can we speak of the one true idea of justice? If so, how do we know what it is? Or is justice at best a contingent and historical idea? In that case, how do we negotiate its meaning and substance? These are critical questions for modern societies. The idea of justice is the foundation of modern constitutional democracies. Yet justice is an inherently ambiguous and contested idea, the site of vehement moral conflict.[13] The contestability of basic normative concepts, like justice and morality, is the underlying source of our culture wars. The ceaseless conservative grievance over "social justice warriors" and "wokeness," for example, reflects different basic instincts about the very idea of justice. The members of the rationalist, empiricist, and idealist schools all proposed various theories of the good, the right, and the just. While they differed in how to approach these foundational concepts, they nonetheless believed in the modernist vision of a society based on public, secular, and rationally defensible standards of moral judgment.

Not everyone accepted or accepts this vision, however. To a certain cynical sensibility, the very idea of public, secular, and rationally defensible standards of moral judgment is a myth, a ruse for the will to power, and therefore something to be exposed and resisted. In its most extreme form, this cynicism devolves into the impulse for trolling. Brandom refers to this absolutist and uncompromising cynicism as genealogy.[14]

Genealogy: A Hermeneutics of Distrust

As discussed in Chapter 5, genealogy is Nietzsche's signature method for demythologizing Western morality. By subjecting the central terms and categories of Western morals to philological analysis, Nietzsche sought to show that the original meanings of these key terms and categories had, over the course of a long and winding history, become obscured and forgotten. He called upon us to see that what we take to be an impersonal and objective set of principles for guiding thought, speech, and action is in fact a noxious and corrosive system of repression, guilt, and self-punishment. Genealogy robs Western morality of its metaphysical power and mystique, thereby freeing us from its normative and psychological grip. Once liberated from this repressive system, argues Nietzsche, we are free to carry out the revaluation of all values. We are free to build a new morality, a *heroic* morality, a morality for a truly post-Christian world.[15]

The brutal and exacting deftness with which Nietzsche wielded the genealogical method has impressed generations of cultural critics, who have found in genealogy an extremely potent weapon for radical critique. Michel Foucault, Gilles Deleuze, Félix Guattari, Edward Said, Judith Butler, and even Daniel

Dennett are just a few such critics who have, in their various ways, adopted, adapted, expanded, and applied the genealogical method to different systems of thought and power—all to devastating effect.[16] Genealogy has proven to be an enormously productive and illuminating critical method. It therefore rightly remains indispensable to the humanities and social sciences.

Yet, for all its impressive analytical power, genealogy risks devolving into a kind of paranoia. When rendered indiscriminate and absolute, when it slides from local to global critique, genealogy comes to regard all normative systems with distrust, finding an invidious will to power wherever it turns. It thus degrades into what Paul Ricoeur called the hermeneutics of suspicion, or what we might also call a hermeneutics of distrust.[17] Genealogy in its global and indiscriminate form moves from worthwhile and purposeful critique of local and specific systems to pointless and generic hostility toward normative systems as such. Brandom regards this paranoid impulse as the principal obstacle to building a spirit of trust.

For Brandom, Nietzsche is the prototypical example of an alienated modern thinker.[18] Brandom understands alienation as a stifling immersion within a foreign system. Alienation is a condition in which "individuals are bound by norms they are not . . . at home with, do not identify with, where, in the image to be interpreted, what binds them does so as something external, alien, or other."[19] Because of the perpetual feeling of being hopelessly out of place, alienation inevitably triggers skepticism and hostility toward the entire surrounding normative edifice. Nietzsche was alienated by more than just Western morality. He was also alienated by reason itself. In Nietzsche's hands, genealogy functions as a universal acid, eating away at both the substance of Western morality and the epistemic force of reason.[20] Nietzsche counted among his enemies both Christ and Socrates—the former the avatar of egalitarianism, the latter the avatar of reason.[21] Nietzsche bitterly resisted to the very end the tantalizing lure of reason, epitomized by the Socratic method of question and answer, the celebrated pedagogical means for reaching a higher truth. For Nietzsche, there was neither a higher truth to be found nor any rational means by which to achieve it. Truth and reason were but illusions, mere guises for the will to power. Nietzsche therefore refused to engage with Socrates on the latter's dialectical terms. Rather, he insisted upon mocking Socrates for his ugliness.[22] In this, Nietzsche might be said to be the first and original troll.

The refusal to engage with, and the impulse to attack, the reasoning subject are the inevitable temptations of genealogy in its indiscriminate and global form. In this respect, Nietzsche may have been the first, but he was hardly the last. He was, rather, the father of a modern tradition of cynicism with many witting and unwitting heirs. The literary critic Stanley Fish is a latter-day example of how an absolute and uncompromising distrust of public standards of truth and justice easily slides into the instinct for trolling. Fish has been for many decades a prominent public intellectual. In the early part of his career, he made a number of critical interventions in literary theory. Fish had taken up the question of whether the text or the reader is the ultimate source of meaning.[23] He argued against the formalist school, which held that the formal structures of a given text are the sole source of its meaning. On the formalist view, meaning is fixed, unchanging, and impervious to the whims and fancies of the reader.

Instead, Fish argued that meaning is created through what he called interpretive communities—local, specific, and delimited readerships whose members are bound by a shared set of practices.[24] Interpretive communities inevitably approach texts through a local and idiosyncratic lens. In developing this idea, Fish put forth a theory of communication, according to which mutual understanding and agreement only occur within interpretive communities. As he put it, "Communication occurs within situations and that to be in a situation is already to be in possession of (or to be possessed by) a structure of assumptions, of practices already understood to be relevant in relation to purposes and goals that are already in place."[25] According to Fish, there is no single, objective, and transcultural meaning to a given text. Rather, there are as many meanings as there are interpretive communities. The consequence of this view is that communication *between* interpretive communities is by definition impossible.

In the later part of his career, Fish branched out of the narrow and exclusive confines of literary criticism and entered the American culture wars. He applied his anti-foundationalist approach to literary criticism to the political realm. Just as he had argued against objective standards in textual interpretation, so, too, did he argue against objective standards in morality and politics. Fish challenged the very idea that public discourse could ever be mediated by shared principles of truth and justice.[26] In his view, principles are illusions of neutrality and impartiality. Fish expressed impatience with and contempt for the very idea of principle. He regarded the commitment to principle as a misguided form of modern piety.

Why the impatience and contempt? "The trouble with principle," Fish wrote, "is that it does not exist."[27] The problem, he argued, is that principles are either so abstract as to be without normative substance or so substantive as to be decidedly partisan. What we call "principles" are nothing more than local biases and prejudices dressed up in the false language of universality, objectivity, and impersonality. Principles are moral fictions serving partisan agendas. The appeal to principle is therefore a form of epistemic authoritarianism, in which the biases and prejudices of some local community are forcibly imposed upon others under false banners like Truth and Justice. The invocation of principles should therefore be fought and resisted. The only standards of truth and justice are local, particular, and idiosyncratic. There is just the truth and justice of this or that community. Inescapably, we inhabit separate and disconnected communal bubbles, self-contained moral universes with internal standards of right and wrong. Internal standards are all we have. The implication is that those who do not inhabit our bubble and who do not subscribe to our local and idiosyncratic beliefs are, by our standards, necessarily in the wrong.[28]

This view has obvious consequences for civic engagement in the public sphere. When we encounter, as Fish puts it, "someone who gives the wrong kind of reasons" or "subscribes to the wrong kind of belief," we should not bother talking to them. On the contrary, says Fish, we "don't give them the time of day," because "they are just obviously the wrong sort." Until they have "gone away and read the right books and taken the right courses"—in other words, until they conform to our idiosyncratic thinking—we don't bother engaging them in "rational discussion." Fish divides the world into "us" and "them." He lambastes anyone purporting to be "non-partisan, non-tribal." As Fish sees it, there are only "tribal" and partisan communities. To those who do not belong to our "tribe," Fish would literally have us say, "You guys are wrong, we're right, and we're not going to listen to you or give you an even break."[29]

The public sphere, on this view, is therefore necessarily a battlefield, an arena of unprincipled ideological warfare, in which open and unapologetic partisanship is the condition of political victory.[30] Fish expresses a common cynicism found across the political spectrum, particularly on the radical right. Despite his high-profile public disagreements with reactionary figures like Dinesh D'Souza on political correctness and universal values, Fish and his conservative interlocutors share the same cynicism toward public reasoning and the same politics of distrust. Indeed, Fish's role in the culture wars has often veered into that of a troll, deploying philosophically dubious arguments for the sole purpose of getting under the skin of his favorite, all-purpose punching bag: "liberals."[31] The entire rationale behind Fish's hermeneutics of distrust, like that of Nietzsche before him, is the unquestioned premise that public reason is always and forever reducible to arbitrary will and power—a clichéd, if stubbornly enduring, idea encountered in one form or another by virtually every graduate student in the humanities. A hermeneutics of distrust is not just the seed of political unreason. It also undermines the very practice of democracy.

Democracy Between Distrust and Trust

At its core, the possibility of democracy hinges upon some basic trust and solidarity.[32] To be American, Canadian, British, or Indian, for example, is not simply to be a citizen of the United States, Canada, Britain, or India, a formal status that confers certain rights and privileges. It is also to possess a political identity, an identity that is the outcome of a specific discursive history. Encoded in this political identity are distinct principles, values, and commitments. Political identities are not natural or set in stone. Rather, they are works in progress. Democratic citizenship requires the ongoing negotiation of the meaning of political identity. To be American, Canadian, British, or Indian is to be part of a public conversation about what it means to be American, Canadian, British, or Indian. This ongoing project of defining and redefining political identity can move in radically different directions.

For Marjorie Taylor Greene and the America First Caucus, America is defined in racially and culturally exclusive terms.[33] Their concept of America is bound up in a reactionary fantasy of Anglo-Saxon racial purity, in which Blacks, Muslims, Jews, and others have no place. By contrast, for Alexandria Ocasio-Cortez, Rashida Tlaib, and Ilhan Omar, America is defined in categorically inclusive terms. Their concept of America is not just that of a land of immigrants but also the possibility of democratic socialism, racial justice, and a green economy.[34] These are two very different concepts of America. Similarly, for the Bharatiya Janata Party, India is defined in religiously exclusive terms. Their concept of India is that of a nation of, by, and for the Hindu majority, a nation in which Muslims, Sikhs, and others have no place.[35] For the Indian National Congress, by contrast, India is defined in secular and pluralistic terms. India for the Indian National Congress is a diverse nation in which Hindus, Muslims, Sikhs, Buddhists, Jains, Christians, and atheists all have a place.[36] The contest over political identity, the struggle over the heart and soul of a nation, is the essence of our culture wars today. America, Canada, Britain, India, and other modern democracies are in the midst of an increasingly violent battle over who they are, what they value, and in what direction they ought to be moving. This includes a battle over the meaning of basic concepts like justice, freedom, and equality, values that lie at the core of their political identities.

How, then, as Charles Taylor asks, can democracies "maintain a real sense of unity around their political identity"? Taylor puts the point as follows:

> It's clear that this requires a kind of trust. . . . Unless party or group *A* is confident about this in relation to *B*, the democratic polity is in danger. If *A* and *B* represent different regions, they may be on the verge of a break-up. But where they are not geographically distributed in this way, something worse can happen. They are liable to enter into a kind of undeclared civil war, in which each is willing to use any means short of violence (because then it would really be a civil war) to win their point.[37]

Interminable disagreements about political identity, about the basic values and commitments that underlie what it means to belong to this or that country, can easily devolve from mere ideological rivalry to rhetorical manipulation to physical violence. The problem with a hermeneutics of distrust, whether in its explicit theoretical form or in its implicit political form, is that it encourages this devolution toward violence. It invites us to look upon fellow citizens as enemies from within and feeds the instincts for trolling ourselves to death. When Trump tells his supporters, "This nation does not belong to them. This nation belongs to you," he echoes Fish when the latter encourages "us" to say, "You guys are wrong, we're right, and we're not going to listen to you or give you an even break."[38] Avoiding a descent into an undeclared civil war requires proactively building what Brandom calls a spirit of trust.

A Hermeneutics of Trust

Genealogy in its global and indiscriminate form rests on a hefty epistemic premise—the thesis, again, that reason is always an instrument of will and power. Brandom recognizes the challenge this view poses to a free and democratic society. It is not enough to brush off this way of thinking as mere theoretical excess and then to purport to carry on with business as usual. If the genealogical view is indeed correct, then it would have material implications for the possibility of a free and democratic society. Public reasoning would necessarily be pointless. Accountability for what we say and do would be incoherent.[39] Brandom therefore interrogates genealogy carefully, asking whether there is any merit to its underlying premise. As a semantic theorist who, like Wittgenstein before him, links meaning to use, Brandom finds that genealogy suffers from a form of "semantic naiveté."[40]

As Brandom observes, genealogy notoriously regards the use of reason through a subordination model of human relationships. The idea is that just as the appeal to the will of God demands subordination, so, too, does the appeal to reason. And just as the Enlightenment sought to liberate us from the chains of *religious* authoritarianism, genealogy similarly seeks to liberate us from the chains of *rational* authoritarianism. But this move, Brandom argues, rests on a naive semantics. It presupposes that the meanings of concepts, once formed, are not publicly negotiable. So, for example, when the concepts of America, Canada, Britain, and India, or of justice, freedom, and equality, get off the ground, so to speak, their meaning is no longer negotiable through public discourse. Rather, they become hardened and immalleable, like the transformation from molten to solid metal. Because concepts, once formed, are non-negotiable, they function as blunt instruments, to be wielded, like chains and hammers, for bending others to our will.[41] The problem with this view, Brandom contends, is that its underlying semantic thesis cannot possibly be right. Concepts *are* publicly negotiable.

Brandom therefore challenges genealogy with a rival semantic theory synthesized from Hegel's *Science of Logic*. As Brandom indicates, this alternative semantic theory regards concepts not as static, dead, and inflexible but rather as organic, living, and evolving phenomena. Concepts, he points out, are like social selves.[42] Concepts do not reside, as Kant had theorized, in a transcendental realm, independent of a semantic ecosystem.[43] Rather, concepts depend for their being on an immersion within a web of concepts and a social environment. The reason concepts like justice, freedom, and equality are so powerful is precisely because they are widely recognized. There is something distinctly *public* about concepts.[44] They are not the private property of a single individual or some exclusive social class. No individual and no social class can arbitrarily dictate the meaning of concepts like justice, freedom, and equality. Nor, for that matter, can anyone arbitrarily dictate the meaning of America, Canada, Britain, or India. We can all, in principle, participate in the ongoing public discourse over political identity. The radically public nature of this process is threatening to people of power and privilege. That concepts should possess a public character does not sit well with those who want the exclusive right to define political identity in exclusive terms.

The tenacity with which political reactionaries cling to dying ideas of political identity indicates an extreme unease with the public and recognitive foundation of concepts. It betrays an unwillingness to allow their cherished images of the nation to evolve through the medium of public discourse. Brandom offers a picture of public discourse in which everyone within a recognitive community is entitled to play a part in shaping the meaning of concepts. The key to understanding the process of conceptual negotiation and evolution is the relationship between concepts and objects, between universals and particulars.[45] When we apply a concept to an object, we make a judgment. The soundness of that judgment depends on the relationship of the one to the other. There is nothing problematic, for example, in my applying the concept "mammal" to my cat. There would, however, be something deeply problematic in my applying the concept "mammal" to my dining table. The former simply does not fit the latter. I cannot force the expansion of the concept of a mammal by applying it to non-mammalian objects. There are instances, however, when the application of a concept to some novel type of object can lead to the expansion and development of that concept.

When, for example, Thomas Jefferson wrote in the Declaration of Independence that "all men are created equal," he not only expressed one of the defining political sentiments of the American Revolution but also formally encoded the value of equality into American political identity. To be an American citizen, according to the Declaration, was to be a member of a society of equals. Jefferson, of course, did not fabricate the concept of equality out of the blue. Rather, he followed the reigning political semantics of his time. Equality for Jefferson, as for his fellow signatories to the Declaration, did not apply to all people or even to all men. Rather, it applied only to educated, propertied, and European men, such as himself. This historically idiosyncratic conception of equality was obviously not going to last, for the simple reason that such a concept of equality was inherently unstable. There was a material tension between the formal idea of equality and the brute social reality of inequality in postrevolutionary America.[46] The poor and the working class, among other groups, had been excluded from the official definition of equality. Legally, this amounted to the denial of the franchise to the propertyless. The early American labor movement therefore highlighted this class gap. Labor activists publicly campaigned for the extension of the franchise. They did so in the name of an expanded concept of equality: universal white male suffrage. As we now know, this movement was successful. By 1856, every state in the Union had granted all white men, regardless of their property-holding status, the right to vote.[47]

From our retrospective standpoint today, the partial extension of the franchise was at once a real historical achievement and an achievement tragically marred by severe political limitations. One of those limitations was soon to become the target of further critique. Before the Civil War, the official meaning of equality only applied to Europeans. It did not apply to Black people. Following Emancipation, Black American political activists made the racial gap in the official meaning of equality explicit. They, too, demanded the right to vote in the name of equality. They, too, undertook public campaigns to challenge the racial gap. Like the white labor movement before them, they were successful in transforming the public understanding of equality. In 1868, Congress passed the Fourteenth Amendment, which extended the franchise to Black men.[48] The public concept of equality thus underwent another crucial stage of historical development, acquiring a racial dimension to the recently recognized class dimension. And just as Black American political activists had highlighted the racial gap, the women's movement highlighted the gender gap. American feminists pointed to the Equal Protection Clause of the Fourteenth Amendment as the operative principle by which they, too, deserved the right to vote, a right that, after more than seventy years of public campaigning, was formally recognized through the passing of the Nineteenth Amendment in 1920.[49] The Equal Protection Clause of the Fourteenth Amendment would also later become the basis on which the civil rights movement, the LGBTQ movement, and the disability rights movement would demand equal protection under the law, effectively expanding the public meaning of equality beyond mere voting rights.[50]

The concept of equality, then, has always lacked a stable and permanent meaning. Rather, its meaning has always been fluid, dynamic, and evolving, always subject to public negotiation.[51] The inescapable indeterminacy, flux, and development of concepts can be both unsettling and empowering. Unsettling, because we lack the existential comforts of a fixed picture of the world; empowering, because we can always hope for a different world, a better world. Herein lies the emancipatory kernel of Hegel's philosophical system, for it leaves open the possibility of breaking free of prevailing systems of thought.[52] No individual can arbitrarily decide the meaning of political concepts. No individual can freeze the meaning of concepts in time or turn back the clock to some golden era, as so many reactionaries would like. The fate of meaning lies in the open-ended practice of public discourse, a practice in which each of us, again, can be a participant. As with playing a game of chess, we need not turn to an external authority, least of all a divine one, to validate our every move in the language game of public discourse. Anyone can, in principle, call out the gaps in our reigning political concepts and make explicit the obdurate blind spots in our political self-image. This is precisely the contribution of movements like Occupy Wall Street, Black Lives Matter, #MeToo, and Every Child Matters. Like the historic political movements before them, these latter-day social justice movements have made explicit the persistent inconsistencies between the intoxicating official celebrations of equality and the sordid reality of widespread inequality on the ground. We have been witnessing in real time the contest over, and evolution of, the concept of equality in the public realm. This ongoing process of making explicit in principle what is implicit in practice, says Brandom, is the essence of public reasoning.[53]

To acknowledge that public reasoning is open-ended and indeterminate, and that no one can claim final and absolute authority over the meaning of concepts is to accept our basic and inescapable fallibility. As Brandom conceives the hermeneutics of trust, we are at the mercy of each other's judgments. We have only each other to hold ourselves accountable. The practice of public reasoning is necessarily messy and imperfect. It is bound to result in flawed judgment. We therefore point out the problems in each other's reasoning not by appeal to scripture or transcendental standards beyond time and history but rather by appeal to contingent and historical principles that are constantly developing in real time. We depend on each other to recognize the gaps and blind spots in our respective judgments.[54]

To accept our mutual dependency upon each other is to enter a relationship of trust, a relationship in which we are prepared both to correct and be corrected by each other. A hermeneutics of trust requires that, as a starting point, we take each other's judgments in good faith, that we see each other as striving to get it right. Hegel calls this attitude *Edelmütigkeit*, or magnanimity. To adopt the attitude of *Edelmütigkeit* is to take a charitable view of each other's words, even if we determine that the other has got things plainly wrong. It means that we each seek in earnest to reconstruct the chain of reasons that led to the other's judgments.[55] *Edelmütigkeit* is the opposite of what Hegel refers to as *Niederträchtigkeit*, or

malice, vileness, and despicableness. *Niederträchtigkeit* is the invidious insist-
ence on seeing the worst possible motives behind everything that others say and
do. *Niederträchtigkeit* means "striving for the low, an impulse to debase."[56] Hegel
thus foresaw the psychology of the troll, a creature whose pathological distrust
of others leads him to public acts of harassment, abuse, degradation, and humiliation. *Niederträchtigkeit* is notably the fallback attitude of reactionaries determined to restore the hierarchies of old by asserting a final and exclusive concept
of the nation and viciously attacking anyone who challenges it.

From Theory to Practice: A Pedagogy of Trust

While Brandom describes in theoretical terms the epistemic architecture of the
structure of trust, we need to ask how this structure might be cultivated in practice to counter mass distrust, cynicism, paranoia, and trolling. How do we create a culture of *Edelmütigkeit* and undo our culture of *Niederträchtigkeit*? Here
I wish to argue that public education has a unique and critical role to play. What
I propose here falls squarely within a familiar tradition of political theory that
upholds public education as one of the foundations of a free and democratic
society. The classical and modern figures of this tradition include Jean-Jacques
Rousseau, Immanuel Kant, Friedrich Schleiermacher, Émile Durkheim, Jane
Addams, and John Dewey.[57] Its more recent and radical figures include Paulo
Freire, bell hooks, Stanley Aronowitz, Henry Giroux, and Jacques Rancière.[58]
Beyond mere critical thinking, this radical branch of the pedagogical tradition
values trust, equality, and solidarity as among the central virtues of public education. Drawing from this tradition, I want to argue that building a spirit of trust
through the classroom can serve as a powerful long-term defense against the
contagion of political trolling.

Public education can do far more for democratic citizenship than teach
mere critical thinking skills for individual autonomy or even, as Postman had
envisioned, media literacy skills for a television age. Public education can
also develop a democratic ethos to resist the antisocial impulses of our heavily atomized, alienated, and jaded social media society. There is a sharp difference between the acquisition of formal civic knowledge, which can be tested on
exams, quizzes, and final papers, and the development of democratic habits, dispositions, virtues, temperaments, and instincts, which can flourish only through
live collective practice. Durkheim notes this difference in *Moral Education*, where
he describes the purpose of public schools as training students to grasp on an
implicit level the basic rules of democratic life that they will later practice on an
explicit level.[59] Dewey presents a similar idea in *Democracy and Education*, where
he sees the purpose of public schools as socializing students into the practice of

democratic communication.[60] Far from being content with mere critical thinking skills for individual autonomy, Durkheim and Dewey call for public education to serve a distinctly social purpose. Schools as they conceive them are social spaces in which students learn through playful practice how to think, reason, speak, deliberate, and cooperate with each other. What they learn through play they will later enact in the public sphere.

Radical pedagogical theorists like Freire, hooks, Aronowitz, Giroux, and Rancière go much further than this. They do not see classrooms as mere training grounds for democracy, where students learn civic skills through mock civic practices, the way they might learn about the justice system through mock trials. Rather, the tradition of radical pedagogy sees classrooms as local sites of democracy, spaces in which democratic practice is intrinsic to the learning process itself, rather than a future goal beyond the classroom. The radical tradition notably challenges authoritarian models of pedagogy, in which teachers talk down to students in hierarchical fashion. Freire famously describes authoritarian styles of pedagogy as the banking model of education.[61] As he describes it, teachers deposit information into the students' minds, which are treated as passive and powerless repositories, from which information is regurgitated as the occasion arises. Freire laments the banking model for reinforcing established hierarchies and obstructing the personal growth and transformation of students. The banking model, he argues, is a means for reproducing relationships of domination and for conditioning students to remain uncritical and obedient in the face of power. Against the authoritarian model, Freire calls for radical equality in education, in which teacher and student participate together in the quest for knowledge and understanding.

Freire defines the purpose of education as "the practice of freedom."[62] By this he means that education is a path toward emancipation. Regardless of one's institutional status, everyone is imperfect and incomplete. For student and teacher alike, education is a process of "*becoming*—as unfinished, uncompleted beings in and with a likewise unfinished reality."[63] Education is therefore the collective project of developing the self through the transformative experience of the classroom. The key to this transformation is what Freire calls "dialogue."[64] Here again, dialogue is not a simulation of real-world political discussion, a kind of harmless exercise with no practical consequence. Rather, dialogue is the medium through which human actors make sense of the world around them and seek to transform it. Dialogue for Freire means critical inquiry—the practice of public reasoning. Like Brandom, Freire sees something radically democratic in dialogue. If dialogue is an investigation into our shared world, then it should be open to everyone. There is no a priori justification for shutting anyone out of dialogue and excluding their perspectives. Dialogue presupposes a fundamental equality between interlocutors. In this respect, dialogue subverts even the most benign forms of paternalistic instruction, in which the teacher has nothing to learn from the student. Rather, dialogue is a collective act of discovery and creation.

Freire identifies six core values in the practice of dialogue. The first value is love, a "profound love for the world and for people."[65] Love is the moral starting point of dialogue. Love rules out economic relationships of social manipulation and sadomasochistic relationships of domination and submission. As Freire puts it, "If I do not love the world—if I do not love life—if I do not love people—I cannot enter into dialogue."[66] The second core value is humility. Dialogue entails a willingness to step down from our perch and see ourselves as members of the same recognitive community. Humility means being open to the possibility that we might learn something from others. Intellectual elitism, the curse of the educated class, is a barrier to knowledge, self-understanding, and dialectical growth and development.[67] The third core value is faith, an "intense faith in humankind." Dialogue presupposes a confidence in others, in their capacity to make sense of the world, to transform both themselves and the world around them. Dialogue is not possible with cynics who, for whatever reason, lack faith in others. Faith is that gesture of interpersonal magnanimity without which our mutual humanity would not be possible.[68]

The fourth core value is trust. While love, humility, and faith are the beginnings of dialogue, trust is its outcome. When we make our intentions plain, when we are open and transparent about our thinking and reasoning, when our words are consistent with our actions, we inspire mutual trust in each other. By creating an environment of trust, we allow for a close partnership for investigating the world.[69] The fifth core value is hope. Dialogue is premised on an optimism about the future, a belief in the realization of our shared humanity. Hopelessness is an obstacle to dialogue. As Freire puts it, "Hopelessness is a form of silence, of denying the world and fleeing from it." Hope, it might be said, is the fighting spirit of dialogue.[70] The sixth core value is critical thinking. Freire defines critical thinking as a dialectical understanding of the world, a view of "reality as process, as transformation, rather than a static entity." To think critically is at once to reject the false certainty of a fixed and unchanging picture of the world, while at the same time understanding how to navigate the world in all its contingency, complexity, and flux. "Only dialogue," says Freire, "is capable of generating critical thinking."[71] Although Freire writes in a more conventional conceptual idiom, his idea of dialogue, with its attendant values of love, humility, faith, trust, hope, and critical thinking, shares the same basic contours as Brandom's idea of trust.

If Freire gives us the general principles for a pedagogy of trust, then bell hooks gives us a powerful example of that pedagogy in practice. In *Teaching to Transgress: Education as the Practice of Freedom*, hooks narrates in vivid biographical detail how she came to practice a radical style of classroom teaching aimed at personal and collective transformation. She describes her formative years as a young student from a Black working-class family in a segregated school in the American South. Her teachers then were compassionate, loving, and nurturing black women, who encouraged their students to become critically engaged scholars and intellectuals. These teachers were dedicated to the cultivation of the mind and self. They took a personal interest in their students, going out of their way to help them realize their "intellectual destiny." Early on, hooks came to see education as a revolutionary practice, "a fundamental way to resist every strategy of white racist colonization."[72] She fondly recalls the exhilaration of being a student at Booker T. Washington:

> Attending school then was sheer joy. I loved being a student. I loved learning. School was the place of ecstasy—pleasure and danger. To be changed by ideas was pure pleasure. But to learn ideas that ran counter to values and beliefs learned at home was to place oneself at risk, to enter the danger zone. Home was the place where I was forced to conform to someone else's image of who and what I should be. School was the place where I could forget that self and, through ideas, reinvent myself.[73]

This joyful and ecstatic experience was tragically lost after desegregation, when Black students were forced to wake up an hour earlier and travel across the city to attend formerly all-white schools. There, white teachers reinforced racist assumptions about Black students through the banking model of education. They expected from Black students strict passivity, conformity, and unquestioning obedience. As a result, hooks lost her love of learning. Her disillusionment with education only worsened during her undergraduate and graduate student years, when she encountered the banking model in course after course, leaving her utterly bored and apathetic about becoming a teacher. Her feelings toward education did not change until she encountered Freire's writings, which presented her with a model of critical pedagogy that spoke to her deep yearning for a living, breathing classroom, where students were animated by the power of ideas, hungry for community, and eager for personal development and transformation.[74]

As a young university teacher, hooks combined her childhood love of learning under the tutelage of uplifting Black women teachers and Freire's radical pedagogy to build a communal space in her classroom. hooks actively worked to cultivate an organic environment. Rather than imposing a fixed and rigid agenda each term, she listened to the mood in the room and encouraged her students to help steer the direction of the class discussion. She worked to establish a democratic and recognitive community, where every student presence was acknowledged and appreciated, where every student was seen in their uniqueness and particularity, where every student opinion was heard and respected, and where every student could play a material role in creating and sustaining the classroom experience. Student contributions to classroom discussion helped create "an open learning community."[75] As hooks soon discovered, her students were not only heartened by the democratic character of the classroom, they also took a personal interest in the success of the classroom experience. "When the classroom is truly engaged," hooks says, "it's dynamic. It's fluid. It's always changing."[76] As hooks observed, it was not just their understanding of ideas that developed and evolved. Their self-concepts developed and evolved, too. They became different people.

hooks repeatedly emphasizes the necessity of fun and excitement in learning.[77] Fun and excitement are the antitheses of the lifeless, suffocating, and mercilessly dispiriting atmosphere of classroom instruction under the banking model. And yet fun and excitement are not the mindless amusement and entertainment that Postman so vehemently deplores. Rather, by "fun" and "excitement," hooks means the thrill and adventure of navigating the terrain of conceptual change and evolution, especially the evolution of the self. For hooks, fun and excitement mean transgression, a "movement beyond accepted boundaries."[78] The classroom is a space in which to make explicit the gaps and blind spots in one another's thinking. It is a space in which to learn from one another. Although hooks does not use Brandom's framework, it is clear that transgression for hooks means the act of making it explicit. Transgression is the practice of public reasoning, a practice in which we make explicit in principle what is implicit in what we say and do. Transgression, making it explicit, allows for the growth and development of our shared concepts, including our individual self-concepts.

hooks takes care to emphasize that classroom excitement is not always warm and cozy. Transgression is not about feeling good inside. As she puts it, "that cozy, good feeling may at times block the possibility of giving students space to feel that there is integrity to be found in grappling with difficult material."[79] Transgression is thus exciting even as it is at times profoundly unsettling. What makes transgression so rewarding is the communal ethos and spirit of solidarity in the classroom. To be recognized as a member of a community, to achieve a sense of belonging, even to a small community like that of a classroom, is to triumph over isolation, loneliness, and alienation—the lived experience of our digital existence today. To accept the invitation to grapple with difficult material together, to undergo, in solidarity with others, the unsettling experience of subjecting our thinking to introspective critique, is to be immersed in the spirit of trust.

The Material Foundations of Trust

While neither Freire nor hooks intended it, their radical pedagogies offer the most promising means of resisting the poison of political trolling. If trolling, as

I have argued in this book, is the outcome of a widespread breakdown in trust, then it is imperative that we turn to a general medium for rebuilding a spirit of trust. Postman was right to point to the powerful role of public education as a means of cultural resistance against the corruption of our public discourse. MacIntyre, too, was right in calling for the construction of local forms of community as another means of cultural resistance. We can synthesize their proposals by turning to classrooms as a powerful public and general medium for building a spirit of trust.

Despite the aggressive assault on public education from political reactionaries—brutal funding cuts, the demonization of teachers and teachers' unions, ideological attacks upon the humanities, and manufactured moral panics over critical race theory and "wokeness"—public education remains an invaluable social institution. It serves as a critical social space in which we can build a spirit of trust and undo a culture of distrust. Creating democratic communities in our classrooms, providing students and teachers alike with a sense of purpose and belonging, recognizing and affirming students as creative and original minds, inviting them to share their thoughts and opinions in classroom discussion, democratizing the experience of classroom learning, practicing critical thinking through public reasoning, and creating an environment of solidarity— in short, building a spirit of trust—can go a long way toward deflating the distrust, cynicism, paranoia, and rage that epitomize the age of social media.

If classrooms offer the promise of building a general spirit of trust, then this has obvious material implications. Building a spirit of trust means investing heavily in public education. It means vigorously defending the arts, the humanities, and the social sciences from ideological attack. It means protecting the labor rights of teachers. It means defending teachers' unions from political assault. It means ensuring that teachers are given fair pay. It means ending the exploitation of precarious faculty and facilitating their transition to permanent teaching positions, so that they may devote adequate time and attention to the classroom. It means recruiting more teachers to allow for smaller class sizes. It means making classrooms more accessible for students and teachers alike. If we care about our students, if we want to facilitate their education, if we want to be as inclusive as possible, then higher education also needs to be feasible. At the very least, this would entail eliminating tuition fees, as has been achieved across much of Europe. It would entail remote learning options for students with disabilities, students from distant communities, and students with parenting responsibilities. It would also entail training teachers in critical pedagogies for creating open learning communities.

Ultimately, building a spirit of trust has even deeper material implications than strengthening public education. If the source of mass distrust, cynicism, and paranoia goes further than the technological media through which we communicate, if these antisocial emotions are the product of a culture of possessive individualism, vicious competition, social alienation, and debilitating loneliness, then building a spirit of trust requires that we work toward a very different political economic order. This would entail a fundamental shift away from an economic system structured around the individual pursuit of private capital and the exploitation of workers and toward an economic system premised on workplace democracy, transparency, accountability, inclusion, and solidarity. If economic exploitation breeds widespread distrust, then ending economic exploitation is necessary to protect and preserve a spirit of trust. It goes without saying that arguments for creating a humane economic system will inevitably confront precisely the kind of deeply ingrained cynicism whose structural and historical roots this book has in part sought to explain. The impulse to dismiss and belittle the call for a more humane society reflects a tragic lack of imagination. This is where public education can play yet another critical role. Classrooms are not just spaces in which to practice democracy and build a spirit of trust. They are also spaces in which to imagine alternatives to the economic ontology of the present.

Conclusion

In the fall of 2020, Netflix released *The Social Dilemma*, a dystopian documentary about the ominous power of social media over our individual lives, our interpersonal relationships, and our political culture. The film notably featured former executives and engineers from the largest social media giants in the game: Facebook, Twitter, Instagram, YouTube, Pinterest, and Google. With their insider knowledge, these former executives disclosed the inner workings, designs, and aims of the algorithms that operate behind the scenes. Like sinners at confession, they acknowledged their complicity in creating platforms whose primary purpose is to turn us into addicts. Every feature of the platform interfaces—the "like" button, the "heart" button, the emojis, the share function, the reply function, the notifications, the reels, the stories—was tweaked and perfected to deliver the notorious dopamine rush to our brains, simulating the effect of a narcotic.

The former executives describe the algorithm as an amoral beast. Its sole purpose is to hack into our minds and keep us hooked on our screens. The beast does not care what grabs our attention. It is just as happy feeding us fake news, conspiracy theories, and racist memes as it is cat photos and food porn. They also reveal that third-party actors, including political parties and foreign governments, have manipulated the algorithms through targeted advertising, enabling them to manufacture public consent, determine election outcomes, and even promote genocide.[1] Whether we are passively scrolling, cheerfully socializing, or aggressively fighting online, the platforms profit all the same. *The Social Dilemma* paints a bleak picture of a digital world in which truth has been lost, free will has been undermined, and democracy has been reduced to a charade. Tristan Harris, a former design ethicist at Google, even predicts a "checkmate for humanity" if we fail to reverse course.[2]

The Social Dilemma has rightly been criticized for exaggerating the nefarious power of digital technology to the neglect of the larger political economic structure that feeds online extremism and the epidemic of screen addiction.[3] This

Trolling Ourselves to Death. Jason Hannan, Oxford University Press. © Oxford University Press 2023.
DOI: 10.1093/oso/9780197557761.003.0008

fundamental shortcoming notwithstanding, *The Social Dilemma* did manage to ignite a long-overdue public debate about the poisonous impact of social media upon our world and what we might do about it. Although it is now common to assert that something is terribly wrong with the platforms, we have no agreement on what that is or what to do about it. Is the central problem the private control of our public sphere?[4] Is it the proliferation of disinformation?[5] Is it the violation of personal privacy and the unregulated extraction of user data?[6] Is it the destruction of social relationships and the rise of political violence?[7] What we take to be the primary problem will determine how we respond. Should we break up the platforms, for example?[8] Should we subject them to government regulation?[9] Should we turn them into public utilities, especially given their role as critical infrastructure for government, healthcare, news, information, education, and commerce?[10] Should we convert the platforms into user-owned and user-governed cooperatives?[11] Should we voluntarily change the way we use social media, moving away from narcissistic self-promotion and focusing instead on educational content?[12] Should we practice other individualized self-care strategies, like turning off our notifications and going on regular social media diets?[13] Or should just we log off, delete the apps, and be done with them already?[14]

The question of what is to be done is further complicated by the evolving nature of our digital environment. The ground is shifting dramatically. Facebook, the quintessential digital network that defined the age of social media, has been caught in a death spiral.[15] Users have been fleeing. Traffic has been plummeting. Revenue has been imploding. Facebook is now something of a ghost town. The ritual of posting almost daily status updates and broadcasting every halfbaked thought that crosses our minds has largely disappeared. There appears to be little appetite either to share or to engage with personal opinion, especially rabid political opinion. The collective exhaustion from years of rage-filled bloviating on the platform is now palpable, like the eerie silence in the aftermath of a battle. Then there's the dismal future of the metaverse. Mark Zuckerberg's fantasy of guiding the entire world into one vast virtual reality, where billions of users would spend the bulk of their waking hours in clunky headsets, attend virtual schools, work in virtual office spaces, and invest real money in virtual real estate, has so far turned out to be a giant flop.[16] In 2022, Meta Platforms, Facebook's parent company, lost $700 billion, prompting Zuckerberg to lay off eleven thousand employees.[17]

Twitter has been a very different story. In March 2022, Elon Musk hinted to the world of his intention to buy Twitter.[18] Then in April, Musk claimed, in his usual grandiloquent rhetoric, to be concerned about "the future of civilization."[19] He suggested that humanity could be saved only by "having a public platform that is maximally trusted and broadly inclusive."[20] He also proudly proclaimed himself a "free speech absolutist."[21] Presumably, the keys to saving human civilization are truth and freedom of speech. How, exactly, Musk planned to balance these contradictory values was never explained. In late October 2022, after dithering for months in the face of a lawsuit from Twitter, Musk finally purchased the platform for $44 billion—a price far above its market value, as many financial analysts noted.[22] Musk marked the occasion by walking into Twitter's headquarters carrying a sink. He later tweeted, "Let that sink in."[23] The entire spectacle, carefully staged and filmed, was Musk's hollow attempt at stunt comedy.

Musk has always fancied himself something of a clever jokester. He has long sought the approval of actual comedians and has desperately wanted to be known as *funny*.[24] In the days following his Twitter takeover, Musk changed his bio to "Chief Twit" and then to "Twitter Complaint Hotline Operator," as if to underscore just how funny he really is.[25] He tweeted, "Comedy is legal again," at once a jab at liberals and a cheap way of positioning himself as a cultural rebel.[26] Almost immediately, Twitter users put Musk's pretensions about comedy and his "free speech absolutism" to the test.[27] They brutally impersonated him through an endless string of parody accounts. Musk responded by suspending some accounts and banning others. Among the casualties of his clampdown were comedians Kathy Griffin and Sarah Silverman, *Mad Men* actor Rich Sommer, and cartoonist Jeph Jacques.[28] Musk then humorlessly declared, "Going forward, any Twitter handles engaging in impersonation without clearly specifying 'parody' will be permanently suspended."[29] In an instant, the aspiring comedian and free speech absolutist morphed, as one observer put it, into "the joke police."[30]

Musk's tenure as "Chief Twit" has been pure pandemonium. On his first day, he fired several key Twitter executives, including CEO Parag Agrawal, CFO Ned Segal, and Vijaya Gadde, Twitter's legal, public policy, and trust and safety lead, a move that required Musk to pay them almost $200 million.[31] He then laid off thirty-five hundred employees, including entire teams responsible for vital operations.[32] He later awkwardly invited some of those teams back.[33] The following week, he fired five thousand contract workers, all without notice.[34] He also banned remote work and ended free on-site lunches, absurdly claiming that Twitter was spending over $400 per lunch for every employee served.[35] In early November, Musk even locked Twitter's remaining thirty-five hundred employees out of the company's headquarters.[36]

One of Musk's first major changes was to overhaul Twitter's verification system. Twitter had offered the highly coveted blue check mark to an exclusive group of users based on strict criteria. The blue check mark certified both the authenticity and the notability of select users: government officials, businesses, nonprofit organizations, journalists, and celebrities. Musk announced the end of blue check mark exclusivity, allowing anyone with $8 to obtain one. To signal the change, he tweeted, "↯↯↯ Power to the People ↯↯↯."[37] With strikingly incoherent logic, Musk sought to establish himself as a populist agitator by converting an instrument for ascertaining authenticity into a revenue stream. The new blue check mark policy turned out to be a nightmare, as the explosion of parody accounts demonstrated.[38] One fake account impersonating pharmaceutical giant Eli Lilly cost the company billions in market capital.[39] The blue check mark option was immediately suspended.[40] Musk then introduced gray check marks for official accounts. He ended those the same day.[41]

Musk's extreme managerial incompetence is only partially responsible for Twitter's chaos. The man's reckless conduct on the platform has also proven to be a financial liability. After a QAnon-obsessed intruder broke into the home of Nancy Pelosi and injured her husband, Paul Pelosi, Musk tweeted an article from a thoroughly discredited news source alleging that Mr. Pelosi was drunk and had gotten embroiled in a physical altercation with a male prostitute.[42] When the *New York Times* published a story about Musk sharing a link from a "site known to publish false news," Musk tweeted a screenshot of the article and added, "This is fake—I did *not* tweet out a link to The New York Times!," a clear nod to Donald Trump's long-standing antipathy for the liberal news organization.[43] When Democratic senator Ed Markey asked Musk on Twitter to explain how a journalist with the *Washington Post* was able to create a fake and verified account impersonating the senator (with Markey's permission), Musk replied, "Perhaps it is because your real account sounds like a parody?" Musk then followed up by asking, "And why does your pp [profile picture] have a mask!?"[44] After firing some eighty-five hundred workers, Musk tweeted a photo of two pranksters posing as former employees leaving Twitter's headquarters. The tweet read, "Ligma Johnson had it coming 👋 ✌."[45] Somehow, a fifty-one-year-old businessman managed to turn mass layoffs affecting thousands of workers and their families into an occasion for the crude sexual humor of a twelve-year-old boy.

After hundreds of thousands of users, appalled at Musk's mismanagement and atrocious conduct, fled to rival social media platform Mastodon, Musk tweeted, "If you don't like Twitter anymore, there is awesome site called Masterbatedone."[46] Musk seems to enjoy trolling both those who left and even those who remain on Twitter. After being inundated with complaints about Twitter's increasing dysfunctionality, Musk tweeted, "I love when people complain about Twitter . . . on Twitter 😂😂."[47] The rolling-on-the-floor-laughing emoji has become a signature item in Musk's increasingly pictographic and logophobic speech. Trolling the entire platform also seems to be a coping mechanism for having to confront Twitter's dire financial calamities.[48] Sensing the general bewilderment, frustration, and despair over his impetuous management style and disastrous decision-making, Musk simply tweeted, "did it 4 da lulz"—a kind of cosmic speech act solidifying his place in history as a 4chan-style mega-troll.[49]

As Musk rolls on the floor, laughing his way into full-blown denial, Twitter's advertisers have been anything but amused. Advertising executives have found

Musk "petulant and thoughtless."[50] His talk of ending content moderation has prompted the NAACP and the Anti-Defamation League to ask Twitter's top advertisers to suspend their advertising on the platform.[51] Fifty of Twitter's top one hundred advertisers have either paused or pulled their advertising.[52] After a dramatic drop in ad revenue, Musk complained about "activist groups . . . trying to destroy free speech in America."[53] In between his endless joking, jesting, teasing, mocking, prodding, and exuberant guffawing, Musk had to warn Twitter's surviving staff members that without sufficient revenue to stay afloat, bankruptcy was not out of the question.[54] After decades of carefully crafting and curating his public image in a saintly light, the man regarded by hordes of adoring fans as a technological genius, a profound philosopher, and the savior of humanity revealed that he has not the foggiest idea how to manage a social media company.

The uncertainty surrounding Twitter's future was only compounded after its arch-troll opened the floodgates to a sea of trolls big and small. Within hours of Musk's takeover, trolls began posting racist messages and Nazi imagery, celebrating the platform's newfound "free speech" direction.[55] One report found that the use of the n-word grew fivefold.[56] Antisemitic slurs soared by 61 percent, while homophobic slurs rose by 63 percent.[57] Twitter notably verified the accounts of white nationalists Jason Kessler, organizer of the deadly 2017 Unite the Right rally, and alt-right figurehead Richard Spencer.[58] The anti-vaccine movement similarly took advantage of Musk's new verification policy to secure blue check marks and aggressively spread COVID-19 disinformation.[59] Encouraged by Musk's lax rules on content moderation, trolls also began ramping up deepfakes: digitally manipulated footage of real people whose facial likeness has been replaced with the likeness and voice of another. Deepfakes have created even more havoc and confusion on Twitter. One deepfake of Sam Bankman-Fried, the disgraced founder of the now-bankrupt cryptocurrency exchange FTX, used a verified account to lure unsuspecting victims into a massive cryptocurrency scam.[60]

According to a 2022 BBC investigation into toxic messaging on Twitter, violent misogyny against women serving in public office has reached intolerable levels. One member of the British Parliament, Flick Drummond of Meon Valley, was forced to quit Twitter because the abuse had gotten out of hand. MP Jess Phillips spoke of "thinly-veiled or completely direct rape and sexual violence threats," while MP Virginia Crosbie reported "several violent threats on social media including threats of being hanged and poisoned."[61] It is also worth noting that Musk's decision to buy Twitter was prompted in part by the suspension of a Christian satire site, the Babylon Bee, after a transphobic tweet about United States assistant secretary for health Rachel Levine.[62] Shortly after his takeover, Musk not only restored the Babylon Bee's account but also transformed Twitter into a haven for transphobia, even banning the account for an activist organization that protects the LGBTQ community from right-wing violence.[63]

As if to certify Twitter's new status as a platform of, by, and for the trolls, Musk ran a poll asking whether Donald Trump's account should be reactivated. Despite earlier vowing to "defeat the spam bots," Musk had no problem with a barrage of bots skewing his own poll result.[64] He took the slim majority voting in favor to justify reactivating Trump's account, absurdly declaring, "Vox Populi, Vox Dei." Musk then sought to woo Trump back to the platform by posting a crude meme of a young woman in a short skirt, her rear end covered with the Twitter logo, and a priest standing behind her, fighting sexual temptation. Days later, Musk ran another poll asking whether all suspended users should be granted a "general amnesty."[65] Once again, he used the occasion to restore suspended accounts as far as the law would permit, effectively dragging the platform into the eighth circle of a digital hell.

It has become clear that Musk never had any intention of keeping Twitter "politically neutral," to use his own words. In June, Musk revealed that he voted for Mayra Flores, a QAnon supporter and January 6 conspiracy theorist, in a south Texas special election. It was, he said, the "first time I ever voted Republican."[66] Musk also announced a "massive red wave in 2022," abandoning even the pretense of political neutrality.[67] On November 7, the day before the 2022 midterm election, Musk flatly called upon "independent-minded voters" to support the Republican Party.[68] He continues to endorse far-right politicians under the gossamer cloak of "centrism."[69] He now openly fraternizes with right-wing trolls on Twitter, groveling for their support. Against his own "free speech absolutism," he has been taking their advice and banning antifascist accounts.[70] As one observer put it, Musk has been "trying on right-wing populism for size." His growing contempt for social justice, his mockery of "wokeness," his disdain for labor unions, his opposition to higher taxes for billionaires and giant corporations like Tesla, and his ruthless and authoritarian management style all reflect the social values and psycho-political sensibilities of the Republican Party. It is therefore no surprise that Musk is turning Twitter into an ideological weapon for class warfare.[71]

Whether Musk will drive Twitter into the ground remains to be seen. His ambition to weaponize the platform for reactionary ends does not imply managerial sagacity. As Twitter rapidly veers further and further toward the right and becomes more hospitable toward hate speech, it is set to clash with both Apple and Google, which may very well drop the platform from their app stores, as they did right-wing app Parler. Musk is also on a collision course with the European Union, which, under the Digital Services Act, requires social media companies to remove hate speech and disinformation from their platforms.[72] Whether Twitter stands or falls will hinge on how Musk responds to these economic challenges.

For now, the problem with Twitter is not so much that the algorithm is eroding our free will or keeping us glued to the screen as that the platform is becoming fascism's new playground. Should it survive, Twitter under Musk will likely be a far greater threat to truth and democracy than it was during Trump's presidency.

As Twitter normalizes the moral cosmology of the far right, it will only encourage what I have called government by trolling. Trump's 2017 Muslim ban and his 2018 child separation policy were designed to shock, scandalize, and exasperate the "liberal" enemy.[73] They set the stage for our current era of performative cruelty in conservative politics. In October 2022, Florida governor Ron DeSantis thought it would be entertaining to lure dozens of Venezuelan migrants with the false promise of housing and jobs and then fly them to Martha's Vineyard, the island destination popular among Democratic Party leaders, where they were dumped and abandoned. It was not beneath DeSantis to use innocent human beings as props to troll Democrats on immigration. This twisted and inhumane political stunt followed similar antics by Texas governor Greg Abbott and Arizona governor Doug Ducey, who sent buses carrying South and Central American migrants to Democratic-governed cities to be similarly dumped and abandoned. These migrants were forced to endure over forty hours of travel with no food or water. Many required medical treatment upon arrival.[74] On Christmas Eve 2022, Abbott sent a bus full of migrants to the home of Vice President Kamala Harris in Washington, D.C., dumping them outside in freezing temperatures.[75] When criticized for this cruel stunt, Abbot aggressively defended his actions. Abbott has boasted of sending some three hundred buses with migrants out of Texas.[76]

Republicans have also sharpened their instincts for punishing and humiliating women. In March 2021, an overwhelming majority of Republicans in Congress opposed reinstating the Violence Against Women Act—just hours after seven women, most of them women of color, were killed in a horrific mass shooting in Atlanta.[77] In July 2022, mere weeks after the fall of *Roe v. Wade*, junior congressman Madison Cawthorn introduced a bill that would prevent anyone from using federal funds to cover travel expenses to obtain an abortion.[78] In September 2022, an all-male group of Republican lawmakers in the Louisiana legislature introduced bill HB 813, which would imprison women and girls for having an abortion, even in cases of rape or life-threatening medical emergencies.[79] Republicans appear to be competing in a new political tournament whose aim is to devise the most sadistic ways to abuse the most vulnerable members of American society. As journalist Adam Serwer aptly describes Trump's effect on the Republican psyche, "The cruelty is the point."[80]

The new generation of MAGA Republicans has also escalated the use of openly violent rhetoric in political campaigns. In May 2022, Republican congressional candidate Cory Mills released a campaign video in which he boasted of his ability to make "liberals" cry.[81] A former advisor to Donald Trump, Mills is co-founder of PACEM Solutions, a company that manufactures tear gas often used by law enforcement against political demonstrators.[82] The campaign video shows footage of "Black Lives Matter protesters," "Antifa rioters," "radical left protesters," "left-wing protestors," and "Hillary Clinton protesters" all being tear-gassed, for which Mills proudly takes credit. "If the media wants to shed some real tears," he says with a defiant grin, "I can help them out with that." In November, Mills was elected to the U.S. House of Representatives in Florida's Seventh Congressional District.[83]

In September 2022, Marjorie Taylor Greene released a campaign video in which she compared Democrats to wild hogs. The video shows Greene boarding a helicopter with a high-powered assault rifle. She shoots a feral hog from the air. The video then jumps to her proudly posing next to the dead animal. Not surprisingly, Greene was condemned for the suggestive subtext that Democrats should be treated like an invasive species through violent culling.[84] At a Trump rally in October 2022, Greene said to the receptive crowd, "We are all targets now though, for daring to push back against the regime. . . . I am not going to mince words with you all. Democrats want Republicans dead and they have already started the killings."[85] As one political commentator noted, the implicit message here is clear: "kill or be killed."[86] Greene has of course used violent rhetoric ever since she first ran for office in 2019. But whereas her fellow Republicans once called her incendiary rhetoric "appalling" and "disgusting," Greene has since become the moral center of the Republican Party.[87] Leading Republicans are increasingly embracing her violent language.[88] Like Mills, Greene won election in the November 2022 midterms.

According to a study by the Center for American Progress, guns were featured in more than a hundred political ads by MAGA Republicans in the 2022 midterm election cycle. A majority of these ads featured sniper rifles, flamethrower, and semiautomatic weapons like those used in mass shootings almost daily across America. At least one-quarter of the ads included explicit threats. Among the targets of these threats were fellow politicians, organizations, political ideologies, and "agendas." Eleven of the ads included threats against the government. Four ads even featured minors with guns. Although most of the ads took aim at "liberals" and "the left," many were aimed at "RINOs" (Republicans in name only), an index of the MAGA movement's lust for violence.[89]

Like all authoritarian populist movements, today's Republican Party thrives on eccentric personalities. The more cartoonish the leader, the fiercer the loyalty. This is yet

another reason social media platforms are so politically dangerous. By design, they are comical environments in which cartoonish personalities are perfectly at home and cult followings are entirely normal. The immediacy of the medium enables the raw speech of charismatic leaders to reach the eyes, ears, hearts, and minds of a great mass of followers, unfiltered by the constricting editorial standards and civic decorum of newspapers, television channels, radio stations, and town halls. Fascism thrives on communicative intimacy, a point that Lewis Mumford insightfully made nearly a century ago.[90] For digital demagogues, every day is a political rally.[91] The platforms invite political whispering, as radio once did for Father Charles Coughlin.[92] It is not a coincidence that the far right is surging in the digital age. Social media have created the conditions for fascism's rebirth. Italian prime minister Giorgia Meloni, whose political party Brothers of Italy is heir to Benito Mussolini's National Fascist Party, relied upon Facebook, Twitter, and Instagram for her rise to political prominence.[93] Republicans have notably turned to Meloni as a model for political communication, just as they have turned to Hungary's Viktor Orbán as a model for autocratic rule.[94]

So, where does this leave us? Reading the historical moment is never an enviable task. The fear of getting things wrong is a powerful inhibitor of honest assessment. At this historical moment, however, political observers with both eyes open are abandoning analytical modesty and sounding the alarm about the growing threat authoritarian populism poses to the culture and institutions of democracy. It would be reckless to dismiss these warnings as exaggerated and alarmist. Our pathological habit of telling ourselves, "It can't happen here," as Sinclair Lewis put it in the title of his 1935 novel about fascism in America, is the political equivalent of climate change denial.

Taking the ascension of political unreason seriously requires acting on multiple fronts. This book zeroes in on one such front: our digital public sphere. Because it rejects both gratuitous pessimism and naive optimism, this book has accepted the moral responsibility of proposing a practical answer to the problem of political trolling. As I have argued, our best hope in the long term for reversing the erosion of our public sphere is building a spirit of trust. I have pointed to public schools as the material site in which to practice a critical pedagogy of trust, community, hope, and solidarity to reverse the culture of distrust, cynicism, and enmity that fuels a reactionary politics. If the emergence of populist governments in Hungary, Poland, Turkey, and India and the disturbing electoral gains of extremist political factions in the United States, Germany, France, Austria, and the Netherlands have taught us anything, it is that democracy can be subverted from within, often through slow and imperceptible means.[95] As Steven Levitsky and Daniel Ziblatt write, "The tragic paradox of the electoral route to authoritarianism is that democracy's assassins use the very institutions of democracy—gradually, and even legally—to kill it."[96] To this, we might add the media of democracy. As Levitsky and Ziblatt caution, those of us who grew up taking democracy for granted no longer have the luxury of being so sanguine and complacent.[97] In our current historical moment, political apathy has grave material consequences. Either we can work to repair our civic culture by building a spirit of trust—with all that that entails economically, institutionally, and culturally—or we can relinquish our politics to the pathogen of unreason and continue trolling ourselves to death.

Notes

Introduction

1. Kim Brunhuber, "Trump's Deportation Delay Defers Pain for Some Migrants, Offers Lifeline for Others," CBC, June 26, 2022.
2. Steven Levitsky and Daniel Ziblatt, *How Democracies Die* (New York: Broadway Books, 2018); Anne Applebaum, *Twilight of Democracy: The Seductive Lure of Authoritarianism* (New York: Doubleday, 2020); Timothy Snyder, *On Tyranny: Twenty Lessons from the Twentieth Century* (New York: Crown, 2017); Masha Gessen, *Surviving Autocracy* (New York: Riverhead Books, 2020); Yascha Mounk, *The People vs. Democracy: Why Our Freedom Is in Danger and How to Save It* (Cambridge, MA: Harvard University Press, 2019); The Writers of *The Atlantic*, *The American Crisis: What Went Wrong, How We Recover* (New York: Simon and Schuster, 2020); Peter Wehner, *The Death of Politics: How to Heal Our Frayed Republic After Trump* (New York: Harper One, 2019); Suzanne Mettler and Robert C. Leiberman, *Four Threats: The Recurring Crises of American Democracy* (New York: St. Martin's Press, 2020); Theo Horesh, *The Fascism This Time and the Global Future of Democracy* (Boulder, CO: Cosmopolis Press, 2020); Astra Taylor, *Democracy May Not Exist, but We'll Miss It When It's Gone* (New York: Metropolitan Books, 2020); Benjamin I. Page and Martin Gilens, *Democracy in America? What Has Gone Wrong and What We Can Do About It* (Chicago: University of Chicago Press, 2020).
3. See, for example, Cass R. Sunstein, *#Republic: Divided Democracy in the Age of Social Media* (Princeton, NJ: Princeton University Press, 2017); Siva Vaidhyanathan, *Antisocial Media: How Facebook Disconnects Us and Undermines Democracy* (New York: Oxford University Press, 2018); Dannagal Goldthwaite Young, *Irony and Outrage: The Polarized Landscape of Rage, Fear, and Laughter in the United States* (New York: Oxford University Press, 2020); Joshua A. Tucker and Nathaniel Persily, eds., *Social Media and Democracy: The State of the Field, Prospects for Reform* (Cambridge, UK: Cambridge University Press, 2020); Chris Bail, *Breaking the Social Media Prism: How to Make Our Platforms Less Polarizing* (Princeton, NJ: Princeton University Press, 2021); Whitney Phillips and Ryan M. Milner, *You Are Here: A Field Guide for Navigating Polarized Speech, Conspiracy Theories, and Our Polluted Media Landscape* (Cambridge, MA: MIT Press, 2021).
4. Marsha Lederman, "The Bullies Are Taking Over Our Politics and Our Culture," *Globe and Mail*, November 4, 2022, https://www.theglobeandmail.com/opinion/article-the-bullies-are-taking-over-our-politics-and-our-culture; Matt Fleming, "American Political Discourse Is Poisoned by Social Media and Hatred," *Orange County Register*, March 25, 2022, https://www.ocregister.com/2022/03/25/american-political-discourse-is-poisoned-by-social-media-and-hatred; Maeve Duggan, "How Platforms Are Poisoning Conversations," *The Atlantic*, May 11, 2017.

5. Michelle Goldberg, "Democracy Grief Is Real," *New York Times*, December 13, 2019, https://www.nytimes.com/2019/12/13/opinion/sunday/trump-democracy.html; Rob Law, "I Have Felt Hopelessness over Climate Change. Here Is How We Move Past the Immense Grief," *The Guardian*, May 9, 2019, https://www.theguardian.com/commentisfree/2019/may/09/i-have-felt-hopelessness-over-climate-change-here-is-how-we-move-past-the-immense-grief; Ashlee Cunsolo and Neville R. Ellis, "Ecological Grief as a Mental Health Response to Climate Change-Related Loss," *Nature Climate Change* 8 (2018): 275–281.

6. The most obvious example is the influence of social media on our perception of the human body. See, for example, Mauro Barone, Annalisa Cogliandro, and Paolo Persichetti, "In Constant Search of 'Like': How Technology and Social Media Influence the Perception of Our Body," *Aesthetic Plastic Surgery* 46, suppl. 1 (2021): 170–171; Hye Min Kim, "What Do Others' Reactions to Body Posting on Instagram Tell Us? The Effects of Social Media Comments on Viewers' Body Image Perception," *New Media and Society* 23, no. 12 (2020): 3448–3465.

7. Larry D. Rosen, Kate Whaling, Sam Rab, L. Mark Carrier, and Nancy A. Cheever, "Is Facebook Creating 'iDisorders'? The Link Between Clinical Symptoms of Psychiatric Disorders and Technology Use, Attitudes and Anxiety," *Computers in Human Behavior* 29, no. 3 (2013): 1243–1254; Julia Brailovskaia, Jürgen Margraf, and Volker Köllner, "Addicted to Facebook? Relationship Between Facebook Addiction Disorder, Duration of Facebook Use and Narcissism in an Inpatient Sample," *Psychiatry Research* 273 (2019): 52–57;

8. Evita March, "Psychopathy, Sadism, Empathy, and the Motivation to Cause Harm: New Evidence Confirms Malevolent Nature of the Internet Troll," *Personality and Individual Differences* 141 (2019): 133–137; Craker, Naomi, and Evita March. "The dark side of Facebook®: The Dark Tetrad, negative social potency, and trolling behaviours." *Personality and Individual Differences* 102 (2016): 79–84.

9. Torill Elvira Mortensen, "Anger, Fear, and Games: The Long Event of# GamerGate," *Games and Culture* 13, no. 8 (2018): 787–806; Noah Berlatsky, "The Comicsgate Movement Isn't Defending Free Speech. It's Suppressing It," *Washington Post*, September 13, 2018; Elizabeth Williamson, *Sandy Hook: An American Tragedy and the Battle for Truth* (New York: Penguin, 2022).

10. Edward Said, *Beginnings: Intention and Method* (New York: Columbia University Press, 1985).

11. Michael Hauben and Ronda Hauben, *Netizens: On the History and Impact of Usenet and the Internet* (Los Alamito, CA: IEEE Computer Society Press, 1997).

12. Hauben and Hauben, *Netizens*, 39.

13. Hauben and Hauben, *Netizens*, 13.

14. Paul Baker, "Moral Panic and Alternative Identity Construction in Usenet," *Journal of Computer-Mediated Communication* 7, no. 1 (2001): JCMC711; Axel Bruns, "Videor Ergo Sum: The Online Search for Disembodied Identity," *M/C Journal* 1, no. 3 (1998).

15. Peter Kollock and Marc Smith, "Managing the Virtual Commons: Cooperation and Conflict in Computer Communities," in *Computer-Mediated Communication*, ed. Susan C. Herring (Philadelphia: Johns Benjamins, 1996), 109–128.

16. Christine B. Smith, Margaret L. McLaughlin, and Kerry K. Osborne, "Conduct Control on Usenet," *Journal of Computer-Mediated Communication* 2, no. 4 (1997): JCMC2410.

17. Susan Herring, Kirk Job-Sluder, Rebecca Scheckler, and Sasha Barab, "Searching for Safety Online: Managing 'Trolling' in a Feminist Forum," *The Information Society* 18, no. 5 (2002): 371–384.

18. Whitney Phillips, *This Is Why We Can't Have Nice Things: Mapping the Relationship Between Online Trolling and Mainstream Culture* (Cambridge, MA: MIT Press, 2015), 15.

19. Judith S. Donath, "Identity and Deception in the Virtual Community," in *Communities in Cyberspace*, ed. Peter Kollack and Marc Smith (London: Routledge, 1998), 43.

20. Gabriella Coleman, *Hacker, Hoaxer, Whistleblower, Spy: The Many Faces of Anonymous* (London: Verso, 2014).

21. Coleman, *Hacker, Hoaxer, Whistleblower*, 4.

22. Coleman, *Hacker, Hoaxer, Whistleblower*, 45–46.

23. Phillips, *This Is Why We Can't Have Nice Things*, 24.

24. Phillips, *This Is Why We Can't Have Nice Things*, 24–26.

25. The classic statement on possessive individualism is, of course, C. B. Macpherson, *The Political Theory of Possessive Individualism* (Oxford: Oxford University Press, 2011).

26. See, for example, Andrew Postman, "My Dad Predicted Trump in 1985—It's Not Orwell, He Warned, It's Brave New World," *The Guardian*, February 2, 2017, https://www.theg uardian.com/media/2017/feb/02/amusing-ourselves-to-death-neil-postman-trump-orw ell-huxley; Ezra Klein, "Amusing Ourselves to Trump: We Are Buried Under Ignorance Disguised as Information," *Vox*, August 5, 2018, https://www.vox.com/policy-and-polit ics/2018/8/6/17599010/neil-postman-trump-amusing-ourselves; Ed McMenamin, "Did Neil Postman Predict the Rise of Trump and Fake News? What We Can Still Learn from His Prophetic Book More than 30 Years Later," *Paste*, January 5, 2017; Megan Garber, "Are We Having Too Much Fun?," *The Atlantic*, April 27, 2017, https://www.theatlantic.com/ entertainment/archive/2017/04/are-we-having-too-much-fun/523143/.

27. Neil Postman, *Amusing Ourselves to Death: Public Discourse in the Age of Show Business* (New York: Penguin, 1985), xix.

28. Aldous Huxley, *Brave New World: And Brave New World Revisited* (New York: HarperPerennial, 2004), 60.

29. George Orwell, *1984* (New York: Signet Classics, 1977), 14.

30. Carla Jones, "'Lock Her Up!': A Biography of a Trump-Era Chant and the Banality of Misogyny," in *Corruption and Illiberal Politics in the Trump Era*, ed. Donna M. Goldstein and Kristen Drybread (New York: Routledge, 2023), 203–218.

31. Nicole A. Cooke, *Fake News and Alternative Facts: Information Literacy in a Post-Truth Era* (Chicago: American Library Association, 2018). The term *doublespeak* is a synthesis of *doublethink* and *newspeak*. See Lutz, William D. "Language, appearance, and reality: Doublespeak in 1984." *ETC: A Review of General Semantics* (1987): 382–391.

32. Alasdair MacIntyre, *After Virtue: A Study in Moral Theory* (Notre Dame, IN: University of Notre Dame Press, 1981), 263.

33. For my interpretation of MacIntyre, see Jason Hannan, *Ethics Under Capital: MacIntyre, Communication, and the Culture Wars* (London: Bloomsbury, 2020). On MacIntyre's Marxism and the Marxist reading of his thought, see Paul Blackledge and Neil Davidson, *Alasdair MacIntyre's Engagement with Marxism: Selected Writings 1953–1974* (Chicago: Haymarket, 2009); John Gregson, *Marxism, Ethics, and Politics: The Work of Alasdair MacIntyre* (New York: Palgrave Macmillan, 2019); Jeffery Nicholas, *Reason, Tradition, and the Good: MacIntyre's Tradition-Constituted Reason and Frankfurt School Critical Theory* (Notre Dame, IN: University of Notre Dame Press, 2012).

34. That story is told in Hegel's *The Phenomenology of Spirit* (Cambridge, UK: Cambridge University Press, 2019).

35. This reading of Hegel is drawn from Robert C. Solomon, *In the Spirit of Hegel* (Oxford: Oxford University Press, 1985), Fredrick Beiser, *Hegel* (New York: Oxford University Press, 2005), and Robert Brandom, *A Spirit of Trust: A Reading of Hegel's* Phenomenology (Cambridge, MA: Harvard University Press, 2019).

36. Fredric Jameson, *The Political Unconscious: Narrative as a Socially Symbolic Act* (Ithaca, NY: Cornell University Press, 1981), 9.

37. The original line, from *A Contribution to the Critique of Political Economy*, reads, "It is not the consciousness of men that specifies their being, but on the contrary their social being that specifies their consciousness." Karl Marx, *Karl Marx: Later Political Writings*, edited by Terrell Carver (Cambridge, UK: Cambridge University Press, 1996), 160.

38. MacIntyre, *After Virtue*, 2.

39. Ian Bogost, "The Age of Social Media Is Ending," *The Atlantic*, November 10, 2022, https://www.theatlantic.com/technology/archive/2022/11/twitter-facebook-social-media-decline/672074.

Chapter 1

1. David Leonhardt and Stuart A. Thompson, "Trump's Lies," *New York Times*, July 21, 2017, https://www.nytimes.com/interactive/2017/06/23/opinion/trumps-lies.html.
2. Glenn Kessler, Salvador Rizzo, and Meg Kelly, "Trump's False or Misleading Claims Total 30,573 over 4 Years," *Washington Post*, January 24, 2021, https://www.washingtonpost.com/politics/2021/01/24/trumps-false-or-misleading-claims-total-30573-over-four-years/.
3. James Ball, "How Can We Fight Back Against Fake News and Post-Truth Politics," *New Statesman*, May 16, 2017, https://www.newstatesman.com/politics/june2017/2017/05/how-can-we-fight-back-against-fake-news-and-post-truth-politics.
4. Hossein Derakhshan, "Social Media Is Killing Discourse Because It's Too Much Like TV," *MIT Technology Review*, November 29, 2016, https://www.technologyreview.com/2016/11/29/155271/social-media-is-killing-discourse-because-its-too-much-like-tv/.
5. The literature on post-truth politics and society includes Ari Rabin-Havt and Media Matters for America, *Lies, Incorporated: The World of Post-Truth Politics* (New York: Penguin, 2016); Jason Hannan, ed., *Truth in the Public Sphere* (Lanham, MD: Lexington, 2016); Ralph Keyes, *The Post-Truth Era: Dishonesty and Deception in Contemporary Life* (New York: St. Martin's Press, 2004); Lee McIntyre, *Post-Truth* (Cambridge, MA: MIT Press, 2018); and Johan Farkas and Jannick Schou, *Post-Truth, Fake News, and Democracy* (New York: Routledge, 2020).
6. Marshall McLuhan, *Understanding Media: The Extensions of Man* (Cambridge, MA: MIT Press, 1994).
7. McLuhan, *Understanding Media*, 7.
8. Neil Postman, *Amusing Ourselves to Death: Public Discourse in the Age of Show Business* (New York: Penguin, 1985), 84.
9. Postman, *Amusing Ourselves to Death*, 85.
10. Postman, *Amusing Ourselves to Death*, 44–63.
11. Postman, *Amusing Ourselves to Death*, 89–98.
12. Postman, *Amusing Ourselves to Death*, 99–113.
13. Postman, *Amusing Ourselves to Death*, 105.
14. Postman, *Amusing Ourselves to Death*, 110.
15. Postman, *Amusing Ourselves to Death*, 107–109.
16. James Katz, Michael Barris, and Anshul Jain, *The Social Media President: Barack Obama and the Politics of Digital Engagement* (New York: Palgrave, 2013).
17. A good case can be made that Obama's rhetoric of "hope" and "change" was little more than a feel-good appeal to a liberal sensibility, as opposed to actual substantive policy positions. See, for example, the critique of the emptiness of Obama's campaign rhetoric in Roger Hodge, *The Mendacity of Hope: Barack Obama and the Betrayal of American Liberalism* (New York: HarperCollins, 2010).
18. This narrative was popularized by Allum Bokhari and Milo Yiannopoulos in their viral essay "An Establishment Conservative's Guide to the Alt-Right," Breitbart, March 29, 2016, https://www.breitbart.com/tech/2016/03/29/an-establishment-conservatives-guide-to-the-alt-right. This narrative would later be reproduced in Angela Nagle's *Kill All Normies: Online Culture Wars from 4chan and Tumblr to Trump and the Alt-Right* (London: Zer0 Books, 2017).
19. Torill Elvira Mortensen. "Anger, Fear, and Games: The Long Event of #GamerGate," *Games and Culture* 13, no. 8 (2018): 787–806.

20. Charlie Warzel, "'A Honeypot for Assholes': Inside Twitter's 10-Year Failure to Stop Harassment," Buzzfeed, August 11, 2016, https://www.buzzfeednews.com/article/charli ewarzel/a-honeypot-for-assholes-inside-twitters-10-year-failure-to-s.

21. See, for example, Mary Papenfuss, "Donald Jr. Says GOP Would Never Get Away with a Northam Scandal; Twitter Lets Him Have It," *HuffPost*, February 2, 2019, https://www. huffpost.com/entry/trump-jr-gop-never-racist-tweet-gets-massive-pushback_n_5c562 dc1e4b09293b204b49a.

22. Ben Collins, "'Back to the Future' Writer: Biff Tannen Is Based on Donald Trump," Daily Beast, April 13, 2017, https://www.thedailybeast.com/back-to-the-future-writer-biff-tan nen-is-based-on-donald-trump.

23. Angelia Wagner, "Tolerating the Trolls? Gendered Perceptions of Online Harassment of Politicians in Canada," *Feminist Media Studies* 22, no. 1 (2022): 32–47.

24. See, for example, Glenn Thrush, "Obama's New Gig: Gleefully Needling Trump," *New York Times*, October 27, 2020, https://www.nytimes.com/2020/10/27/us/politics/obama-trump-biden.html. As Thrush writes, "Former President Barack Obama bounded off the stage in Philadelphia last week after his debut as Joseph R. Biden Jr.'s 2020 battering ram and pronounced himself pumped—and even a bit delighted at the chance to troll his troll, President Trump."

25. David Weigel, "Government by Trolling," *Slate*, October 10, 2013, https://slate.com/ news-and-politics/2013/10/government-by-trolling.html.

26. HJR 31, "Declare Central Park a Wilderness Area," Alaska State Legislature, 2012.

27. HJ0013, "Resolution in Support of Central Park Wilderness," State of Wyoming Legislature, 2012, http://legisweb.state.wy.us/2012/Introduced/HJ0013.pdf.

28. HB150, "An Act to Provide That for All Official Purposes Within the State of Mississippi, the Body of Water Located Directly South of Hancock, Harrison, and Jackson Counties Shall Be Known as the 'Gulf of America,'" Mississippi State Legislature, 2012, https://legis can.com/MS/bill/HB150/2012.

29. Erin Gloria Ryan, "Brilliant Democratic State Senator Tacks 'Every Sperm Is Sacred' Clause to Oklahoma's Personhood Bill," Jezebel, February 7, 2012, https://jezebel.com/brilliant-democratic-state-senator-tacks-every-sperm-is-5883026.

30. Cassie Murdoch, "Brilliant State Senator Attaches Rectal Exam to Anti-Abortion Bill," Jezebel, January 13, 2012, https://jezebel.com/brilliant-state-senator-attaches-rectal-exam-to-anti-ab-5880775.

31. Jamie Gumbrecht, "Georgia Democrats Propose Limitations on Vasectomies for Men," CNN, February 22, 2012, https://www.cnn.com/2012/02/22/us/georgia-democrats-propose-limitations-on-vasectomies-for-men.

32. Tom Dart, "Texas Lawmaker Ridicules Anti-Abortion Measures by Filing Anti-Masturbation Bill," *The Guardian*, March 13, 2017, https://www.theguardian.com/us-news/2017/mar/13/texas-masturbation-bill-abortion-jessica-farrar.

33. Alex Zielenski, "How Lawmakers Use Satirical Bills to Troll Anti-Abortion Legislation," ThinkProgress, February 16, 2016, https://archive.thinkprogress.org/how-lawmakers-use-satirical-bills-to-troll-anti-abortion-legislation-9e8b61bc163a/.

34. Nicholas Vincour, "Marine Le Pen's Internet Army," Politico, February 2, 2017, https://www.politico.eu/article/marine-le-pens-internet-army-far-right-trolls-social-media/.

35. Henry Samuel, "Emmanuel Macron Files Defamation Complaint Against Marine Le Pen over Bahamas Account Allegation," *The Telegraph*, May 4, 2017, https://www.telegraph.co.uk/news/2017/05/04/emmanuel-macron-files-defamation-complaint-marine-le-pen-offshore/.

36. Benjamin Kentish, "Barack Obama Is a 'Loathsome Creature' Who 'Can't Stand Britain,' Says Nigel Farage," *The Independent*, November 10, 2016, https://www.independent.co.uk/news/uk/politics/nigel-farage-barack-obama-loathsome-creature-donald-trump-us-elect ion-ukip-a7409236.html.

37. Barbara Tasch, "Some British Politicians Have a Skewed Idea of How the Top EU Officials Come to Power—Here Is How It Happens," Insider, March 8, 2016, https://www.business insider.com/is-the-eu-undemocratic-2016-3.
38. Anoosh Chakelian, "How Much of Our Law Is Made in Brussels?," *New Statesman*, June 16, 2016, https://www.newstatesman.com/politics/uk/2016/06/how-much-our-law-made-brussels.
39. Jon Henley, "Why Vote Leave's £350m Weekly EU Cost Claim Is Wrong," *The Guardian*, June 10, 2016, https://www.theguardian.com/politics/reality-check/2016/may/23/does-the-eu-really-cost-the-uk-350m-a-week.
40. Gatestone Institute, https://www.gatestoneinstitute.org/
41. Lee Fang, "Islamophobic U.S. Megadonor Fuels German Far-Right Party with Viral Fake News," The Intercept, September 22, 2017, https://theintercept.com/2017/09/22/german-election-afd-gatestone-institute/.
42. https://www.bloomberg.com/news/articles/2023-06-13/german-far-right-overtakes-chancellor-scholz-s-spd-in-forsa-poll.
43. Adam Frisk, "'Madman' vs. 'Dotard': A Timeline of War of Words Between Donald Trump, Kim Jong Un," Global News, September 22, 2017, https://globalnews.ca/news/3763142/donald-trump-kim-jong-un-timeline-of-words/.
44. Frisk, "'Madman' vs. 'Dotard,'" 7.
45. Frisk, "'Madman' vs. 'Dotard,'" 7.
46. Amanda Taub, "The Real Story About Fake News Is Partisanship," *New York Times*, January 11, 2017, https://www.nytimes.com/2017/01/11/upshot/the-real-story-about-fake-news-is-partisanship.html.

Chapter 2

1. Alasdair MacIntyre, *After Virtue: A Study in Moral Theory* (Notre Dame, IN: University of Notre Dame Press, 1981), 6.
2. MacIntyre, *After Virtue*, 8.
3. MacIntyre, *After Virtue*, 8.
4. MacIntyre *After Virtue*, 51–61.
5. MacIntyre, *After Virtue*, 36–50.
6. W. R. Ward, *Christianity Under the Ancien Régime, 1648–1789* (Cambridge, UK: Cambridge University Press, 2012), 1–33.
7. Robert Filmer, *Patriarcha and Other Writings*, ed. Johann P. Sommerville (Cambridge, UK: Cambridge University Press, 1991), 1–63.
8. Filmer, *Patriarcha and Other Writings*, 1–10.
9. Filmer, *Patriarcha and Other Writings*, 34–63.
10. Matthias Range, "*Dei Gratia* and the 'Divine Right of Kings': Divine Legitimization or Human Humility?," in *The Routledge History of Monarchy*, ed. Elena Woodacre, Lucinda H. S. Dean, Chris Jones, Zita Rohr, and Russell Martin (New York: Routledge, 2019), 130–145.
11. John Mahoney, *The Making of Moral Theology* (Oxford, UK: Clarendon, 1989).
12. Peter Gay, *The Enlightenment: An Interpretation* (New York: W. W. Norton, 1977).
13. John Locke, *Two Treatises of Government*, ed. Peter Laslett (Cambridge, UK: Cambridge University Press, 2012), 137.
14. On the influence of Hobbes and Grotius on Locke, see Jeffrey R. Collins, *In the Shadow of Leviathan: John Locke and the Politics of Conscience* (Cambridge, UK: Cambridge University Press, 2020); James Tully, *A Discourse on Property: John Locke and His Adversaries* (Cambridge, UK: Cambridge University Press, 1980), 80–94; Knud Haakonssen, "Hugo Grotius and the History of Political Thought," *Political Theory* 13, no. 2 (May 1985): 239–265.
15. Locke, *Two Treatises of Government*, 323.

16. Locke, *Two Treatises of Government*, 299.

17. Locke, *Two Treatises of Government*, 398–340.

18. This limitation only concerns the "guards and fences" necessary for the protection of private property.

19. Thomas L. Pangle, *The Spirit of Modern Republicanism: The Moral Vision of the American Founders and the Philosophy of John Locke* (Chicago: University of Chicago Press, 1988); Jerome Huyler, *Locke in America: The Moral Philosophy of the Founding Era* (Lawrence: University Press of Kansas, 1995).

20. Bronislaw Baczko, "The Social Contract of the French: Sieyès and Rousseau," *Journal of Modern History* 60 (1988): 98–125.

21. MacIntyre, *After Virtue*, 36.

22. R. G. Collingwood, *The Idea of Nature* (Oxford, UK: Oxford University Press, 1960), 113–120.

23. David Hume, *An Enquiry Concerning Human Understanding*, ed. Stephen Buckle (Cambridge, UK: Cambridge University Press, 2007), 76.

24. For Hume's classic treatment of the problem of "ought" and "is," see David Hume, *A Treatise of Human Nature*, ed. David Fate Norton and Mary J. Norton (Oxford, UK: Oxford University Press, 2000), 301–303.

25. For Kant's classic statement on moral theory, see Immanuel Kant, *Groundwork of the Metaphysics of Morals*, ed. Mary Gregor and Jens Timmerman (Cambridge, UK: Cambridge University Press, 2012).

26. Kant, *Groundwork of the Metaphysics of Morals*, 31.

27. Immanuel Kant, "On a Supposed Right to Lie from Philanthropy," in *Immanuel Kant: Practical Philosophy*, ed. Allen Wood and Mary J. Gregor (Cambridge, UK: Cambridge University Press, 1996), 605–616.

28. Kant, *Groundwork of the Metaphysics of Morals*, 45.

29. MacIntyre, *After Virtue*, 51–62.

30. Aristotle, *Nicomachean Ethics*, ed. Roger Crisp (Cambridge, UK: Cambridge University Press, 2000).

31. Aristotle, *Nicomachean Ethics*, 20–21.

32. MacIntyre, *After Virtue*, 51–53. See also my overview of MacIntyre's historical argument in *Ethics Under Capital: MacIntyre, Communication, and the Culture Wars* (London, UK: Bloomsbury, 2020), 21–66.

33. MacIntyre, *After Virtue*, 53.

34. MacIntyre, *After Virtue*, 53–61.

35. MacIntyre, *After Virtue*, 226–243.

36. MacIntyre, *After Virtue*, 239–240. Although he does not cite Marx or Engels, MacIntyre's description of the corrosive effects of factories upon social life was undoubtedly influenced by his earlier Marxism and very likely by Engels's *The Condition of the Working Class in England*.

37. MacIntyre, *After Virtue*, 227.

38. John Locke, *Second Treatise*, in Locke, *Two Treatises of Government*, ed. Peter Laslett (Cambridge, UK: Cambridge University Press, 1988), 295. See also C. B. Macpherson, *The Political Theory of Possessive Individualism: Hobbes to Locke* (Oxford, UK: Clarendon, 1962).

39. John Durham Peters, "John Locke, the Individual, and the Origin of Communication," *Quarterly Journal of Speech* 74, no. 4 (1989): 387–399.

40. Locke, *Two Treatises of Government*, 323. On Locke as an early bourgeois political theorist, see Macpherson, *The Political Theory of Possessive Individualism*, 250–251. For a different reading of Locke, with criticisms of Macpherson's interpretation, see Tully, *A Discourse on Property*.

41. On the transition of liberal individualism from mere idea to institutional reality, see Charles Taylor, "Modern Social Imaginaries," *Public Culture* 14, no. 1 (2002): 91–124.

42. As John Rawls puts it, "Justice as fairness . . . does not look behind the use which persons make of the rights and opportunities available to them in order to measure, much less to maximize, the satisfactions they achieve. Nor does it try to evaluate the relative merits of different conceptions of the good. Instead, it is assumed that the members of society are rational persons able to adjust their conceptions of the good to their situation. There is no necessity to compare the worth of the conceptions of different persons once it is supposed they are compatible with the principles of justice. Everyone is assured an equal liberty to pursue whatever plan of life he pleases as long as it does not violate what justice demands." *A Theory of Justice* (Cambridge, MA: Harvard University Press, 1971), 80–81.

43. MacIntyre, *After Virtue*, 23.

44. Edward L. Bernays, "The Engineering of Consent," *Annals of the American Academy of Political and Social Science* 250, no. 1 (1947): 113–120.

45. MacIntyre, *After Virtue*, 10–22.

46. W. H. F. Barnes, "A Suggestion About Value," *Analysis* 1, no. 3 (1934): 45–46; C. L. Stevenson, "The Emotive Meaning of Ethical Terms," *Mind* 46, no. 181 (1937): 14–31; C. L. Stevenson, *Ethics and Language* (New Haven, CT: Yale University Press, 2011). In more recent work in metaethics, the term for emotivism is "expressivism." See, for example, Allan Gibbard, "An Expressivistic Theory of Normative Discourse," *Ethics* 96, no. 3 (1986): 472–485; Allan Gibbard, *Thinking How to Live* (Cambridge, MA: Harvard University Press, 2009), 179–198.

47. On this point, see Huw Price, "Truth as Convenient Friction," *Journal of Philosophy* 100, no. 4 (2003): 167–190.

48. Ann Coulter quoted in Mark Dery, *I Must Not Think Bad Thoughts: Drive-By Essays on American Dread, American Dreams* (Minneapolis: University of Minnesota Press, 2012).

49. Paul Ricoeur, *Freud and Philosophy: An Essay on Interpretation* (New Haven, CT: Yale University Press, 1970), 32.

50. MacIntyre, *After Virtue*, 71; emphasis in the original.

51. Jessica Dawson, "Shall Not Be Infringed: How the NRA Used Religious Language to Transform the Meaning of the Second Amendment," *Palgrave Communications* 5 (2019): art. 58; Helena Rosenblatt, "No, There Isn't a Constitutional Right to Not Wear a Mask," *Washington Post*, August 20, 2020, https://www.washingtonpost.com/outl ook/2020/08/20/no-there-isnt-constitutional-right-not-wear-masks/; Jeffrey Flocken, "Trophy Hunting: 'Killing Animals to Save Them Is Not Conservation,'" CNN, January 4, 2018, https://www.cnn.com/2015/05/19/opinions/trophy-hunting-not-conservat ion-flocken/index.html; Mikayla Lewis, "Robertson Co. Man Says He Has the Right to Fly Swastika Flag," Fox17 WZTV Nashville, February 17, 2017, https://fox17.com/ news/local/robertson-co-man-says-he-has-the-right-to-fly-swastika-flag; Hiroko Tabuchi, "'Rolling Coal' in Diesel Trucks, to Rebel and Provoke," *New York Times*, September 4, 2016, https://www.nytimes.com/2016/09/05/business/energy-environment/rolling-coal-in-diesel-trucks-to-rebel-and-provoke.html.

52. For Marx's classic statements on rights, see "On the Jewish Question" and "Critique of the Gotha Program," in *The Marx-Engels Reader*, ed. Robert Tucker, 2nd ed. (New York: W. W. Norton, 1978), 26–52, 525–541.

53. Alasdair MacIntyre, *Three Rival Versions of Moral Enquiry: Encyclopaedia, Genealogy, and Tradition* (Notre Dame, IN: University of Notre Dame Press, 1990), 185. For a more recent version of this argument, see Jamal Greene, *How Rights Went Wrong: Why Our Obsession with Rights Is Tearing America Apart* (New York: Houghton Mifflin, 2021).

54. Naomi Klein, "Greta Thunberg on the Climate Fight: 'If We Can Save the Banks, Then We Can Save the World,'" The Intercept, September 13, 2019, https://theintercept.com/ 2019/09/13/greta-thunberg-naomi-klein-climate.

55. Evan Osnos, *Wildland: The Making of America's Fury* (New York: Macmillan, 2021).

Chapter 3

1. William F. Buckley, *God and Man at Yale* (Washington, DC: Regnery, 2021); William F. Buckley, *McCarthy and His Enemies* (Washington, DC: Regnery, 1954); William F. Buckley, *Up from Liberalism* (New York: Ivan Obolensky, 1959).

2. Douglas Martin, "William F. Buckley Jr. Is Dead at 82," *New York Times*, February 27, 2008, https://www.nytimes.com/2008/02/27/business/media/27cnd-buckley.html.

3. For an excellent intellectual and political biography, see Carl T. Bogus, *William F. Buckley Jr. and the Rise of American Conservatism* (London: Bloomsbury, 2011).

4. Nina Burleigh, "Trump Speaks at Fourth-Grade Level, Lowest of Last 15 U.S. Presidents, New Analysis Finds," *Newsweek*, January 8, 2018, https://www.newsweek.com/trump-fire-and-fury-smart-genius-obama-774169; David A. Graham, "The President Who Doesn't Read," *The Atlantic*, January 5, 2018, https://www.theatlantic.com/politics/archive/2018/01/americas-first-post-text-president/549794/; Maggie Haberman, Glenn Thrush, and Peter Baker, "Inside Trump's Hour-by-Hour Battle for Self-Preservation," *New York Times*, December 9, 2017, https://nytimes.com/2017/12/09/us/politics/donald-trump-presid ent.html; Marina di Marzo, "How Often Does Trump Misspell Words on Twitter? These Researchers Have an Answer," CNN Business, November 3, 2019, https://www.cnn.com/2019/11/03/media/trump-twitter-typos.

5. Adam Edelman, "A Guide to Trump's Nicknames and Insults About the 2020 Democratic Field," NBC News, April 25, 2019, https://www.nbcnews.com/politics/2020-election/everything-trump-has-said-about-2020-field-insults-all-n998556; Daniel Strauss, "Donald Trump Campaign Repeatedly Doctoring Videos for Social Media Ads," *The Guardian*, September 4, 2020, https://www.theguardian.com/us-news/2020/sep/04/donald-trump-campaign-doctoring-joe-biden-videos-manipulated-media-twitter.

6. Christopher Buckley, "What Would William F. Buckley Have Made of Donald Trump?," *Vanity Fair*, December 5, 2016, https://www.vanityfair.com/news/2016/12/what-would-william-f-buckley-have-made-of-donald-trump.

7. George Will, "It's All Just One Giant Act of Trolling," *Washington Post*, October 10, 2018, https://www.washingtonpost.com/opinions/trumps-presidency-is-one-giant-act-of-troll ing/2018/10/10/d6aa4632-cbe6-11e8-920f-dd52e1ae4570_story.html.

8. David Frum, *Trumpocalypse: Restoring American Democracy* (New York: Harper Collins, 2020).

9. Rick Wilson, "How the Tea Party Got Hijacked by Trump's Troll Party," Daily Beast, April 14, 2017, https://www.thedailybeast.com/how-the-tea-party-got-hijacked-by-tru mps-troll-party.

10. Eric Sorenson, "Meet the Republican Strategists Who Have Crossed Over to Oppose Trump," Global News, July 26, 2020, https://globalnews.ca/news/7184494/republicans-against-trump/.

11. For a similar argument and an excellent historical account of conservative thought, see Matthew McManus, *The Rise of Post-Modern Conservatism: Neoliberalism, Post-Modern Culture, and Reactionary Politics* (Cham, Switzerland: Palgrave Macmillan, 2020).

12. John Cassidy, "An Inconvenient Truth: It Was George W. Bush Who Bailed Out the Automakers," *New Yorker*, March 16, 2012, https://www.newyorker.com/news/john-cass idy/an-inconvenient-truth-it-was-george-w-bush-who-bailed-out-the-automakers.

13. Amanda Macias, "Trump Signs $738 Billion Defense Bill. Here's What the Pentagon Is Poised to Get," CNBC, December 20, 2019, https://www.cnbc.com/2019/12/21/trump-signs-738-billion-defense-bill.html; Alice Miranda Olstein, "Republican Graham Introduces Bill That Would Restrict Abortions Nationwide," Politico, September 13, 2022, https://www.politico.com/news/2022/09/13/republicans-graham-bill-restrict-aborti ons-nationwide-00056404.

14. Clara Long, "Written Testimony: 'Kids in Cages: Inhumane Treatment at the Border,'" Human Rights Watch, July 11, 2019, https://www.hrw.org/news/2019/07/11/written-testimony-kids-cages-inhumane-treatment-border.

15. Melissa Gira Grant, "Republicans' Criminalization of Protest and Cops' Crackdown on Journalists Go Hand in Hand," *New Republic*, April 20, 2021, https://newrepublic.com/article/162104/desantis-protest-riot-george-floyd-police; Brooke Migdon, "What Is DeSantis's 'Stop WOKE Act'?," *The Hill*, August 19, 2022, https://thehill.com/changing-america/respect/diversity-inclusion/3608241-what-is-desantiss-stop-woke-act/.

16. Jim Tankersley and Emily Cochrane, "US Budget Deficit Set to Top $1tn as Trump's Tax Cuts and Spending Force Rise in Borrowing," *The Independent*, August 22, 2019, https://www.independent.co.uk/news/business/news/trump-budget-deficit-borrowing-tax-cuts-us-economy-a9074531.html.

17. Theodore Schleifer, "Donald Trump Defends Racial Profiling In Wake of Bombings," CNN, September 20, 2016, https://www.cnn.com/2016/09/19/politics/donald-trump-racial-profiling.

18. This has been the standard view for decades. As Samuel Huntington put it, "All the analysts of conservatism, moreover, unite in identifying Edmund Burke as the conservative archetype and in assuming that the basic elements of his thought are the basic elements of conservatism." See Samuel Huntington, "Conservatism as an Ideology," *American Political Science Review* 51, no. 2 (1957): 454–473. See also Russell Kirk, *The Conservative Mind: From Burke to Eliot* (Washington, DC: Regnery, 1985).

19. For a general account of Burke's thought as a defense of tradition over revolution, see C. B. Macpherson, *Burke* (Oxford, UK: Oxford University Press 1980). See also Roger Paden, "Reason and Tradition in Burke's Political Philosophy," *History of Philosophy Quarterly* 5, no. 1 (1988): 63–77. On the place of tradition within conservatism broadly, see Roger Scruton, *The Meaning of Tradition* (South Bend, IN: St. Augustine's Press, 2002), 30–36.

20. Edmund Burke, *Speech on Conciliation with America*, ed. George Rice Carpenter (New York: Longman, Green, 1917), 44.

21. As E. J. Payne put it in his introduction to a classic collection of Burke's speeches, Burke "led the way in Reform while raising his voice against innovation. The spirit of Conservatism and the spirit of Reform are really the necessary complements of each other." See Edmund Burke, *Thoughts on the Present Discontents: The Two Speeches on America*, ed. E. J. Payne (Oxford, UK: Clarendon, 1878), xxvi)

22. Edmund Burke, *Burke: Revolutionary Writings*, ed. Ian Hampsher-Monk (Cambridge, UK: Cambridge University Press, 2014), 27.

23. Edmund Burke, *Thoughts on the Present Discontents, and Speeches* (London: Cassell, 1892), 157.

24. Edmund Burke, *The Correspondence of Edmund Burke: Volume IV, July 1778–June 1782*, ed. John A. Woods (Cambridge, UK: Cambridge University Press, 1963), 115.

25. Burke, *Burke*, 96.

26. Edmund Burke, *The Works of the Right Honorable Edmund Burke* (Boston: Little, Brown, 1869), 344.

27. Burke, *Burke*, 90.

28. Burke, *The Correspondence of Edmund Burke*, 96.

29. Burke, *Burke*, 20.

30. Burke, *Burke*, 79.

31. Burke, *Burke*, 79

32. Don Herzog, *Poisoning the Minds of the Lower Orders* (Princeton, NJ: Princeton University Press, 1998), 25.

33. Burke, *Burke*, 79.

34. Edmund Burke, *The Works of the Right Honorable Edmund Burke, Vol. IV* (Boston: Little, Brown, 1869), 174.

35. Herzog, *Poisoning the Minds of the Lower Orders*, 30–31.

36. Herzog, *Poisoning the Minds of the Lower Orders*, 31.

37. Herzog, *Poisoning the Minds of the Lower Orders*, 30.

38. Samuel Horseley, *The Speeches in Parliament* (Dundee, UK: J. Ballantyne, 1813), 176.

39. James Boswell, *The Life of Johnson*, ed. R. W. Chapman (Oxford, UK: Oxford University Press, 1998), 514.

40. Boswell, *The Life of Johnson*, 924.

41. John Bowles, *A Protest Against T. Paine's "The Rights of Man"* (Edinburgh: J. Dickson and J. and J. Fairbain, 1792), 22.

42. Bowles, *A Protest Against T. Paine's "The Rights of Man,"* 22.

43. William Cowper, *The Life and Letters of William Cowper, Esq., with Remarks on Epistolary Writers* (London: Longman, Rees, 1835), 402.

44. Burke, *Burke*, 101.

45. Alexander Pope, *The Poetical Works of Alexander Pope* (New York: Macmillan, 1893), 199.

46. Arthur Lovejoy, *The Great Chain of Being: A Study of the History of an Idea* (Cambridge, MA: Harvard University Press, 1964).

47. Lovejoy, *The Great Chain of Being*, 183–241.

48. On the influence of the idea of the Great Chain of Being upon English thought, see Anthony Fletcher and John Stevenson, eds., *Order and Disorder in Early Modern England* (Cambridge, UK: Cambridge University Press, 1985), 1–5, 31–40.

49. Burke, *Burke*, 81.

50. Burke, *Burke*, 81. For commentary on the threat that popular literacy posed to the English aristocracy, see Patrick Brantlinger, *The Reading Lesson: The Threat of Mass Literacy in Nineteenth Century British Fiction* (Bloomington: Indiana University Press, 1998). See also Roland Bartel, "Shelley and Burke's Swinish Multitude," *Keats-Shelley Journal* 18 (1969): 4–9.

51. Corey Robin, *The Reactionary Mind: Conservatism from Edmund Burke to Donald Trump* (Oxford, UK: Oxford University Press, 2017), 49.

52. Robin, *The Reactionary Mind*, 49.

53. Robin, *The Reactionary Mind*, 53.

54. Robin, *The Reactionary Mind*, 35.

55. Richard Hofstadter, *The Paranoid Style in American Politics* (New York: Vintage, 2008).

56. Hofstadter, *The Paranoid Style in American Politics*, 13.

57. Hofstadter, *The Paranoid Style in American Politics*, 19.

58. Hofstadter, *The Paranoid Style in American Politics*, 20–21.

59. Hofstadter, *The Paranoid Style in American Politics*, 23.

60. Hans-Georg Betz, "Politics of Resentment: Right-Wing Radicalism in West Germany," *Comparative Politics* 23, no. 1 (1990): 45–60; Hans-George [*sic*] Betz, "The New Politics of Resentment: Radical Right-Wing Populist Parties in Western Europe," *Comparative Politics* 25, no. 4 (1993): 413–427; David Jacobs and Daniel Tope, "The Politics of Resentment in the Post–Civil Rights Era: Minority Threat, Homicide, and Ideological Voting in Congress," *American Journal of Sociology* 112, no. 5 (2007): 1458–1494; Katherine J. Cramer, *The Politics of Resentment: Rural Consciousness in Wisconsin and the Rise of Scott Walker* (Chicago: University of Chicago Press, 2016); Jeremy Engels, *The Politics of Resentment: A Genealogy* (University Park, PA: Penn State University Press, 2015);

61. Giulia Carbonaro, "Dana Loesch Doesn't Care If Herschel Walker Paid 'Skank' for Abortion," *Newsweek*, October 5, 2022, https://www.newsweek.com/dana-loesch-doesnt-care-herschel-walker-paid-skank-abortion-1749023.

62. Kristen Clarke, "Voter Intimidation Is Surging in 2020. Fight for the Right That Begets All Other Rigths," *USA Today*, October 27, 2020, https://www.usatoday.com/story/opin ion/2020/10/27/voter-intimidation-surging-2020-protect-minority-voters-column/604 3955002/.

63. Lois Beckett and Alexandra Villareal, "Biden Campaign Says Trump Supporters Tried to Force Bus off Highway," *The Guardian*, November 1, 2020, https://www.theguardian.com/us-news/2020/oct/31/biden-harris-bus-texas-trump-supporters-highway.

64. Aliyya Swaby, "'These Patriots Did Nothing Wrong,' Trump Says of Supporters Who Surrounded Biden Bus," *Texas Tribune*, November 1, 2020, https://www.texastribune.org/2020/11/01/trump-biden-bus/.

65. Aristotle, *Aristotle: The Art of Rhetoric*, trans. John Henry Freese (Cambridge, MA: Harvard University Press, 2006), 201.
66. Aristotle, *Aristotle: The Art of Rhetoric*, 203.
67. Aristotle, *Aristotle: The Art of Rhetoric*, 205.
68. Corey Robin, *Fear: The History of a Political Idea* (Oxford, UK: Oxford University Press, 2004), 3.
69. David L. Atheide, *Creating Fear: News and the Construction of Crisis* (New York: Aldine de Gruyter, 2002).
70. Ruth Wodak, *The Politics of Fear: What Right-Wing Populist Discourses Mean* (Thousand Oaks, CA: Sage, 2015).
71. Wodak, *The Politics of Fear*, 79.
72. Wodak, *The Politics of Fear*, 151–155.
73. Kathryn Ruud, "Lcfiberal Parasites and Other Creepers: Rush Limbaugh, Ken Hamblin, and the Discursive Construction of Group Identities," in *At War with Words*, ed. Mirjana N. Dedaic and Daniel N. Nelson (New York: Mouton de Gruyter, 2003), 27–62.
74. For an overview of Limbaugh's media revolution, see Kathleen Hall Jamieson and Joseph N. Cappella, *Rush Limbaugh and the Conservative Media Establishment* (Oxford, UK: Oxford University Press, 2008).
75. Richard Corliss, "A Man. A Legend. A What? Raging Against Commie Libs and Femi-Nazis, Rush Limbaugh Is Bombastic, Infuriating, and Nearly Irresistable," *Time*, September 23, 1991, http://content.time.com/time/subscriber/article/0,33009,973851-2,00.html.
76. Emma Nolan, "Fact Check: Did Rush Limbaugh Read a List of Gay Men Who Died as an 'AIDS Update'?," *Newsweek*, February 18, 2021, https://www.newsweek.com/fact-check-did-rush-limbaugh-mock-aids-death-radio-show-1570282.
77. David Montgomery, "Limbaugh Mocks Michael J. Fox Political Ad," NBC News, October 25, 2006, https://www.nbcnews.com/id/wbna15408508.
78. Maggie Fazeli Fard, "Sandra Fluke, Georgetown Student Called a 'Slut' by Rush Limbaugh," *Washington Post*, March 2, 2012, https://www.washingtonpost.com/blogs/the-buzz/post/rush-limbaugh-calls-georgetown-student-sandra-fluke-a-slut-for-advocating-contraception/2012/03/02/gIQAvjfSmR_blog.html.
79. Jen Doll, "Rush Limbaugh Is Trolling Us," *The Atlantic*, March 2, 2012, https://www.theatlantic.com/national/archive/2012/03/rush-limbaugh-uber-troll/331031/.
80. Robert D. McFadden and Michael M. Grynbaum, "Rush Limbaugh Dies at 70; Turned Talk Radio into a Right-Wing Attack Machine," *New York Times*, February 17, 2021, https://www.nytimes.com/2021/02/17/business/media/rush-limbaugh-dead.html.
81. Laura M. Holson, "Outflanked on Right, Coulter Seeks New Image," *New York Times*, October 8, 2020, https://www.nytimes.com/2010/10/10/fashion/10coulter.html.
82. John Cloud, "Ms. Right: Ann Coulter," *Time*, April 17, 2005, http://content.time.com/time/subscriber/article/0,33009,1050304,00.html.
83. Richard Bernstein, "Letter from America: A Conservative Pundit, or Is It Just Showtime?," *New York Times*, November 3, 2006, https://www.nytimes.com/2006/12/03/world/americas/03iht-letter.3760135.html.
84. Bruce Cheadle, "Watch Your Mouth, Ann Coulter Warned for Canadian Tour," *Toronto Star*, March 22, 2010, https://www.thestar.com/news/canada/2010/03/22/watch_your_mouth_ann_coulter_warned_for_canadian_tour.html.
85. Ann Coulter, "That Was No Lady—That Was My Husband," Townhall, June 28, 2007, https://anncoulter.com/2007/06/28/that-was-no-lady-that-was-my-husband/.
86. Bernstein, "Letter from America."
87. Scott Eric Kaufman, "Ann Coulter: Mexican Culture 'Is Obviously Deficient,' and Hispanics Are 'Not Black, So Drop the Racism Crap,'" *Salon*, May 27, 2015, https://www.salon.com/2015/05/27/ann_coulter_mexican_culture_is_obviously_deficient_and_hispanics_are_not_black_so_drop_the_racism_crap/.
88. Carson Jerema, "Ann Coulter Responds," *Maclean's*, March 23, 2010, https://www.macleans.ca/education/uniandcollege/ann-coulter-responds/.

89. Chris Sosa, "Let's All Laugh at Ann Coulter, Right-Wing Performance Artist," *Salon*, October 24, 2013, https://www.salon.com/2013/10/24/lets_all_laugh_at_ann_coulter_right_wing_performance_artist/.

90. Amanda Marcotte, "Ann Coulter Is Not a Satirist," *Slate*, October 24, 2013, https://slate.com/human-interest/2013/10/ann-coulter-is-not-a-satirist-but-means-all-those-horrible-things-she-says.html.

Chapter 4

1. Andrew Marantz, "The Stylish Socialist Who Is Trying to Save YouTube from Alt-Right Domination," *New Yorker*, November 19, 2018, https://www.newyorker.com/culture/persons-of-interest/the-stylish-socialist-who-is-trying-to-save-youtube-from-alt-right-domination.

2. Arwa Mahdawi, "He, She, They . . . Should We Now Clarify Our Preferred Pronouns When We Say Hello?," *The Guardian*, September 19, 2019, https://www.theguardian.com/lifeandstyle/2019/sep/13/pronouns-gender-he-she-they-natalie-wynn-contrapoints.

3. Jessie Earl, "What Does the ContraPoints Controversy Say About the Way We Criticize?," Pride, October 21, 2019, https://www.pride.com/firstperson/2019/10/21/what-does-contrapoints-controversy-say-about-way-we-criticize.

4. ContraPoints, "Opulence," YouTube, October 12, 2019, https://youtu.be/jD-PbF3ywGo.

5. Earl, "What Does the ContraPoints Controversy Say."

6. Earl, "What Does the ContraPoints Controversy Say."

7. ContraPoints, "Canceling," YouTube, January 2, 2020, https://youtu.be/OjMPJVmXxV8.

8. Ari Paul, "Panic over 'Cancel Culture' Is Another Example of Right-Wing Projection," FAIR, October 23, 2020, https://fair.org/home/panic-over-cancel-culture-is-another-example-of-right-wing-projection/.

9. Evan Smith, "The Conservatives Have Been Waging Their 'War on Woke' for Decades," *The Guardian*, April 21, 2021, https://www.theguardian.com/commentisfree/2021/apr/21/conservatives-war-on-woke-loony-left-political-correctness.

10. Katie Herzog, "Cancel Culture: What Exactly Is This Thing?," The Stranger, September 17, 2019, https://www.thestranger.com/slog/2019/09/17/41416013/cancel-culture-what-exactly-is-this-thing.

11. Loretta Ross, "I'm a Black Feminist. I Think Call-Out Culture Is Toxic," *New York Times*, August 17, 2019, https://www.nytimes.com/2019/08/17/opinion/sunday/cancel-culture-call-out.html.

12. Jessica Bennett, "What if Instead of Calling People Out, We Called Them In?," *New York Times*, November 19, 2020, https://www.nytimes.com/2020/11/19/style/loretta-ross-smith-college-cancel-culture.html.

13. Friedrich Nietzsche, "'Good and Evil,' 'Good' and 'Bad,'" in Friedrich Nietzsche, *On the Genealogy of Morals* and *Ecce Homo*, ed. and trans. Walter Kaufmann (New York: Vintage Books, 1989), 24–56.

14. Friedrich Nietzsche, "'Guilt,' 'Bad Conscience,' and the Like," in Friedrich Nietzsche, *On the Genealogy of Morals* and *Ecce Homo*, ed. and trans. Walter Kaufmann (New York: Vintage Books, 1989), 57–96.

15. Nietzsche, "'Guilt,' 'Bad Conscience,' and the Like," 62–63.

16. Nietzsche, "'Guilt,' 'Bad Conscience,' and the Like," 61.

17. Nietzsche, "'Guilt,' 'Bad Conscience,' and the Like," 61.

18. Nietzsche, "'Guilt,' 'Bad Conscience,' and the Like," 61.

19. Nietzsche, "'Guilt,' 'Bad Conscience,' and the Like," 62.

20. Nietzsche, "'Guilt,' 'Bad Conscience,' and the Like," 64.

21. Nietzsche, "'Guilt,' 'Bad Conscience,' and the Like," 64.

22. Nietzsche, "'Guilt,' 'Bad Conscience,' and the Like," 65.

23. Nietzsche, "'Guilt,' 'Bad Conscience,' and the Like," 65.

24. Nietzsche, "'Guilt,' 'Bad Conscience,' and the Like," 69.
25. Nietzsche, "'Guilt,' 'Bad Conscience,' and the Like," 71.
26. Nietzsche, "'Guilt,' 'Bad Conscience,' and the Like," 71.
27. Nietzsche, "'Guilt,' 'Bad Conscience,' and the Like," 71.
28. Nietzsche, "'Guilt,' 'Bad Conscience,' and the Like," 28.
29. Nietzsche, "'Guilt,' 'Bad Conscience,' and the Like," 93.
30. Nietzsche, "'Guilt,' 'Bad Conscience,' and the Like," 85.
31. Nietzsche, "'Guilt,' 'Bad Conscience,' and the Like," 85.
32. Nietzsche, "'Guilt,' 'Bad Conscience,' and the Like," 70.
33. David Graeber, *Debt: The First 5,000 Years* (New York: Melville House, 2014), 77, emphasis added.
34. Graeber, *Debt*, 78–79, emphasis added.
35. Walter Benjamin, "Capitalism as Religion," in *Walter Benjamin: Selected Writings, Vol. 1*, ed. Michael W. Jennings, Howard Eiland, and Gary Smith (Cambridge, MA: Belknap, 2005), 288–291.
36. Benjamin, "Capitalism as Religion," 288.
37. Samuel Weber, "The Debt of the Living," *Postmodern Culture* 23, no. 3 (2013): n.p.
38. Benjamin, "Capitalism as Religion," 288.
39. For examples of Democrats and Republicans treating capitalism as a religion, see Sam Raskin, "Nancy Pelosi to Leftist NYU Student: We're Capitalists, Deal with It," NYULocal, February 1, 2017, https://nyulocal.com/nancy-pelosi-to-leftist-nyu-student-were-capi talists-deal-with-it-abf1e8e04e46; Lois Becket, "Older People Would Rather Die than Let Covid-19 Harm US Economy—Texas Official," *The Guardian*, March 24, 2020, https:// www.theguardian.com/world/2020/mar/24/older-people-would-rather-die-than-let-covid-19-lockdown-harm-us-economy-texas-official-dan-patrick; James Osborne, "Perry Says Texans Willing to Suffer Blackouts to Keep Feds out of Power Market," *Houston Chronicle*, February 17, 2021, https://www.houstonchronicle.com/business/energy/arti cle/Perry-says-Texans-wiling-to-suffer-blackouts-to-15956705.php.
40. Benjamin, "Capitalism as Religion," 288.
41. Benjamin, "Capitalism as Religion," 288.
42. Benjamin, "Capitalism as Religion," 288.
43. Benjamin, "Capitalism as Religion," 288.
44. Michael Löwy, "Capitalism as Religion: Walter Benjamin and Max Weber," *Historical Materialism* 17 (2009): 64.
45. Lowy, "Capitalism as Religion," 64. Examples of this "iron destiny" abound. As just one example, see Lora Jones, "I Was Working 72 Hours a Week—It Was Cult-Like," BBC, March 24, 2021, https://www.bbc.com/news/business-56496883.
46. Benjamin, "Capitalism as Religion," 289.
47. Benjamin, "Capitalism as Religion," 289.
48. Benjamin, "Capitalism as Religion," 289.
49. Max Weber, *The Protestant Ethic and the Spirit of Capitalism* (London: Routledge, 2005), 114–115.
50. Alice Marwick, *Status Update: Celebrity, Publicity, and Branding in the Social Media Age* (New Haven, CT: Yale University Press, 2013).
51. Marwick, *Status Update*, 207–213.
52. Marwick, *Status Update*, 210.
53. Marwick, *Status Update*, 13–14.
54. Marwick, *Status Update*, 112–117.
55. Tim Denning, "The Crippling Guilt of Being Away from Social Media," Medium, December 30, 2019, https://medium.com/swlh/the-crippling-guilt-of-being-away-from-social-media-74411e5eecb0.
56. Denning, "The Crippling Guilt," emphasis added.

57. Richard C. MacKinnon, "Searching for the Leviathan in Usenet," in *CyberSociety*, ed. Steve Jones (Thousand Oaks, CA: Sage, 1995), 119.

58. Michel Foucault, *Discipline and Punish: The Birth of the Prison* (New York: Vintage, 1977), 1.

59. Foucault, *Discipline and Punish*, 29.

60. Foucault, *Discipline and Punish*, 47.

61. Foucault, *Discipline and Punish*, 48.

62. Foucault, *Discipline and Punish*, 48.

63. Foucault, *Discipline and Punish*, 23.

64. Foucault, *Discipline and Punish*, 49.

65. Foucault, *Discipline and Punish*, 43–46.

66. Foucault, *Discipline and Punish*, 47.

67. The concept of technological rationality is taken from Herbert Marcuse, "Some Social Implications of Modern Technology," *Zeitschrift für Sozialforschung* 9, no. 3 (1941): 414–439.

68. Nietzsche, " 'Good and Evil,' 'Good' and 'Bad,' " 49, emphasis in the original.

69. Ute Frevert, *The Politics of Humiliation: A Modern History* (Oxford, UK: Oxford University Press, 2020).

70. Frevert, *The Politics of Humiliation*, 3.

71. Frevert, *The Politics of Humiliation*, 4.

72. Frevert, *The Politics of Humiliation*, 4.

73. Frevert, *The Politics of Humiliation*, 5.

74. For more on the practice of lurking and its constitutive role in digital spaces, see Gina Sipley, *Just Here for the Comments: Lurking as Literacy Practice* (Bristol, UK: Bristol University Press, forthcoming).

75. Martha Nussbaum, *Hiding from Humanity: Disgust, Shame, and the Law* (Princeton, NJ: Princeton University Press, 2004).

76. Nussbaum, *Hiding from Humanity*, 230.

77. Nussbaum, *Hiding from Humanity*, 230.

78. Nussbaum, *Hiding from Humanity*, 230.

79. Elisha Lim, "The Protestant Ethic and the Spirit of Facebook: Updating Identity Economics," *Social Media + Society* 6, no. 2 (2020): 1–8.

80. Weber, *The Protestant Ethic and the Spirit of Capitalism*, 74–75.

81. Weber, *The Protestant Ethic and the Spirit of Capitalism*, 75.

82. Weber, *The Protestant Ethic and the Spirit of Capitalism*, 75.

83. Nussbaum, *Hiding from Humanity*, 232–233.

84. Jon Ronson, *So You've Been Publicly Shamed* (New York: Riverhead Books, 2015).

85. David Matthews, "Online 'Intimidation' of 'Left-Biased' Academics Spreads Worldwide," *Times Higher Education*, January 3, 2019, https://www.timeshighereducation.com/news/online-intimidation-left-biased-academics-spreads-worldwide.

86. Ronson, *So You've Been Publicly Shamed*, 276.

Chapter 5

1. Erika Ibrahim, "Ottawa Doctor Pleads for Help from the Prime Minister After Death Threat," CTV News, November 11, 2021, https://ottawa.ctvnews.ca/ottawa-doctor-pleads-for-help-from-the-prime-minister-after-death-threat-1.5662499.

2. Rory Cellan-Jones, "Coronavirus: Fake News Is Spreading Fast," BBC, February 26, 2020; Tom Warren, "British 5G Towers Are Being Set on Fire Because of Coronavirus Conspiracy Theories," The Verge, April 4, 2020, https://www.theverge.com/2020/4/4/21207927/5g-towers-burning-uk-coronavirus-conspiracy-theory-link.

3. Olga Khazan, "How a Bizarre Claim About Masks Has Lived on for Months," *The Atlantic*, October 9, 2020, https://www.theatlantic.com/politics/archive/2020/10/can-masks-make-you-sicker/616641/.

4. Bruce Y. Lee, "Newsmax Reporter Claims Covid-19 Vaccines Have 'Luciferase' to Track You," *Forbes*, November 2, 2021, https://www.forbes.com/sites/brucelee/2021/11/02/newsmax-reporter-claims-covid-19-vaccines-have-luciferase-to-track-you/.

5. Katie Camero, "No, COVID Vaccines Don't Make You Magnetic. Experts Debunk Social Media Videos," *Miami Herald*, August 3, 2021, https://www.miamiherald.com/news/coronavirus/article251955083.html.

6. Anastasia Berg, "Giorgio Agamben's Coronavirus Cluelessness," *Chronicle of Higher Education*, March 23, 2020, https://www.chronicle.com/article/giorgio-agambens-coronavirus-cluelessness/; Christopher Caldwell, "Meet the Philosopher Who Is Trying to Explain the Pandemic," *New York Times*, August 21, 2020, https://www.nytimes.com/2020/08/21/opinion/sunday/giorgio-agamben-philosophy-coronavirus.html.

7. Connor Friedersdorf, "The Conservatives Who'd Rather Die than Not Own the Libs," *The Atlantic*, September 24, 2021, https://www.theatlantic.com/ideas/archive/2021/09/breitbart-conservatives-john-nolte-vaccine/620189/.

8. Carly M. Goldstein, Eleanor J. Murray, Jennifer Beard, Alexandra M. Schnoes, and Monica L. Wang, "Science Communication in the Age of Misinformation," *Annals of Behavioral Medicine* 54, no. 12 (2020): 985–990; Jacky Habib, "Meet the Man Working to Get COVID-19 Conspiracy Theorists Banned from Social Media," Global Citizen, December 10, 2021, https://www.globalcitizen.org/en/content/worlds-best-shot-Imran-Ahmed/; Center for Countering Digital Hate, "Failure to Act: How Tech Giants Continue to Defy Calls to Rein In Vaccine Misinformation," August 2020, https://252f2edd-1c8b-49f5-9bb2-cb57bb47e4ba.filesusr.com/ugd/f4d9b9_8d23c70f0a014b3c9e2cfc334d4472dc.pdf.

9. Jennifer L. Osterhage and Katherine Rogers-Carpenter, "Combatting Misinformation Through Science Communication Training," *American Biology Teacher* 84, no. 7 (2022): 390–395.

10. Rebecca Heilweil, "Twitter Joins Facebook and YouTube in Banning Covid-19 Vaccine Misinformation," *Vox*, December 16, 2020, https://www.vox.com/recode/22179145/twitter-misinformation-covid-19-vaccines-pfizer-moderna. Note that after taking over Twitter, Musk decided to end its COVID misinformation policy. Donie O'Sullivan, "Twitter Is No Longer Enforcing Its Covid Misinformation Policy," CNN, November 29, 2022, https://www.cnn.com/2022/11/29/tech/twitter-covid-misinformation-policy/index.html.

11. Helen Innes and Martin Innes, "De-platforming Disinformation: Conspiracy Theories and Their Control," *Information, Communication and Society* 26, no. 6 (2021): 1262–1280.

12. Chris Yuill, "Forgetting and Remembering Alienation Theory," *History of the Human Sciences* 24, no. 2 (2011): 103–119.

13. Georg Wilhelm Friedrich Hegel, *Phenomenology of Spirit*, trans. Arnold V. Miller, ed. J. N. Findlay (Oxford, UK: Clarendon Press, 1977), 119–139, 294–328.

14. Georg Wilhelm Friedrich Hegel, *Lectures on the Philosophy of World History*, trans. Hugh Barr Nisbet, ed. Duncan Forbes, Cambridge Studies in the History and Theory of Politics (Cambridge, UK: Cambridge University Press, 1975); Georg Wilhelm Friedrich Hegel, *Lectures on the Philosophy of Religion: The Lectures of 1827*, ed. Peter Hodgson (Berkeley: University of California Press, 2021).

15. Karl Marx, *Economic and Philosophic Manuscripts of 1844*, trans. and ed. Martin Milligan (Mineola, NY: Dover, 2007), 67–83.

16. As many critics have noted, this third conception of alienation implies not just a human-animal dualism but more importantly a straightforward hierarchy of humanity over animality. Marx here falls back upon the residual anthropocentrism and species narcissism so characteristic of Christian theology and Renaissance humanism. For a thorough critique of this unfortunate, though by no means essential, feature of Marx's theory of capital and alienation, see Ted Benton, "Humanism = Speciesism: Marx on Humans and Animals," *Radical Philosophy* 50 (1988): 4–18; reprinted in Ted Benton, *Natural Relations: Ecology, Animal Rights, and Social Justice* (London: Verso, 1993), 23–57.

17. Marx, *Economic and Philosophic Manuscripts*, 76–77, 80.

18. Charles Taylor, "Atomism," in *Essays in Honour of C. B. Macpherson*, ed. Alkis Kontos (Toronto: University of Toronto Press, 1979).

19. Thomas Hobbes and W. G. Pogson Smith, *Leviathan* (Oxford, UK: Clarendon Press, 1965), 94–95.

20. Hobbes, *Leviathan*, x.

21. Hobbes, *Leviathan*, 96–97.

22. John Locke, *Two Treatises of Government and A Letter Concerning Toleration*, ed. Ian Shapiro (New Haven, CT: Yale University Press, 2003), 111.

23. Locke, *Two Treatises*, 111.

24. Locke, *Two Treatises*, 112.

25. Charles Taylor, *Modern Social Imaginaries* (Durham, NC: Duke University Press, 2004).

26. The classic statement of the distinction between *Gemeinschaft* and *Gesellschaft* is Ferdinand Tönnies, *Community and Society* (Mineola, NY: Dover, 2002).

27. C. B. Macpherson, *The Political Theory of Possessive Individualism* (Oxford, UK: Oxford University Press, 1962).

28. Taylor, *Modern Social Imaginaries*.

29. See, for example, Jean M. Twenge, "Have Smartphones Destroyed a Generation?," *The Atlantic*, September 2017, https://www.theatlantic.com/magazine/archive/2017/09/has-the-smartphone-destroyed-a-generation/534198/. See also Jean M. Twenge, *iGen: Why Today's Super-Connected Kids Are Growing Up Less Rebellious, More Tolerant, Less Happy—and Completely Unprepared for Adulthood—and What That Means for the Rest of Us* (New York: Simon and Schuster, 2017).

30. John T. Cacioppo and Stephanie Cacioppo, "The Growing Problem of Loneliness," *The Lancet* 391, no. 10119 (2018): 426.

31. Gillian Orr, "Britain Has Been Voted the Loneliness Capital of Europe—So How Did We Become So Isolated?," *The Independent*, July 3, 2014, https://www.independent.co.uk/life-style/health-and-families/features/britain-has-been-voted-the-loneliness-capital-of-eur ope-so-how-did-we-become-so-isolated-9566617.html; Ceylan Yeginsu, "U.K. Appoints a Minister for Loneliness," *New York Times*, January 17, 2018, https://www.nytimes.com/2018/01/17/world/europe/uk-britain-loneliness.html.

32. Fay Bound Alberti, *A Biography of Loneliness: The History of an Emotion* (Oxford, UK: Oxford University Press, 2019).

33. Alberti, *A Biography of Loneliness*, 18.

34. Samuel Johnson, *A Dictionary of the English Language: An Anthology*, ed. David Crystal (London: Penguin, 2006), 154.

35. Alberti, *A Biography of Loneliness*, 21.

36. Alberti, *A Biography of Loneliness*, 19–21.

37. Alberti, *A Biography of Loneliness*, 31.

38. Alberti here draws from Taylor's historical account of this inward turn. See Charles Taylor, *Sources of the Self: The Making of Modern Identity* (Cambridge, MA: Harvard University Press, 1992).

39. Fay Bound Alberti, "This 'Modern Epidemic': Loneliness as an Emotion Cluster and a Neglected Subject in the History of Emotions," *Emotion Review* 10, no. 3 (2018): 242–254.

40. Alberti, *A Biography of Loneliness*, 34.

41. Because of its exclusive focus on the mind, psychoanalysis has met significant criticism from trauma specialists who regard the psychoanalytic method, along with much of modern psychiatry and psychology generally, as predicated upon a badly antiquated mind-body dualism. See, for example, Bessel van der Kolk, *The Body Keeps the Score: Brain, Mind, and Body in The Healing of Trauma* (New York: Penguin, 2015), 232–239.

42. Mary Shelley, *Frankenstein: The 1818 Text* (New York: Penguin, 2018), 135.

43. T. S. Eliot, *The Cocktail Party* (New York: Harcourt Brace, 1978), 134.

44. For an insightful commentary on the nightmare of solipsism as a backdrop for modern theorizing about communication, see John Durham Peters, *Speaking into the Air: A History of the Idea of Communication* (Chicago: University of Chicago Press, 1999), 84–85, 88–89.

45. Virginia Woolf, *Mrs. Dalloway*, ed. Elaine Showalter (New York: Penguin, 2021), 5.

46. Virginia Woolf, *A Writer's Diary* (New York: Houghton Mifflin Harcourt, 1981), 129.

47. Woolf, *A Writer's Diary*, 129.

48. Hans Herlof Grelland, "Edvard Munch: The Painter of *The Scream* and His Relation to Kierkegaard," in *Kierkegaard's Influence on Literature, Criticism, and Art: Tome III: Sweden and Norway*, ed. Jon Stewart (Surrey, UK: Ashgate, 2013), 177–193.

49. David J. Chalif, "The Death of Casagemas: Early Picasso, the Blue Period, Mortality, and Redemption," *Neurosurgery* 61, no. 2 (2007): 404–417; Harold P. Blum, "Picasso's Prolonged Adolescence, His Blue Period, and Blind Figures," in *Art in Psychoanalysis*, ed. Gabriela Golstein (London: Routledge, 2021), 39–55.

50. Gail Levin, "Edward Hopper's Loneliness," *Social Research: An International Quarterly* 88, no. 3 (2021): 747–770; Tom Slater, "Fear of the City 1882–1967: Edward Hopper and the Discourse of Anti-urbanism," *Social and Cultural Geography* 3, no. 2 (2002): 135–154.

51. Hannah Arendt, *The Origins of Totalitarianism* (New York: Harcourt, 1971), 460.

52. Arendt, *The Origins of Totalitarianism*, 461–466.

53. Arendt, *The Origins of Totalitarianism*, 470–471.

54. Arendt, *The Origins of Totalitarianism*, 471.

55. Arendt, *The Origins of Totalitarianism*, 474.

56. George Herbert Mead and Charles W. Morris, *Mind, Self, and Society* (Chicago: University of Chicago Press, 2015).

57. Arendt, *The Origins of Totalitarianism*, 475. Arendt's distinction between *homo faber* and *animal laborans* is presented in fuller detail in *The Human Condition*, 2nd ed. (Chicago: University of Chicago Press, 1998), 144–158. Although Arendt critiques Marx for what she regards as his overtly subjectivist thinking, it is impossible to overlook the influence of Marx's theory of alienation upon Arendt's description of loneliness.

58. Arendt, *The Origins of Totalitarianism*, 475.

59. Arendt, *The Origins of Totalitarianism*, 477.

60. Alasdair MacIntyre, *After Virtue: A Study in Moral Theory* (Notre Dame, IN: University of Notre Dame Press, 1984).

61. MacIntyre, *After Virtue*, 217.

62. David Carr, *Time, Narrative, and History* (Bloomington: Indiana University Press, 1986), 87.

63. Carr, *Time, Narrative, and History*, 87–88.

64. Carr, *Time, Narrative, and History*, 88.

65. Carr, *Time, Narrative, and History*, 97.

66. MacIntyre, *After Virtue*, 217.

67. James Sosnoski, "Hyper-Readers and Their Reading Engines," in *Passions, Pedagogies, and Twenty-First Century Technologies*, ed. Gail E. Hawisher and Cynthia L. Selfe (Urbana, IL: National Council of Teachers of English, 1999), 161–177; N. Katherine Hayles, "Hyper and Deep Attention: The Generational Divide in Cognitive Modes," *Profession*, 2007, 187–199; N. Katherine Hayles, "How We Read: Close, Hyper, Machine," *ADE Bulletin* 150, no. 18 (2010): 62–79; N. Katherine Hayles, *How We Think: Digital Media and Contemporary Technogenesis* (Chicago: University of Chicago Press, 2012).

68. Mattha Busby, "Social Media Copies Gambling Methods 'To Create Psychological Cravings,'" *The Guardian*, May 8, 2018, https://www.theguardian.com/technology/2018/may/08/social-media-copies-gambling-methods-to-create-psychological-cravings.

69. Hailey G. Holmgren and Sarah M. Coyne, "Can't Stop Scrolling! Pathological Use of Social Networking Sites in Emerging Adulthood," *Addiction Research and Theory* 25, no. 5 (2017): 375–382; Simone Cunningham, Chloe C. Hudson, and Kate Harkness, "Social Media and Depression Symptoms: A Meta-analysis," *Research on Child and Adolescent Psychopathology* 49, no. 2 (2021): 241–253.

70. Fredric Jameson, *Postmodernism: or, The Cultural Logic of Late Capitalism* (Durham, NC: Duke University Press, 1991), 26.

71. Jameson, *Postmodernism*, 26.

72. Jameson, *Postmodernism*, 27. Jameson's argument is similar to that of Jean Baudrillard; see Baudrillard's *In the Shadow of the Silent Majorities, or, The End of the Social and Other Essays* (Cambridge, MA: MIT Press, 1983).

73. Jameson, *Postmodernism*, 27.

74. Jameson, *Postmodernism*, 27.

75. Jameson, *Postmodernism*, 27.

76. Edmund Burke, *A Philosophical Enquiry into the Sublime and Beautiful: And Other Pre-Revolutionary Writings*, ed. David Womersley (New York: Penguin, 1998); Immanuel Kant, *Observations on the Feeling of the Beautiful and Sublime* (Berkeley, CA: University of California Press, 1960).

77. Jameson, *Postmodernism*, 34.

78. Carr, *Time, Narrative, and History*, 93.

79. As Donovan Schaefer insightfully observes, conspiracy theory "clicks" for the believer. Conspiracy theory is less a matter of understanding than of feeling. When things click, the believer feels reassured. Conspiracy theorists, as Schaefer argues, are addicted to the clicks. See Schaefer's *Wild Experiment: Feeling, Science, and Secularism After Darwin* (Durham, NC: Duke University Press, 2022), 33–56.

80. See, for example, Ali Breland, "How Lin Wood and His QAnon Fans Tried to Force a Hospital to Use Ivermectin," *Mother Jones*, September 13, 2021, https://www.motherjones.com/politics/2021/09/lin-wood-veronica-wolski-ivermectin/.

81. Adrienne LaFrance, "The Prophecies of Q," *The Atlantic*, June 2020, https://www.theatlantic.com/magazine/archive/2020/06/qanon-nothing-can-stop-what-is-coming/610567/; see also the interview with LaFrance in Dave Davies, "Journalist Enters the World of QAnon: 'It's Almost Like a Bad Spy Novel,'" NPR, August 20, 2020, https://www.npr.org/2020/08/20/904237192/journalist-enters-the-world-of-qanon-it-s-almost-like-a-bad-spy-novel.

82. Michael Barkun, "Failed Prophecies Won't Stop Trump's True Believers," *Foreign Policy*, November 8, 2018, https://foreignpolicy.com/2018/11/08/failed-prophecies-wont-stop-trumps-true-believers/; Paris Martineau, "I Helped Uncover QAnon. Failed Prophecies Won't Kill It," The Information, January 23, 2021, https://www.theinformation.com/articles/i-helped-uncover-qanon-failed-prophecies-wont-kill-it.

83. Mike Rothschild, *The Storm Is upon Us: How QAnon Became a Movement, Cult, and Conspiracy Theory of Everything* (New York: Melville House, 2021), 141–158, 186.

84. Justin Ling, "5G and QAnon: How Conspiracy Theorists Steered Canada's Anti-vaccine Trucker Protest," *The Guardian*, February 8, 2022, https://www.theguardian.com/world/2022/feb/08/canada-ottawa-trucker-protest-extremist-qanon-neo-nazi.

85. Zack Beauchamp, "The Canadian Trucker Convoy Is an Unpopular Uprising," *Vox*, February 11, 2022, https://www.vox.com/policy-and-politics/22926134/canada-trucker-freedom-convoy-protest-ottawa.

86. Simon Little, "Vancouver Hospital Workers Told Not to Wear Scrubs, ID Outside During COVID-19 Protests," Global News, February 4, 2022, https://globalnews.ca/news/8597044/vancouver-hospital-workers-told-not-to-wear-scrubs-id-outside-during-covid-19-protests/.

87. Michael Jensen and Sheehan Kane, "QAnon Offenders in the United States," National Consortium for the Study of Terrorism and Responses to Terrorism, February, 2021, https://www.start.umd.edu/pubs/START_PIRUS_QAnon_Feb2021.pdf.

88. Jensen and Kane, "QAnon Offenders in the United States."

89. Sophia Moskalenko and Mia Bloom, "Why QAnon Followers Are Like Opioid Addicts, and Why That Matters," NBC News, August 22, 2021, https://www.nbcnews.com/think/opinion/why-qanon-followers-are-opioid-addicts-why-matters-ncna1277323. On the relationship between trauma and addiction, see Gabor Maté, *In the Realm of Hungry Ghosts: Close Encounters with Addiction* (Toronto: Alfred Knopf, 2008).

90. This is the recommendation in Mia Bloom and Sophia Moskalenko, *Pastels and Pedophiles: Inside the Mind of QAnon* (Stanford, CA: Stanford University Press, 2021).

Chapter 6

1. Neil Postman, *Amusing Ourselves to Death: Public Discourse in the Age of Show Business* (New York: Penguin, 1985), 155.
2. Postman, *Amusing Ourselves to Death*, 161.
3. Postman, *Amusing Ourselves to Death*, 161.
4. Postman, *Amusing Ourselves to Death*, 162.
5. Alasdair MacIntyre, *After Virtue: A Study in Moral Theory* (Notre Dame, IN: University of Notre Dame Press, 1984), 256.
6. MacIntyre's critique here concerns vanguard party revolutionary strategy, which he contends relies not on collective moral principles but rather upon the private will and individual judgment of self-appointed revolutionary leaders. See MacIntyre, *After Virtue*, 256–263. See also Rosa Luxemburg, *The Russian Revolution and Leninism or Marxism?* (Ann Arbor: University of Michigan Press, 1961) and Maurice Brinton, *The Bolsheviks and Workers Control* (Montreal: Black Rose Books, 1972).
7. MacIntyre, *After Virtue*, 263.
8. Robert Brandom, *A Spirit of Trust: A Reading of Hegel's* Phenomenology (Cambridge, MA: Harvard University Press, 2019).
9. Immanuel Kant, *Prolegomena to Any Future Metaphysics*, ed. Gary Hatfield (Cambridge, UK: Cambridge University Press, 2004), 34–45.
10. Immanuel Kant, *Critique of Pure Reason*, trans. and ed. Paul Guyer and Allen Wood (Cambridge, UK: Cambridge University Press, 1998).
11. Georg Wilhelm Friedrich Hegel, *The Science of Logic*, trans. and ed. George Di Giovanni (Cambridge, MA: Cambridge University Press, 2010), 2:507–753; Georg Wilhelm Friedrich Hegel, *Phenomenology of Spirit*, trans. A. V. Miller, ed. J. N. Findlay (Oxford, UK: Oxford University Press, 1977).
12. Brandom, *A Spirit of Trust*, 636.
13. Amartya Sen, *The Idea of Justice* (Cambridge, MA: Harvard University Press, 2009).
14. Brandom, *A Spirit of Trust*, 560–569; Robert Brandom, "Reason, Genealogy, and the Hermeneutics of Magnanimity," Howison Lectures in Philosophy Series, University of California, Berkley, 2013, https://sites.pitt.edu/~rbrandom/Texts/Reason_Geneal ogy_and_the_Hermeneutics_of.pdf.
15. Friedrich Nietzsche, *The Twilight of the Idols and the Anti-Christ: or How to Philosophize with a Hammer*, trans. R. J. Hollingdale, ed. Michael J. Tanner (New York: Penguin, 1990).
16. Michel Foucault, "Nietzsche, Genealogy, History," in Michel Foucault, *The Foucault Reader*, ed. Paul Rabinow (New York: Pantheon, 1984), 76–100; Michel Foucault, *Discipline and Punish: The Birth of the Prison*, trans. Alan Sheridan (New York: Vintage, 1977); Gilles Deleuze and Félix Guattari, *Anti-Oedipus* (London: Bloomsbury, 2004); Edward W. Said, *Orientalism* (New York: Vintage, 2014); Judith Butler, *Gender Trouble: Feminism and the Subversion of Reality* (London: Routledge, 1999); Daniel Dennett, *Darwin's Dangerous Idea: Evolution and the Meaning of Life* (New York: Simon and Schuster, 1995).
17. Paul Ricoeur, *The Conflict of Interpretations: Essays in Hermeneutics* (Evanston, IL: Northwestern University Press, 2007), 331.
18. Brandom, *A Spirit of Trust*, 555.
19. Brandom, *A Spirit of Trust*, 473.
20. The concept of a universal acid here is taken from Dennett, *Darwin's Dangerous Idea*, 63.
21. Nietzsche, *The Twilight of the Idols*; Friedrich Nietzsche, *The Birth of Tragedy: Out of the Spirit of Music*, ed. Michael J. Tanner (New York: Penguin, 1993). For commentary on Nietzsche's antagonistic relationship to Socrates, see Werner J. Dannhauser, *Nietzsche's View of Socrates* (Ithaca, NY: Cornell University Press, 2019).
22. Nietzsche writes, "Socrates belonged, in his origins, to the lowest orders: Socrates was rabble. One knows, one sees for oneself, how ugly he was. But ugliness, an objection itself, is among the Greeks almost a refutation. Was Socrates Greek at all?" For the full condescending reflection, see Nietzsche, *The Twilight of the Idols*, 40–41.

23. Stanley Fish, "Interpreting the Variorum," *Critical Inquiry* 2, no. 3 (1976): 465–485.

24. Stanley Fish, *Is There a Text in This Class? The Authority of Interpretive Communities* (Cambridge, MA: Harvard University Press, 1980).

25. Fish, *Is There a Text in This Class?*, 318.

26. Stanley Fish, *The Trouble with Principle* (Cambridge, MA: Harvard University Press, 1999); Stanley Fish, *There's No Such Thing as Free Speech: And It's A Good Thing, Too* (Oxford, UK: Oxford University Press, 1994); Stanley Fish, "Boutique Multiculturalism, or Why Liberals Are Incapable of Thinking About Hate Speech," *Critical Inquiry* 23, no. 2 (1997): 378–395; Stanley Fish, "Liberalism Doesn't Exist," *Duke Law Journal* 1987, no. 6 (1987): 997–1001.

27. Fish, *The Trouble with Principle*, 2.

28. Stanley Fish, "Faith Before Reason," in *The Trouble with Principle* (Cambridge, MA: Harvard University Press, 1999), 263–275.

29. Stanley Fish, "Citing Chapter and Verse: Which Scripture is the Right One," *New York Times*, March 26, 2012.

30. Stanley Fish, "Why We Can't All Just Get Along," in *The Trouble with Principle* (Cambridge, MA: Harvard University Press, 1999), 243–262.

31. For a perceptive critique of Fish, see Martha Nussbaum, "Sophistry About Conventions," *New Literary History* 17, no. 1 (1985): 129–139.

32. Mark E. Warren, ed., *Democracy and Trust* (Cambridge, MA: Cambridge University Trust, 1999).

33. Haley Talbot and Sahil Kapur, "Hard-Right Republicans Forming New Caucus to Protect 'Anglo-Saxon Political Traditions,'" NBC News, April 16, 2021, https://www.nbcnews.com/politics/congress/hard-right-republicans-forming-new-caucus-protect-anglo-saxon-political-n1264338.

34. Raina Lipsitz, *The Rise of a New Left: How Young Radicals Are Shaping the Future of American Politics* (London: Verso, 2022); Ilhan Omar, *This Is What America Looks Like: My Journey from Refugee to Congresswoman* (London: C. Hurst, 2020).

35. Christophe Jaffrelot, *Hindu Nationalism: A Reader* (Princeton, NJ: Princeton University Press, 2007); Lars Tore Flåten, *Hindu Nationalism, History and Identity in India: Narrating a Hindu Past Under the BJP* (New York: Routledge, 2016).

36. David Taylor, "The Indian National Congress: A Hundred-Year Perspective," *Journal of the Royal Asiatic Society* 119, no. 2 (1987): 289–305.

37. Charles Taylor, "Brandom's Hegel," in *Reading Brandom: On A Spirit of Trust*, ed. Gilles Bouché (New York: Routledge, 2020), 206.

38. Peter Wehner, "Trump Supporters Think They're in a Fight to the Death," *The Atlantic*, August 1, 2022, https://www.theatlantic.com/ideas/archive/2022/08/trump-america-first-speech-analysis-gop/671004/.

39. On the political implications of Nietzsche's thought, see Fredrick Appel, *Nietzsche Contra Democracy* (Ithaca, NY: Cornell University Press, 2019).

40. Brandom, "Reason, Genealogy, and the Hermeneutics of Magnanimity."

41. It is worth noting here that Nietzsche defines truth through the metaphor of metal. As he puts it, truth can be understood as "illusions about which one has forgotten that this is what they are; metaphors which are worn out and without sensuous power; coins which have lost their pictures and now matter only as metal, no longer as coins." That metal should function as a metaphor for truth indicates that, for Nietzsche, concepts *do* change, but only because their origins have been forgotten and enshrouded in myth, not because they have been publicly negotiated. See Nietzsche, "On Truth and Lies in An Extra-Moral Sense," in Friedrich Nietzsche, *The Portable Nietzsche*, ed. Walter Kaufmann (New York: Penguin, 1976), 42–46.

42. Brandom, *A Spirit of Trust*, 235–261; Brandom, "Some Pragmatist Themes in Hegel's Idealism: Negotiation and Administration in Hegel's Account of the Structure and Content of Conceptual Norms," *European Journal of Philosophy* 7, no. 2 (1999): 164–189.

43. See Kant's discussion of the derivation of concepts in *Critique of Pure Reason* (London: Penguin, 2008), 94–169.

44. Brandom, *A Spirit of Trust*, 298–305.

45. Brandom, *A Spirit of Trust*, 133–197.

46. This tension is what Jean-Luc Nancy, in his short study of Hegel, refers to as "restlessness." See Jean-Luc Nancy, *Hegel: The Restlessness of the Negative* (Minneapolis: University of Minnesota Press, 2002).

47. Chilton Williamson, *American Suffrage: From Property to Democracy, 1760–1860* (Princeton, NJ: Princeton University Press, 1960), 138–157.

48. On Black political activism in shaping the public understanding of equality, see Martha S. Jones, *Birthright Citizens: A History of Race and Rights in Antebellum America* (Cambridge, UK: Cambridge University Press, 2018).

49. On the role of suffragist journalism and media activism in shaping the public understanding of equality, see Linda Steiner, Carolyn Kitch, and Brooke Kroeger, eds., *Front Pages, Front Lines: Media and the Fight for Women's Suffrage* (Urbana: University of Illinois Press, 2020).

50. Judith Baer, *Equality Under the Constitution: Reclaiming the Fourteenth Amendment* (Ithaca, NY: Cornell University Press, 2018).

51. On the instability of the idea of equality, see Amartya Sen, "Equality of What?," in *Inequality Reexamined* (Cambridge, MA: Harvard University Press, 1992), 12–28, and Celeste Michelle Condit and John Louis Lucaites, *Crafting Equality: America's Anglo-African Word* (Chicago: University of Chicago Press, 1993).

52. Italo Testa, "Hegelian Pragmatism and Social Emancipation: An Interview with Robert Brandom," *Constellations* 10, no. 4 (2003): 554–570.

53. Robert Brandom, *Making it Explicit: Reasoning, Representing, and Discursive Commitment* (Cambridge, MA: Harvard University Press, 1994).

54. Brandom, *A Spirit of Trust*, 583–635.

55. Brandom, *A Spirit of Trust*, 547.

56. Brandom, *A Spirit of Trust*, 547–548; Brandom, "Reason, Genealogy, and the Hermeneutics of Magnanimity."

57. Jean-Jaques Rousseau, *Emile, or, On Education*, trans. and ed. Allan David Bloom (New York: Penguin, 1991); Immanuel Kant, "Lectures on Pedagogy," in Immanuel Kant, *Anthropology, History, and Education*, ed. Robert B. Louden and Günter Zöller (Cambridge, UK: Cambridge University Press, 2007), 434–485; Friedrich Schleiermacher, Norm Friesen, and Karsten Kenklies, *F. D. E. Schleiermacher's Outlines of the Art of Education: A Translation and Discussion* (New York: Peter Lang, 2023); Emile Durkheim, *Moral Education: A Study in the Theory and Application of the Sociology of Education* (New York: Free Press, 1973); Jane Addams, *Jane Addams on Education*, ed. Ellen Condliffe Lagemann (New York: Routledge, 2017); John Dewey, *Democracy and Education: An Introduction to the Philosophy of Education* (New York: Macmillan, 1916).

58. Paulo Freire, *Pedagogy of the Oppressed* (New York: Penguin, 2017); bell hooks, *Teaching to Transgress: Education as the Practice of Freedom* (New York: Routledge, 1994); Jaques Rancière, *The Ignorant Schoolmaster: Five Lessons in Intellectual Emancipation*, trans. Kristin Ross (Stanford, CA: Stanford University Press, 1991); Henry Giroux, *Theory and Resistance in Education: Towards a Pedagogy for the Opposition* (Westport, CT: Bergin & Garvey, 2001); Stanley Aronowitz, *Against Schooling: For an Education That Matters* (New York: Routledge, 2015).

59. Durkheim, *Moral Education*.

60. Dewey, *Democracy and Education*.

61. Freire, *Pedagogy of the Oppressed*, 44–59.

62. Freire, *Pedagogy of the Oppressed*, 54.

63. Freire, *Pedagogy of the Oppressed*, 57.

64. Freire, *Pedagogy of the Oppressed*, 60–66.

65. Freire, *Pedagogy of the Oppressed*, 62.

66. Freire, *Pedagogy of the Oppressed*, 63.
67. Freire, *Pedagogy of the Oppressed*, 63.
68. Freire, *Pedagogy of the Oppressed*, 63–64.
69. Freire, *Pedagogy of the Oppressed*, 64.
70. Freire, *Pedagogy of the Oppressed*, 64.
71. Freire, *Pedagogy of the Oppressed*, 65.
72. hooks, *Teaching to Transgress*, 2.
73. hooks, *Teaching to Transgress*, 3.
74. hooks, *Teaching to Transgress*, 3–6.
75. hooks, *Teaching to Transgress*, 8.
76. hooks, *Teaching to Transgress*, 158.
77. hooks, *Teaching to Transgress*, 7.
78. hooks, *Teaching to Transgress*, 7.
79. hooks, *Teaching to Transgress*, 154.

Conclusion

1. The most egregious case of political manipulation of Facebook's algorithms involves the now-defunct digital consulting firm Cambridge Analytica, which assisted Donald Trump's presidential campaign in the 2016 U.S. general election. For an account of the Cambridge Analytica scandal, see Christopher Wylie, *Mindf*ck: Cambridge Analytica and the Plot to Break America* (New York: Random House, 2019).
2. *The Social Dilemma*, directed by Jeff Orlowski (Boulder, CO: Exposure Labs, 2020).
3. Richard Seymour, "No, Social Media Isn't Destroying Civilization," *Jacobin*, September 22, 2020, https://jacobin.com/2020/09/the-social-dilemma-review-media-documentary.
4. Christian Fuchs, "Social Media and the Public Sphere," *tripleC* 12, no. 1 (2014): 57–101.
5. Philip M. Napoli, *Social Media and the Public Interest: Media Regulation in the Disinformation Age* (New York: Columbia University Press, 2019).
6. Daniel Trottier, *Social Media as Surveillance: Rethinking Visibility in a Converging World* (London: Routledge, 2016); Sebastian Sevignani, *Privacy and Capitalism in the Age of Social Media* (New York: Routledge, 2015).
7. Lisa Schirch, ed., *Social Media Impacts on Conflict and Democracy: The Techtonic Shift* (New York: Routledge, 2021); Mette Mortensen and Ally McCrow-Young, eds., *Social Media Images and Conflicts* (New York: Routledge, 2022).
8. Chris Hughes, "It's Time to Break Up Facebook," *New York Times*, May 9, 2019, https://www.nytimes.com/2019/05/09/opinion/sunday/chris-hughes-facebook-zuckerberg.html.
9. Philip M. Napoli, *Social Media and the Public Interest: Media Regulation in the Disinformation Age* (New York: Columbia University Press, 2019).
10. Nick Srnicek, *Platform Capitalism* (New York: John Wiley & Sons, 2017).
11. Evan Malmgren, "Socialized Media: What Will It Take to Remake Facebook and Twitter in the Public's Interest?," *The Baffler*, September 19, 2018, https://thebaffler.com/latest/socialized-media-malmgren.
12. Meagan Day, "Unfortunately, We Can't Log Off," *Jacobin*, December 6, 2018, https://www.jacobinmag.com/2018/12/log-off-social-media-twitter-organizing-facebook.
13. Monideepa Tarafdar, "Social Media: Six Steps to Take Back Control," The Conversation, May 4, 2018, https://theconversation.com/social-media-six-steps-to-take-back-control-95814.
14. Jaron Lanier, *Ten Arguments for Deleting Your Social Media Accounts Right Now* (New York: Henry Holt, 2018); Benjamin Fong, "Log Off," *Jacobin*, November 29, 2018, https://www.jacobinmag.com/2018/11/log-off-facebook-twitter-social-media-addiction.
15. Jonathan Vanian, "Facebook Scrambles to Escape Stock's Death Spiral as Users Flee, Sales Drop," CNBC, September 30, 2022, https://www.cnbc.com/2022/09/30/facebook-scrambles-to-escape-death-spiral-as-users-flee-sales-drop.html.

16. Ramenda Cyrus, "Why Meta's Virtual Worlds Are Failing," *American Prospect*, October 24, 2022, https://prospect.org/culture/why-metas-virtual-worlds-are-failing/.

17. Aimee Picchi, "Meta's Value Has Plunged by $700 Billion. Wall Street Calls It a 'Train Wreck,'" CBS News, October 28, 2022, https://www.cbsnews.com/news/meta-stock-down-earnings-700-billion-in-lost-value/; Jon Haworth, "Mark Zuckerberg Announces Meta Will Lay Off 11,000 Employees," ABC News, November 9, 2022, https://abcnews.go.com/Business/mark-zuckerberg-announces-meta-layoff-11000-employees/story?id=92974784.

18. Scott Nover, "A Detailed Timeline of Elon Musk Buying Twitter," *Quartz*, May 20, 2022, https://qz.com/2167563/an-annotated-history-of-elon-musk-buying-twitter.

19. Quint Forgey, "'Extremely Important to the Future of Civilization': Musk Describes a Twitter Remade in His Own Image," Politico, April 14, 2022, https://www.politico.com/news/2022/04/14/elon-musk-offer-buy-twitter-00025229.

20. Forgey, "'Extremely Important to the Future of Civilization.'"

21. Michel Martin, "Elon Musk Calls Himself a Free Speech Absolutist. What Could Twitter Look Like Under His Leadership?," NPR, October 8, 2022, https://www.npr.org/2022/10/08/1127689351/elon-musk-calls-himself-a-free-speech-absolutist-what-could-twitter-look-like-un.

22. Kate Conger and Lauren Hirsch, "Elon Musk Completes $44 Billion Deal to Own Twitter," *New York Times*, October 27, 2022, https://www.nytimes.com/2022/10/27/technology/elon-musk-twitter-deal-complete.html; Will Daniel, "Elon Musk's $44 Billion Twitter Purchase Is 'One of the Most Overpaid Tech Acquisitions in History,' Wedbush's Dan Ives Says. Twitter's Fair Value Is Only $25 Billion," *Fortune*, October 27, 2022, https://fortune.com/2022/10/27/elon-musk-twitter-purchase-most-overpaid-tech-history-dan-ives-wedbush/.

23. Maya Yang, "Elon Musk Makes Splashy Visit to Twitter Headquarters Carrying Sink," *The Guardian*, October 26, 2022, https://www.theguardian.com/technology/2022/oct/26/elon-musk-twitter-visit-sink.

24. Joseph Bernstein, "Elon Musk Has the World's Strangest Social Calendar," *New York Times*, October 11, 2022, https://www.nytimes.com/2022/10/11/style/elon-musk-social-calendar.html.

25. Ryan Mac, "Facing a Tide of Criticism, Elon Musk Is Tweeting Through It," *New York Times*, November 7, 2022, https://www.nytimes.com/2022/11/07/technology/elon-musk-twitter-spree.html.

26. Elon Musk (@elonmusk), "Comedy is now legal on Twitter," Twitter, October 28, 2022, https://twitter.com/elonmusk/status/1586104694421659648?lang=en.

27. Dan Milmo, "How 'Free Speech Absolutist' Elon Musk Would Transform Twitter," *The Guardian*, April 14, 2022, https://www.theguardian.com/technology/2022/apr/14/how-free-speech-absolutist-elon-musk-would-transform-twitter.

28. Jon Blistein, "Twitter Bans Sarah Silverman, Kathy Griffin for Parodying Alleged Comedy Lover Elon Musk," *Rolling Stone*, November 7, 2022, https://www.rollingstone.com/culture/culture-news/twitter-suspends-accounts-parodying-elon-musk-1234625867/; Philip Drost, "This Cartoonist Was Banned from Twitter for Impersonating Elon Musk," CBC, November 11, 2022, https://www.cbc.ca/radio/day6/elon-musk-twitter-impersonations-1.6648071.

29. Lora Kolodny, "Elon Musk Bans Impersonation Without Parody Label on Twitter Raising Questions About Free Speech Commitment," CNBC, November 7, 2022, https://www.cnbc.com/2022/11/07/elon-musk-unlabeled-twitter-parody-accounts-risk-permanent-suspension.html.

30. Jason Zinoman, "Hey, Elon Musk, Comedy Doesn't Want to Be Legal," *New York Times*, November 11, 2022, https://www.nytimes.com/2022/11/11/arts/elon-musk-twitter-parody.html.

31. Chris Isidore, "Elon Musk Will Have to Pay Three Fired Twitter Executives Nearly $200 Million," CNN, October 28, 2022, https://www.cnn.com/2022/10/28/tech/elon-musk-twitter-golden-parachutes.

32. Charisma Madarang, "Elon Musk to Slash 50 Percent of Twitter Staff, Remaining Employees to Return to Office," *Rolling Stone,* November 2, 2022, https://www.rollingst one.com/culture/culture-news/elon-musk-slash-50-percent-twitter-staff-employees-ret urn-office-1234623653/.

33. Kurt Wagner and Edward Ludlow, "Twitter Now Asks Some Fired Workers to Please Come Back," Bloomberg, November 6, 2022, https://www.bloomberg.com/news/artic les/2022-11-06/twitter-now-asks-some-fired-workers-to-please-come-back.

34. Kurt Wagner, Kamaron Leach, and Maxwell Adler, "Musk Fires More Twitter Sales Workers After 'Hardcore' Purge," Bloomberg, November 21, 2022, https://www.bloomberg.com/ news/articles/2022-11-21/twitter-s-musk-fires-more-sales-workers-after-hardcore-purge.

35. Li Goldstein, "Elon Musk's $13 Million (?!) Lunch Problem, Explained," *Bon Appétit,* November 18, 2022, https://www.bonappetit.com/story/elon-musk-twitter-400-staff-lunches.

36. James Clayton and Peter Hoskins, "Twitter Locks Staff Out of Offices Until Next Week," BBC, November 18, 2022, https://www.bbc.com/news/business-63672307.

37. Sara Morrison, "The Ridiculous but Important Twitter Check Mark Fiasco, Explained," Vox, November 11, 2022, https://www.vox.com/recode/2022/11/4/23438917/twitter-verifications-blue-check-elon-musk.

38. Ryan Mac, Benjamin Mullin, Kate Conger, and Mike Isaac, "A Verifiable Mess: Twitter Users Create Havoc by Impersonating Brands," *New York Times,* November 14, 2022, https://www.nytimes.com/2022/11/11/technology/twitter-blue-fake-accounts.html.

39. Kevin Jiang, "Eli Lilly Loses Billions in Market Cap After 'Verified' Twitter Impostor Promises Free Insulin," *Toronto Star,* November 11, 2022, https://www.thestar.com/busin ess/technology/2022/11/11/eli-lilly-loses-billions-in-market-cap-after-verified-twitter-impostor-promises-free-insulin.html.

40. Nivedita Balu, "Musk Halts Twitter's Coveted Blue Check amid Proliferation of Imposters," Reuters, November 12, 2022, https://www.reuters.com/technology/musk-says-his-com panies-will-remain-well-positioned-2023-2022-11-11/.

41. Corinne Reichert, Queenie Wong, and Sean Keane, "Twitter Briefly Added Gray Check Marks for Official Accounts. Then Musk 'Killed It,'" CNET, November 9, 2022, https:// www.cnet.com/news/social-media/twitter-briefly-adds-gray-check-marks-for-official-accounts-until-elon-musk-killed-it/.

42. Victoria Bekiempis, "Musk Posts Baseless Conspiracy Theory About Paul Pelosi Attack on Twitter," *The Guardian,* October 30, 2022, https://www.theguardian.com/technology/ 2022/oct/30/elon-musk-twitter-baseless-conspiracy-theory-paul-pelosi-attack.

43. Ariel Zilber, "Elon Musk Trolls New York Times with 'False News' Tweet," *New York Post,* October 31, 2022, https://nypost.com/2022/10/31/elon-musk-trolls-new-york-times-with-false-news-tweet/.

44. Ryan Lizza, "Sen. Markey vs. Musk's Twitter: The Freed Bird Might Get Its Wings Clipped," Politico, November 18, 2022, https://www.politico.com/news/2022/11/18/ed-markey-deep-dive-00069221.

45. Elon Musk (@elonmusk), "Ligma Johnson had it coming 🖐 ✌," Twitter, October 28, 2022, https://twitter.com/elonmusk/status/1586108809772089345.

46. Brian McGleenon, "What Is Mastodon? The 'Twitter Killer' Attracting Hundreds of Thousands After Musk's Takeover," Yahoo News, November 8, 2022, https://ca.news. yahoo.com/mastodon-twitter-killer-elon-musk-takeover-060002299.html.

47. Elon Musk (@elonmusk), "I love when people complain about Twitter . . . on Twitter 😂 😂," Twitter, November 10, 2022, https://twitter.com/elonmusk/status/159075550611 2823296.

48. Mark Maurer, "How Elon Musk's Twitter Faces Mountain of Debt, Falling Revenue and Surging Costs," *Wall Street Journal*, November 21, 2022, https://www.wsj.com/articles/how-elon-musks-twitter-faces-mountain-of-debt-falling-revenue-and-surging-costs-1166 9042132.

49. Mike Masnick, "It's Not Anyone in the Senate's Job to Save Twitter from Elon Musk," TechDirt, November 14, 2022, https://www.techdirt.com/2022/11/14/its-not-anyone-in-the-senates-job-to-save-twitter-from-elon-musk/.

50. Ben Smith, "A Top Ad Exec Says Elon Musk Is Being 'Petulant and Thoughtless,'" Semafor, November 6, 2022, https://www.semafor.com/article/11/06/2022/a-top-ad-exec-says-elon-musk-is-being-petulant-and-thoughtless.

51. Nikki McCann Ramirez, "NAACP, ADL, Other Orgs Call for Advertisers to Boycott Twitter," *Rolling Stone*, November 4, 2022, https://www.rollingstone.com/politics/polit ics-news/naacp-adl-coalition-call-for-advertisers-boycott-twitter-1234625113/.

52. Suzanne Vranica and Patience Haggin, "General Mills, Audi and Pfizer Join Growing List of Companies Pausing Twitter Ads," *Wall Street Journal*, November 3, 2023, https://www.wsj.com/articles/general-mills-audi-and-pfizer-join-growing-list-of-companies-pausing-twit ter-ads-11667507765.

53. Megan Cerullo, "Elon Musk Says Activists Want to 'Destroy Free Speech' as Advertisers Flee Twitter," CBC News, November 4, 2022, https://www.cbsnews.com/news/elon-musk-twitter-advertisers-massive-drop-in-revenue/.

54. Kelly Rissman, "Elon Musk Cautions Twitter Could Go Bankrupt Without More Cash," *Vanity Fair*, November 12, 2022, https://www.vanityfair.com/news/2022/11/elon-musk-cautions-twitter-could-go-bankrupt.

55. Drew Harwell, Taylor Lorenz, and Cat Zakrzewski, "Racist Tweets Quickly Surface After Musk Closes Twitter Deal," *Washington Post*, October 28, 2022, https://www.washingtonp ost.com/technology/2022/10/28/musk-twitter-racist-posts/.

56. Aisling Murphy, "Use of N-Word, Racial Slurs Up More than 500% on Twitter Post-Musk, Says New Report," *Toronto Star*, October 31, 2022, https://www.thestar.com/business/2022/10/31/use-of-n-word-racial-slurs-up-more-than-500-on-twitter-post-musk-says-new-report.html.

57. Sheera Frenkel and Kate Conger, "Hate Speech's Rise on Twitter Is Unprecedented, Researchers Find," *New York Times*, December 2, https://www.nytimes.com/2022/12/02/technology/twitter-hate-speech.html.

58. Jason Wilson, "Twitter Blesses Extremists with Paid 'Blue Checks,'" Southern Poverty Law Center, November 16, 2022, https://www.splcenter.org/hatewatch/2022/11/16/twitter-blesses-extremists-paid-blue-checks.

59. Melody Schreiber, "'Verified' Anti-Vax Accounts Proliferate as Twitter Struggles to Police Content," *The Guardian*, November 21, 2022, https://www.theguardian.com/technology/2022/nov/21/twitter-anti-vax-health-misinformation.

60. Matthew Gault, "FTX Founder Deepfake Offers Refund to Victims in Verified Twitter Account Scam," Vice, November 21, 2022, https://www.vice.com/en/article/v7vj9a/sam-bankman-fried-deepfake-offers-refund-to-victims-in-verified-twitter-account-scam.

61. Paul Lynch, Pete Sherlock, and Paul Bradshaw, "Scale of Abuse of Politicians on Twitter Revealed," BBC, November 9, 2022, https://www.bbc.com/news/uk-63330885.

62. Patrick McHale, "Elon Musk Opined About Buying Twitter After Babylon Bee Ban," Bloomberg, April 5, 2022, https://www.bloomberg.com/news/articles/2022-04-05/elon-musk-opined-about-buying-twitter-after-babylon-bee-ban.

63. Melissa Gira Grant, "Elon Musk's Anti-Trans Twitter Regime," *New Republic*, November 22, 2022, https://newrepublic.com/article/169112/elon-musk-anti-trans-twitter-john-br.

64. Christiano Lima, "Elon Musk Wants to 'Defeat the Spam Bots' but Faces a Free Speech Problem," *Washington Post*, April 27, 2022, https://www.washingtonpost.com/polit ics/2022/04/27/elon-musks-plan-defeat-spam-bots-has-free-speech-problem;   Noah Schachtman and Adam Rawnsley, "Musk's Beloved Twitter Polls Are Bot-Driven Bullsh!t,

Ex-Employees Say," *Rolling Stone*, December 1, 2022, https://www.rollingstone.com/cult ure/culture-news/elon-musk-twitter-polls-are-bot-driven-bullsht-1234639288/.

65. Dan Milmo, "Elon Musk Offers General Amnesty to Suspended Twitter Accounts," *The Guardian*, November 24, 2022, https://www.theguardian.com/technology/2022/nov/ 24/elon-musk-offers-general-amnesty-to-suspended-twitter-accounts.

66. Adrian Carrasquillo, "Vicente Gonzalez: Mayra Flores 'Unqualified,' a 'Pawn' of GOP," *Newsweek*, June 22, 2022, https://www.newsweek.com/vicente-gonzalez-mayra-flores-unqualified-pawn-gop-1718115.

67. Jared Gans, "Musk Predicts 'Massive Red Wave,' Teases Creation of 'Super Moderate Super PAC,'" The Hill, June 15, 2022, https://thehill.com/policy/technology/3524401-musk-teases-creating-a-super-moderate-super-pac/.

68. Kelly Garrity and Rebecca Kern, "Musk Backs Republicans Ahead of Midterms," Politico, November 7, 2022, https://www.politico.com/news/2022/11/07/elon-musk-independe nts-vote-republican-midterms-twitter-00065412.

69. Joshua Bote and Gabe Lehman, "Elon Musk Signals His Support for Ron DeSantis in 2024 on Twitter," SF Gate, November 26, 2022, https://www.sfgate.com/tech/article/musk-twitter-chaos-live-updates-17610826.php.

70. Kaitlin Lewis, "Activists Accuse Elon Musk of Banning 'Anti-Fascist Accounts' on Twitter," *Newsweek*, November 23, 2022, https://www.newsweek.com/activists-accuse-elon-musk-banning-anti-fascist-accounts-twitter-1761957.

71. Zeeshan Aleem, "Elon Musk Sees Twitter as a Political Weapon," MSNBC, November 22, 2022, https://www.msnbc.com/opinion/msnbc-opinion/elon-musk-trump-twitter-acco unt-republican-rcna57861.

72. Caroline Cauffman and Catalina Goanta, "A New Order: The Digital Services Act and Consumer Protection," *European Journal of Risk Regulation* 12, no. 4 (2021): 758–774; Jillian Deutsch, "How EU Could Frustrate Musk's Plans for Twitter," *Washington Post*, November 26, 2022, https://www.washingtonpost.com/business/how-eu-could-frustr ate-musks-plans-for-twitter/2022/11/24/8f6eabba-6c04-11ed-8619-0b92f0565592_st ory.html.

73. Ediberto Roman and Ernesto Sagas, "A Domestic Reign of Terror: Donald Trump's Family Separation Policy," Florida International University Legal Studies Research Paper 21–11, 2021, 66–109; Saba Hamedy, "Everything You Need to Know About the Travel Ban: A Timeline," CNN, June 26, 2018, https://www.cnn.com/2018/06/26/politics/timeline-travel-ban/index.html.

74. Rodrique Ngowi, "Florida, Texas Escalate Flights, Buses to Move Migrants," AP News, September 15, 2022, https://apnews.com/article/florida-immigration-ron-desantis-char lie-baker-4fe96d293de4b189299a372b85c95add; Zach Schonfeld, "Attorneys for Migrant Families Flown to Martha's Vineyard Urge Investigation into 'Political Stunt,'" The Hill, September 18, 2022, https://thehill.com/latino/3648390-attorneys-for-migrant-famil ies-flown-to-marthas-vineyard-urge-investigation-into-political-stunt/; Jason Opal, "The Republican Party's Cruel Migrant Stunts Have Very Deep Roots," The Conversation, September 21, 2022, https://theconversation.com/the-republican-partys-cruel-migrant-stunts-have-very-deep-roots-190893.

75. Mariam Khan and Adam Carlson, "Greg Abbott Pushes Back on Criticism After Busing Migrants to VP's Home on Freezing Christmas Eve," ABC News, December 27, 2022, https://abcnews.go.com/Politics/greg-abbott-pushes-back-criticism-after-busing-migrants/.

76. Shawna Chen, "Texas Has Now Sent 300 Buses of Migrants out of State, Abbott Says," Axios, November 10, 2022, https://www.axios.com/2022/11/11/texas-migrants-abbott-busses.

77. Bridget Read, "172 Republicans Vote to Oppose Violence Against Women Act," The Cut, March 19, 2021, https://www.thecut.com/2021/03/172-republicans-vote-to-oppose-violence-against-women-act.html.

78. John Bowden, "Madison Cawthorn Introduces Bill to Prevent Federal Funds Being Used to Pay for Abortion Travel Expenses," *The Independent*, July 18, 2022, https://www.independent.co.uk/news/world/americas/us-politics/madison-cawthorn-bill-abortion-travel-b2125995.html.

79. Blake Ellis and Melanie Hicken, "These Male Politicians Are Pushing for Women Who Receive Abortions to Be Punished with Prison Time," CNN, September 21, 2022, https://www.cnn.com/2022/09/20/politics/abortion-bans-murder-charges-invs.

80. Adam Swerver, *The Cruelty Is the Point: The Past, Present, and Future of Trump's America* (New York: One World, 2021).

81. Xander Landen, "Ex-Trump Adviser Brags About Creating Products Used to Deter Protesters," *Newsweek*, May 6, 2022, https://www.newsweek.com/ex-trump-adviser-brags-about-creating-products-used-deter-protesters-1704258.

82. Brittany Gibson and Daniel Lippman, "GOP Hopeful Sold Tear Gas Used on Black Lives Matter Protesters," Politico, April 14, 2022, https://www.politico.com/news/2022/04/14/mills-congress-tear-gas-black-lives-matter-protesters-00025269.

83. Kristina Peterson, "Republican Cory Mills Wins Open Florida House Seat," *Wall Street Journal*, November 8, 2022, https://www.wsj.com/livecoverage/election-midterms-2022/card/republican-wins-open-florida-house-seat-UIrtJLLVkj1pCnM0Camn.

84. Johanna Chisholm, "Marjorie Taylor Greene Mocked for Hog Hunting Contest as She's Seen Slaying Animals from Chopper with Rifle," *The Independent*, September 28, 2022, https://www.independent.co.uk/news/world/americas/us-politics/marjorie-taylor-greene-hog-hunting-video-b2177402.html.

85. Sravasti Dasgupta, "Marjorie Taylor Greene Under Fire for Incendiary Comments at Trump Rally," *The Independent*, October 2, 2022, https://www.independent.co.uk/news/world/americas/us-politics/marjorie-taylor-greene-trump-rally-democrats-killings-b2190854.html.

86. Jay Bookman, "Top Republicans Embrace Marjorie Taylor Greene's Violent Rhetoric," New Jersey Monitor, October 20, 2022, https://newjerseymonitor.com/2022/10/20/top-republicans-embrace-marjorie-taylor-greenes-violent-rhetoric/.

87. Melanie Zanona and Ally Mutnick, "Republicans Called Her Videos 'Appalling' and 'Disgusting.' But They're Doing Little to Stop Her," Politico, August 9, 2020, https://www.politico.com/news/2020/08/09/republicans-marjorie-taylor-greene-392735.

88. Bookman, "Top Republicans Embrace Marjorie Taylor Greene's Violent Rhetoric."

89. Will Ragland, Ryan Koronowski, and Danielle Dietz, "Guns and Political Violence Play Central Role in MAGA Republican Campaign Ads," Center for American Progress, July 13, 2022, https://www.americanprogressaction.org/article/guns-and-political-violence-play-central-role-in-maga-republican-campaign-ads/.

90. Lewis Mumford, *Technics and Civilization* (New York: Harcourt Brace, 1963), 239–242.

91. Christian Fuchs. *Digital Demagogue: Authoritarian Capitalism in the Age of Trump and Twitter* (London: Pluto Press, 2018).

92. Donald Warren, *Radio Priest: Charles Coughlin, the Father of Hate Radio* (New York: Free Press, 1996).

93. Vernon Silver, "This Far-Right Italian Politician Is Relying on Social Media to Spread Her Message," Bloomberg, February 14, 2018, https://www.bloomberg.com/news/articles/2018-02-15/italy-first-politician-giorgia-meloni-turns-to-social-media?leadSource=uverify%20wall.

94. Chico Harlan, "In Midterms, Trump Republicans Turn to Giorgia Meloni as Model of Success," *Washington Post*, November 4, 2022, https://www.washingtonpost.com/world/2022/11/04/giorgia-meloni-trump-right-maga/.

95. Steven Levitsky and Daniel Ziblatt, *How Democracies Die* (New York: Viking, 2018), 2.

96. Levitsky and Ziblatt, *How Democracies Die*, 8.

97. Levitsky and Ziblatt, *How Democracies Die*, 231.

Index

For the benefit of digital users, indexed terms that span two pages (e.g., 52–53) may, on occasion, appear on only one of those pages.